NS 27.95

KT-433-066

FINANCIAL
MANAG...
for the Sma...

FINANCIAL MANAGEMENT
for the Small Business
The Daily Telegraph Guide

Colin Barrow

**Kogan
Page**

Copyright © Colin Barrow 1984

All rights reserved

First published in Great Britain in 1984
by Kogan Page Limited
120 Pentonville Road
London N1 9JN

Reprinted 1985 (twice), 1986

British Library Cataloguing in Publication Data

Barrow, Colin
    Financial management for the small business
    1. Small business — Great Britain — Finance
    I. Title
    658.1'592'0941   HG4027.7

    ISBN 0-85038-750-7
    ISBN 0-85038-751-5 Pbk

Printed in Great Britain by
Billing and Sons Limited, Worcester

Contents

Preface

This book is intended to help those who find business finance confusing. A heavy fog seems to descend as soon as anyone approaches this field for the first time. Whether running or setting up a business, getting a first taste of responsibility accounts or taking a business course, the first steps towards an understanding of finance are the most difficult. The consequences of failing to understand business finance are not the same for everyone. The student simply fails an exam, while the businessman all too often loses his business, and the executive gets fired. Competition is generally greater today and the margin for mistakes smaller. Indeed, the first years of this decade have seen the trend of business failures rising rapidly. The largest number of failures are in the early years, and the single most common cause is poor financial control. People running small businesses frequently leave financial questions to their accountants to sort out at the year end. They often have the mistaken belief that keeping the books is an activity quite divorced from the 'real' task of getting customers or making products.

By the time the first set of figures is prepared most small businesses are already too far down the road to financial failure to be saved. The final accounts become all too final and a good business proposition has been ruined by financial illiteracy. The few businessmen who do ask the way, perhaps of an accountant or bank manager, often do not understand the terms being used to explain the situation.

The book starts off with an introduction to the key financial statements. All too often these vital building blocks are missed out by those trying to come to grips with the problems of poor profits and a negative cash flow.

With this foundation, the tools of financial analysis are explained in Part 2, and these are the key to controlling a business successfully. If you can imagine trying to drive a car without any instruments at all, you will have some impression how unsatisfactory it would be to run a business without financial controls.

Part 3 covers the field of business planning and budgeting. Most new ventures cannot get off the ground without a sound business plan and existing businesses cannot grow without one.

Much of the material in this book has been used with business and academic audiences in the UK and mainland Europe over the past five years. I should like to record my appreciation of those 'students' who helped me to focus on these key financial issues and to sharpen up my thinking generally. In particular, I am grateful to the participants of the Graduate Enterprise Programme at Stirling University; those on the Small Business Programmes at Thames Polytechnic; and people attending the Royal Borough of Kensington and Chelsea's new business courses. I am also grateful to directors, executives and managers of the following companies whose financial training programmes have included much of this material: Abbott Laboratories, Ash and Lacy, Dorada Holdings, Englehard Industries, Johnson & Johnson, Leyland Paints, Seddon Atkinson, Seagram Distillers, Trust House Forte, Schwarzkopf, Ruberoid, Brooke Bond Oxo, the Mangers Group of Companies and Manders Paints.

Finally, I thank Jackie Severn FCA and Paul Barrow FCA for checking the manuscript and Gail Montague for typing from my rough drafts.

Colin Barrow
November 1983

Part 1 Understanding Key Financial Statements

Chapter 1

The Balance Sheet — Where we are now

There is a much told Irish story of the driver lost on his travels between Dublin and Cork. He stopped to ask the way of a passing farmer, who replied, 'If I were going to Cork I wouldn't start from here.'

For people in business this is an all too pertinent answer. We nearly always need a good idea of where we are now if we are to have any chance of reaching our goal. But either through pressures of more immediate tasks, or the nagging feeling that we will not like the answers, sizing up the financial situation is a job relegated to the bottom of the pile.

Even in our private lives it is helpful to 'strike a balance' when important financial issues are at stake. Questions such as should we move house, buy a boat, a new car, or take a holiday, involve us in an informal sizing up of the situation before making a decision.

A personal experience

This example looks at the finances of Terry Brown. She has become a little confused by the complexity of her financial affairs and has decided to get things sorted out. In short, she wants to know where she is.

If you were to summarise your present financial position it would contain, at least, some elements of the following example:

Terry Brown — Financial position today (28 March) 1

	£
Cash	50
House	15,000
Mortgage	10,000
Money owed by sister (Jackie)	135
Overdraft	100
Car	1,000
Credit cards	50
Jewellery and paintings	350
Hire purchase (on various goods)	500
Furniture, hi-fi etc	500

13

This information tells us something of Terry's circumstances, but until we organise the information we cannot really understand her true financial position.

Terry believes that in money matters, things divide neatly into two: things you have and things you owe, with the latter usually exceeding the former. So, using this concept and slightly different words, we could show the same information in the following manner. On the right-hand side we have made a list of Terry's *Assets:* what she has done with the money she has had. On the left is listed where she got the money from to pay for these assets: the *Liabilities and Claims* against her.

Terry Brown — Financial position today (28 March) 2

Liabilities and Claims (Where I got the money from)	£	*Assets* (What I have done with the money)	£
Overdraft	100	Cash	50
Mortgage	10,000	House	15,000
Hire purchase	500	Car	1,000
Credit cards	50	Jewellery and paintings	350
Total claims by other people	10,650	Money owed by sister	135
My Capital	6,385	Furniture, hi-fi etc	500
Total of my and other people's money	17,035	My Assets	17,035

You may have got a little lost towards the bottom of the left-hand column. This is simply because we have to try and show the complete picture of Terry's financial affairs. She has acquired £17,035's worth of assets and must have provided an identical sum from one source or another. We can find only £10,650 owed to other people. The only reasonable assumption is that Terry herself must have put in the balance over the past years. In other words, she has put her past salary or wages towards buying the assets.

Now while Terry might be happy with the help we have given her so far, it is unlikely she will be completely satisfied. Like the rest of us, she probably considers events as long- or short-term in nature. Even though we have shown a fairly dazzling picture of £17,000+ of assets, she knows she is short of cash for day-to-day living. So once again we could restructure the information on her financial position to give a clearer picture.

Terry Brown — Financial position today (28 March) 3

Liabilities (long term) (Where I got the money from)	£	Fixed Assets (long term) (What I have done with the money)	£
Mortgage	10,000	House	15,000
Hire purchase	500	Car	1,000
		Furniture, hi-fi etc.	500
My Capital	6,385	Jewellery and paintings	350
	16,885		16,850
Current Liabilities (short term)		Current Assets (short term)	
Overdraft	100	Money owed by sister	135
Credit cards	50	Cash	50
	150		185
Total Liabilities	17,035	Total Assets	17,035

For example, we can now see that her short-term financial position is dominated by the money her sister owes her. If that is safe, then all current liabilities can be met. If it is not safe, and that money is unlikely to be repaid quickly, the position is not so good. There is an accounting convention according to which 'current' liabilities are those that we will have to pay within a year. Similarly, 'current' assets will turn into cash within a year.

We are getting very close to having a *Balance Sheet* of Terry's financial position. One further adjustment will reveal all. It is vital that both the long- and short-term financial positions are readily visible to the examiner. Terry's day-to-day assets and liabilities need to be clearly highlighted. What we are looking for is the net position: how much she currently owes, subtracted from how much she has.

By re-drafting the financial position, we shall see the whole picture much more clearly. £16,850 is tied up in *fixed assets* and £35 is tied up in *net current assets*. All these assets have been *financed by* £6,385 of Terry's capital and £10,500 has been provided by a mortgage and a hire purchase company.

The public picture

Terry Brown found it useful to have a clear picture of her current financial position. A business will find such a picture essential. While most people are responsible only to themselves and their families, businesses have a wider audience. Partners,

Terry Brown — Balance Sheet at 28 March 198X

Fixed Assets	£	£
House		15,000
Car		1,000
Furniture, hi-fi etc		500
Jewellery and paintings		350
		16,850
Current Assets		
Money owed by sister		135
Cash		50
		185
Less Current Liabilities		
Overdraft		100
Credit cards		50
		150
So, Net Current Assets		35
Total Assets		16,885
Financed by		
My Capital		6,385
Mortgage	10,000	
Hire purchase	500	10,500
Total		16,885

shareholders, financial institutions, Customs and Excise and the Inland Revenue are only a few of the possible interested parties, apart from the owners' and managers' interest in the financial situation which is taken for granted.

All these interested parties keep track of a business's financial performance by having a series of reports, or statements, prepared. In effect a business acts as a steward of other people's money and it is to give account of this stewardship that these financial records are prepared. While these 'figure' statements provide useful evidence, it is as well to remember that the evidence is only partial: nothing in Terry's Balance Sheet has told us that she is shapely, 27 years old and currently sporting a carrot-red head of hair.

Another important limitation on these financial statements is the reliability of the figures themselves. The cash in hand figure is probably dead right, but can the same be said of the furniture and hi-fi values? Accountants have their own rules on how these figures are to be arrived at, but they do not pretend to anything better than an approximation. Every measuring device has inherent inaccuracies, and financial controls are no exception.

Not all the information that we need to prepare a financial statement is always readily on hand. For example, Terry has not had a statement on her credit card account since February (the preceding month), so despite the incomplete data, she has made an educated guess at the current position.

With these questions of reliability in mind, let us now look at how a business monitors and controls its financial position.

The structure of the business Balance Sheet

You might have noticed that we stopped calling Terry's statement a financial position, and called it a Balance Sheet in the last example. This is one of the principal business control reports. It is designed to show what assets the business is using at a particular time, and where it got the money to finance those assets. The Balance Sheet is usually a statement of the present position, but of course, once a business has been in existence for some time there will be historical balance sheets. These can be used to compare performance in one year (period) with another. This use of the Balance Sheet will be examined in the chapters on financial control.

It is also possible to prepare a projected Balance Sheet to show what the future financial picture might look like, given certain assumptions. We shall look at this aspect in more detail in the chapters on planning and budgeting.

You will notice a number of differences between the business Balance Sheet overleaf and the personal one we looked at before. But there are also many basic similarities.

First, you will notice the date at the top. This is essential, as the Balance Sheet is a picture of the business at a particular moment in time. The picture could look quite different tomorrow if, for example, some of the £400 cash was spent on further fixtures and fittings. There are three columns of £s simply to make the arithmetic of the subtotals easier to calculate and understand.

You can also see that some different terms are used for the account categories. Before looking at the main elements of this Balance Sheet it will be useful to describe the key terms, assets and liabilities. Other terms, such as debtors, creditors and stock are described in the glossary.

A Balance Sheet for a small business might look something like this:

Balance Sheet at 31 December 198X

Net Assets employed	£	£	£
Fixed Assets			
Shop premises		9,000	
Fixtures and fittings		3,800	12,800
Current Assets			
Stock	700		
Debtors	700		
Cash	400	1,800	
Less Current Liabilities			
Creditors		900	
Net Current Assets			
(Working Capital)			900
			13,700
Financed by			
Owner's Capital introduced	6,500		
Add net profit for year	5,000		
	11,500		
Less drawings	4,500		7,000
10-year loan from bank			6,700
			13,700

ASSETS

Accountants describe assets as 'valuable resources, owned by a business, which were acquired at a measurable money cost'. You can see that there are three key points in the definition:

1. To be valuable the resource must be cash, or of some use in generating current or future profits. For example, a debtor (someone who owes a business money for goods or services provided) usually pays up. When he does, the debtor becomes cash and so meets this test. If there is no hope of getting payment then you can hardly view the sum as an asset.
2. Ownership, in its legal sense, can be seen as being different from possession or control. The accounting use of the word is similar but not identical. In a business, possession and control are not enough to make a resource an asset.

For example, a leased machine may be possessed controlled by a business but be owned by the leasing co pany. So not only is it not an asset, it is a regular expense. (More about expenses in the next chapter.)

3. Most business resources are bought for a 'measurable money cost'. Often this test is all too painfully obvious. If you pay cash for something, or promise to pay at a later date, it is clearly an asset. If the resource was manufactured by the business then money was paid in wages, materials etc during that process. There may be problems in deciding exactly what money figure to put down, but there is no problem in seeing that money has been spent.

The asset 'goodwill' is one important grey area of particular interest to those buying or selling a small business. This term is defined in the glossary.

Ranking of Assets

There is a useful convention that recommends listing assets in the Balance Sheet in their order of permanence, that is, starting out with the most difficult to turn into cash and working down to cash itself. This structure is very practical when you are looking at someone else's Balance Sheet, or comparing Balance Sheets. It can also help you to recognise obvious information gaps quickly.

LIABILITIES

These are the claims by people outside the business. In our example only creditors are shown, but they could include such items as: tax; accruals; deferred income; overdrafts etc. These are also described either in the glossary or elsewhere in an appropriate place. The 'financed by' section of our example balance sheet is also considered in part as liabilities.

CURRENT

This is the term used with both assets and liabilities to show that they will be converted into cash, or have a short life (under one year).

Now let's go through the main elements of the Balance Sheet.

NET ASSETS EMPLOYED

This is the 'What have we done with the money?' section. A

...e things with funds:

assets, such as premises, machinery and ...ese are assets that the business intends to ...ie longer term. They will be used to help make ...it will not physically vanish in the short term ...sold and replaced, like motor cars, for example). ...ey can be tied up in *working capital,* that is, 'things' ...mediately involved in the business's products (or services), that will vanish in the short term. Stocks get sold and are replaced; debtors pay up, and creditors are paid; and cash circulates. Working capital is calculated by subtracting the current liabilities from the current assets. This is the net sum of money that a business has to find to finance the working capital. In the Balance Sheet this is called the *net current assets,* but on most other occasions the term working capital is used.

3. Finally a business can put money aside over the longer term, perhaps in local government bonds or as an investment in someone else's business venture. In the latter case this could be a prelude to a takeover. In the former it could be a cash reserve for future capital investment. The account category is called *investments.* It is not shown in this example as it is a fairly rare phenomenon in new or small businesses, who are usually cash hungry rather than rich.

FINANCED BY

This section of the balance sheet shows where the money came from. It usually has at least three subheadings, although larger companies can have many more.

1. The *owner's capital introduced* shows the money put into the business by the proprietor. If this was the Balance Sheet of a limited company it would be called *share capital.* There could then follow a list of different types of share, for example, preference and ordinary shares.
2. The second source of funds are the *profits* ploughed back into the business to help it grow. In this example the £5,000 profit was reduced to £500 after the owner had taken his drawings — or wages — out. So £500 was *retained* and this is the term often used to describe this ploughed-back profit. Another term in common use is *Reserves,* which conjures up pictures of sums of cash stored away for a rainy day. It

is important to remember that this is not necessarily so. The only cash in a business is that shown under that heading in the current assets. The reserves, like all the other funds, are used to finance a business and are tied up in the fixed assets and working capital.

3. The final source of money to finance a business is long-term *loans* from outside parties. These loans could be in the form of debentures, a mortgage, hire purchase agreements or long-term loans from a bank. The common features of all such loans are that businesses have to pay interest on the money, and eventually repay the capital whether or not the business is successful. Conversely, if the business is a spectacular success the lenders, unlike the shareholders, will not share in the extra profits.

The ground rules, concepts and conventions

Accounting is certainly not an exact science. Even the most enthusiastic member of the profession would not make that claim. As we have already seen, there is considerable scope for interpretation and educated guesswork. Obviously, if this were to go on unbridled no one inside or outside the business would place any reliance on the figures, so certain ground rules have been laid down by the profession to help get a level of consistency into accounting information.

1. *Money measurement.* In accounting, a record is kept only of the facts that can be expressed in money terms. For example, the state of the managing director's health, or the fact that your main competitor is opening up right opposite in a more attractive outlet, are important business facts. No accounting record of them is made, however, and they do not show up on the Balance Sheet, simply because no objective monetary value can be assigned to these facts.

Expressing business facts in money terms has the great advantage of providing a common denominator. Just imagine trying to add typewriters and motor cars, together with a 4,000 square foot workshop, and then arriving at a total. You need a common term to be able to carry out the basic arithmetical functions, and to compare one set of accounts with another.

There is one great danger with expressing things in money terms. It suggests that all the pounds are identical. This is not always so. Pounds currently shown as cash in a Balance Sheet are not exactly the same, for example, as debtors' pounds that may not be turned into cash for many months. The ways of examining this changing value of money over time are looked at in Chapter 7.

2. *Business entity.* The accounts are kept for the business itself, rather than for the owner(s), workers, or anyone else associated with the firm. If an owner puts a short-term cash injection into his business, it will appear as a loan under current liabilities in the business account. In his personal account it will appear as an asset — money someone else owes him. So depending on which point of view you take, the same sum of money can be an asset or a liability. And as in this example, the owner and the business are substantially the same person, the possibilities of confusion are considerable. This source of possible confusion must be cleared up and the business entity concept does just that.

The concept states that assets and liabilities are always defined from the business's viewpoint. Once again it is this idea of stewardship that forces us to see the business as an entity separate from *all* outside parties.

3. *Cost concept.* Assets are usually entered into the accounts at cost. For a variety of reasons, the real 'worth' of an asset will probably change over time.

The worth, or value, of an asset is a subjective estimate which no two people are likely to agree on. This is made even more complex, and artificial, because the assets themselves are usually not for sale. So in the search for objectivity, the accountants have settled for cost as the figure to record. It does mean that a balance sheet does not show the current worth, or value of a business. That is not its intention. Nor does it mean that the 'cost' figure remains unchanged forever. For example a motor car costing £6,000 may end up looking like this after two years:

Year 1		*Year 2*	
Fixed Assets	£	Fixed Assets	£
Motor car	6,000	Motor car	6,000
Less cumulative depreciation	1,500	Less cumulative depreciation	3,000
Net Asset	4,500	Net Asset	3,000

The depreciation is how we show the asset being 'consumed' over its working life. It is simply a book-keeping record to allow us to allocate some of the cost of an asset to the appropriate time period. The time period will be determined by such factors as how long the working life of the asset is. The Inland Revenue does not allow depreciation as a business expense — but it does allow tax relief on the capital expenditure.

Other assets, such as freehold land and buildings, will be revalued from time to time, and stock will be entered at cost, or market value, whichever is the lower, in line with the principle of conservatism (explained on page 25).

4. *Going concern.* Accounting reports always assume that a business will continue trading indefinitely into the future — unless there is good evidence to the contrary. This means that the assets of the business are looked at simply as profit generators and not as being available for sale.

Look again at the motor car example above. In year 2, the net asset figure in the accounts, prepared on a 'going concern' basis, is £3,000. If we knew that the business was to close down in a few weeks, then we would be more interested in the car's resale value than its 'book' value: the car might fetch only £2,000 which is quite a different figure.

Once a business stops trading, we cannot realistically look at the assets in the same way. They are no longer being used in the business to help generate sales and profits. The most objective figure is what they might realise in the market place. Anyone who has been to a sale of machinery will know the difference between book and market value!

5. *Dual aspect.* To keep a complete record of any business transaction we need to know both where money came from, and what has been done with it. It is not enough simply to say, for example, that someone has put £1,000 into their business. We have to see how that money has been used.

Take a look at the example overleaf. Column 1 has in it the figures we inherited before the owner put an extra £1,000 into the business. Column 2 shows what happened to the 'financed by' section of the Balance Sheet at the moment more money was put in. But as you can see, the Balance Sheet does not balance. It is also logically clear that we must have done something with that £1,000 the moment we received it. Column 3 shows exactly how we have used the

Example: Balance Sheet changes

Net Assets employed	1		2		3	
	£	£	£	£	£	£
Fixed Assets		12,800		12,800		12,800
Current Assets						
Stock	700		700		700	
Debtors	700		700		700	
Cash	400		400		1,400	
	1,800		1,800		2,800	
Less Current Liabilities						
Creditors	(900)		(900)		(900)	
Net Current Assets		900		900		1,900
		13,700		13,700		14,700
Financed by						
Owner's Capital (less drawings)		7,000		8,000		8,000
10-year loan from bank		6,700		6,700		6,700
		13,700		14,700		14,700

money. It is tied up in cash. It could just have easily been used to finance more customers (debtors) or to buy more stock, or even to pay off a bill, ie, reduce creditors.

However, the essential relationship of Assets = Capital + Liabilities has to be maintained. That is the basis of double entry book-keeping. You can think of it as the accounting equivalent of Newton's third law, 'For every force there is an equal and opposite reaction'.

There are two other important accounting concepts, realisation and accrual, but they can be better dealt with when the next accounting report is looked at.

ACCOUNTING CONVENTIONS
These concepts provide a useful set of ground rules, but they are open to a range of possible interpretations. Over time, a generally accepted approach to how the concepts are applied has been arrived at. This approach hinges on the use of three conventions: conservatism, materiality and consistency.

Conservatism

Accountants are often viewed as merchants of gloom, always prone to taking a pessimistic point of view. The fact that a point of view has to be taken at all is the root of the problem. The convention of conservatism means that, given a choice, the accountant takes the figure that will result in a lower end profit. This might mean, for example, taking the higher of two possible expense figures. Few people are upset if the profit figure at the end of the day is higher than earlier estimates. The converse is never true.

Materiality

A strict interpretation of depreciation (see cost concept, item 3, above) would lead to all sorts of trivial paperwork. For example, pencil sharpeners, staplers and paperclips, all theoretically items of fixed assets, should be depreciated over their working lives. This is obviously a useless exercise and in practice these items are written off when they are bought.

Clearly, the level of 'materiality' is not the same for all businesses. A multinational may not keep meticulous records of every item of machinery under £1,000. For a small business this may represent all the machinery it has.

Consistency

Even with the help of these concepts and conventions, there is a fair degree of latitude in how you can record and interpret financial information. You should choose the methods that give the fairest picture of how the firm is performing and stick with them. It is very difficult to keep track of events in a business that is always changing its accounting methods. This does not mean that you are stuck with one method for ever. Any change, however, is an important step.

The Balance Sheet shown earlier, though very simple, is complete enough to demonstrate the key principles involved. A much larger or more complex business may have more account categories, but the main sections of its Balance Sheet will be much the same, and you will now be able to recognise them.

Questions

These questions may help you to make sure of your understanding of the Balance Sheet.

1. Draw up your own personal Balance Sheet, using the four stages of the Terry Brown example as your guide.

2. A friend has brought round the following information about his business, and asked for your help. Put together a balance sheet for him.

The situation today (Sunday 24 April 198X)

	£
Debtors	1,400
Creditors	1,800
Factory premises	18,000
Cash in hand	800
Tax due to be paid	700
(should have gone out last week)	
Equipment and machinery	7,600
Money I put in at start	18,700
Long-term loan	12,000
Money I have drawn out so far	4,000
Stock	1,400

Chapter 2
The Profit and Loss Account —
Where we have been

The Balance Sheet shows the financial position of a business at a particular moment in time. Over time that picture will change, just as pictures of you, first as a baby, then as a teenager and lastly as an adult, will all be different — but nevertheless true likenesses of you. The 'ageing' process that changes a business's appearance is an event called a transaction. This takes place when anything is done that can be represented in money terms. For example, if you buy in stock, sell out to a customer or take credit, these are all events that can be expressed in money.

Dealing with transactions

Let us take a very simple example. On 6 April a new business called High Finance Limited is started. The initial share capital is £10,000 and on day 1, this money is held in the company's bank. The balance sheet would look something like this:

Balance Sheet for High Finance Ltd at 6 April 198X

Assets employed	£
Cash at Bank	10,000
Financed by	
Share Capital	10,000

Not very profound, but it does show the true picture at that date. On 7 April things begin to happen.

Balance Sheet for High Finance Ltd at 7 April 198X

Assets employed	£	£
Current Assets		
Cash at Bank A and in hand	£15,000	
Less Current Liabilities		
Overdraft (Bank B)	5,000	
Net Current Assets		10,000
Financed by		
Share Capital		10,000

27

High Finance borrows £5,000 on an overdraft from another bank, taking the money out immediately in cash. This event is an accounting transaction and the new balance sheet is shown on page 27.

You can see that the asset, 'cash', has gone up, while the liability, 'overdraft', has also risen. Any financial event must have at least two effects on the balance sheet.

On 8 April, High Finance buys in stock for resale, at a cost of £2,000, paying cash.

Balance Sheet for High Finance Ltd at 8 April 198X

Assets employed	£	£
Current Assets		
Cash at Bank and in hand	13,000	
Stock	2,000	
	15,000	
Less Current Liabilities		
Overdraft	5,000	
Net Current Assets		10,000
Financed by		
Share Capital		10,000

The working capital has been changed, not in total, but in content. Cash has been reduced to pay for stock. However, a new asset, stock, has been acquired.

On 9 April, High Finance sells for £300 cash, stock that cost it £200.

Balance Sheet for High Finance Ltd at 9 April 198X

Assets employed	£	£
Current Assets		
Cash at Bank and in hand	13,300	
Stock	1,800	
	15,100	
Less Current Liabilities		
Overdraft	5,000	
Net Current Assets		10,100
Financed by		
Share Capital	10,000	
Retained Earnings (reserves)	100	
		10,100

In this case cash has been increased by £300, the money received from a customer. Stocks have been reduced by £200, the amount sold. Finally, a 'profit' has been made and this can be shown, at least in this example, as Retained Earnings (or reserves).

The residual effect of *all* trading transactions is an increase or decrease in the worth of the business to the owners (shareholders in this case). Income from sales tends to increase the worth of a business. Expenses incurred in generating sales tend to decrease the worth. These events are so vital to the business that they are all monitored in a separate accounting report — the Profit and Loss Account.

So to summarise: the Balance Sheet shows the financial picture of a business at a particular moment in time. The Profit and Loss Account monitors income and expenditure over a particular period of time. The time intervals can be a week, a month, an accounting period, or a year. While we are very interested in all the components of income and expense, it is the result, the net profit (or loss), that we are most interested in. This shows the increase (or decrease) in the business's worth, over the time in question.

Some more ground rules

Before looking at the structure of the Profit and Loss Account, it would be helpful to look at the accounting concepts that apply to it. These are numbered 6 and 7 to follow on from the five concepts given in Chapter 1.

6. *The realisation concept.* A particularly prudent sales manager once said that an order was not an order until the customer's cheque had cleared: he had consumed the product; had not died as a result; and finally, he had shown every indication of wanting to buy again.

Most of us know quite different salesmen who can 'anticipate' the most unlikely volume of sales. In accounting, income is usually recognised as having been earned when the goods (or services) are despatched and the invoice sent out. This has nothing to do with when an order is received, or how firm an order is, or how likely a customer is to pay up promptly.

It is also possible that some of the products despatched may be returned at some later date — perhaps for quality reasons. This means that income, and consequently profit, can be brought into the business in one period, and have to be removed later on. Obviously, if these returns can be estimated accurately, then an adjustment can be made to income at the time.

So the 'Sales Income' figure that is seen at the top of a Profit and Loss Account is the value of the goods despatched and invoiced to customers in the period in question.

7. *The accrual concept.* The Profit and Loss Account sets out to 'match' income and expenditure to the appropriate time period. It is only in this way that the profit for the period can be realistically calculated. Suppose, for example, that you are calculating one month's profits when the quarterly telephone bill comes in. The picture might look like this:

Profit and Loss Account for January 198X

	£
Sales Income for January	4,000
Less Telephone Bill (last quarter)	800
Profit	3,200

This is clearly wrong. In the first place, three months' telephone charges have been 'matched' against one month's sales. Equally wrong is charging anything other than January's telephone bill against January's income. Unfortunately, bills such as this are rarely to hand when you want the accounts, so in practice the telephone bill is 'accrued' for. A figure (which may even be absolutely correct if you have a meter) is put in as a provision to meet this liability when it becomes due.

With these two additional concepts we can now look at a business Profit and Loss Account.

Profit and Loss Account for a manufacturing business

Hardcourt Ltd
Profit and Loss Account for the year ended 31 December 198X

	£
Sales	100,000
Cost of Goods Sold	65,000
Gross Profit	35,000
Selling Expenses	5,000
Administrative Expenses	14,000
Total Expenses	19,000
Net Profit before Tax	16,000
Taxation	6,400
Net Profit after Tax	9,600

This is a simplified P and L Account for a small manufacturing company. A glance at it will show that we have at least three sorts of profit to measure in the Profit and Loss Account. The first, *gross profit,* is the difference between the sales income that we have generated and all the costs that have gone into making the goods.

COST OF GOODS SOLD\
Now you may consider that everything you have spent in the business has gone into 'making' the product, but to calculate the cost of goods sold only costs strictly concerned with making are considered. These will include the cost of all materials and the cost of manufacturing labour.

Blowing up the cost of goods sold section of Hardcourt's P and L Account, it could look like this:

Hardcourt Ltd
Profit and Loss Account for the year ended 31 December 198X

	£	£	£
Sales			100,000
Manufacturing Costs			
Raw materials opening stock	30,000		
Purchases in period	25,000		
	55,000		
Less Raw materials closing stock	15,500		
Cost of Materials used		39,500	
Direct Labour Cost		18,000	
Manufacturing Overhead Cost			
Indirect Labour	4,000		
Workshop Heat, Light and Power	3,500		
Total Manufacturing Costs		7,500	
Cost of Goods Sold			65,000
Gross Profit			35,000

This is not a complete list of items we would find in the cost of goods sold section of a manufacturer's P and L Account. For example, work in progress, plant depreciation etc, have been ignored to keep the example clear enough for the principle to be established.

NET PROFIT BEFORE AND AFTER TAX
The second type of profit we have to measure is net profit

before tax (NPBT). This is arrived at by deducting all the other expenses from the gross profit. The final item to be deducted is tax, which leaves the last profit to be measured, net profit after tax (NPAT), or the much referred to 'bottom line'.

Clearly we could arrive at net profit after tax by simply deducting all the expenses for the period from all the income. The reason for 'organising' the information is to help us analyse and interpret that information: in other words, to see how we made a certain profit or loss in a particular trading period.

Profit and Loss Account for a service business

All the basic principles and practices of the manufacturing business apply to a service or professional business. The main area of difference will be in the calculation of gross profit. For example, a consultancy organisation's P and L Account could look as follows:

Thames Consultants

	£	£
Sales	65,000	
Fees paid to consultants	30,000	
Profit before Expenses (Gross Profit)		35,000
Expenses etc (as for any other business)		..

or a travel agency's account might look like this:

Sunburn Travel

	£
Sales	200,000
Payments to Carriers	130,000
Net Commission Income (Gross Profit)	70,000
Expenses etc (as for any other business)	..

You can see that the basic principle of calculating the gross profit, or the margin that is left after the cost of 'producing' the service has been met, is being maintained.

SALES ANALYSIS

It may be useful to show the sales revenue by each major product group, and by home and export sales, if appropriate. It would be even more useful to show the gross margin by major product.

Domestic Furniture Ltd.

Sales:	£	£
Tables	50,000	
Chairs	20,000	
Repairs etc	10,000	
		80,000
Cost of Goods Sold		50,000
Gross Profit		30,000
Less Expenses (as for any other business)		..

The structure of a Profit and Loss Account

Once a business has been trading for a few years it will have taken on a wide range of new commitments. For example, as well as the owner's money, there may be a long-term loan to be serviced (interest and capital repayments), or part of the work-shop or offices may be sublet. Now the business Profit and Loss Account will include most of the elements listed below.

Like any accounting report it should be prepared in the best form for the user. The elements of this example are explained below.

(a) Sales (and any other revenue from operations).
(b) Cost of sales (or cost of goods sold). (At the moment a product is sold and its income is 'realised', so too are its costs.) See fuller explanation of cost of goods sold on page 31.

	£
Opening Stock	18,000
Plus Purchases	74,000
Equals Goods Available for Sale	92,000
Less Closing Stock	22,000
Cost of Goods Sold	70,000

(c) Gross profit — the difference between sales and cost of sales.
(d) Operating expenses: selling — administration and general.
(e) Operating profit: the difference between gross profit and operating expense.
(f) Non-operating revenues — other revenues including interest — rent etc.
(g) Non-operating expenses — financial costs and other expenses not directly related to the running of the business.

(h) Profit before income tax.
(i) Provision for income tax.
(j) Net income — or profit and loss.

Just to make sure you understand the process and structure of the Profit and Loss Account, work through the examples at the end of the chapter.

Profit and Loss Account

		£	£
1.	Sales		140,000
2.	Cost of Sales		
	Opening Stock	18,000	
	Purchases	74,000	
		92,000	
	Less Closing Stock	22,000	
	Cost of Goods Sold		70,000
3.	Gross Profit		70,000
4.	Operating Expenses		
	Selling	12,500	
	Administration	12,500	
	General	30,000	
	Total Expenses		55,000
5.	Operating (or Trading) Profit		15,000
6.	Non-operating Revenue		
	Investment Interest	1,000	
	Rents	500	
	Total		1,500
			16,500
7.	Non-operating Expenses		
	Loan Interest Paid		3,000
8.	Profit before Income Tax		13,500
9.	Tax		5,400
10.	Profit after Tax		8,100

Accounting requirements of the Companies Acts

A very sizeable majority of small businesses are either sole traders or partnerships. There is no obligation for them to prepare accounts in any particular way, but obviously they would be prudent to follow guidelines such as those in these first two chapters.

Limited companies do have to prepare accounts and file them with the Registrar of Companies. The Companies Act 1981 lays down standard Balance Sheet and Profit and Loss Account formats. These are similar to those we have been looking at, but by no means as clear and understandable to the layman, as they are really designed for company auditors' use.

Fortunately, small companies are exempted from following the Companies Act guidelines, so throughout this book they have been largely ignored.

Questions

1. Record the effects of the following events on the Balance Sheet, noting the changes you would make to existing figures, or by adding new items as necessary. Remember every transaction must have at least two effects on the Balance Sheet. Look back at the dual aspect concept on page 23 to remind yourself how this works. After you have finished recording the events, prepare a closing Balance Sheet.

High Finance Ltd
Balance Sheet at 10 April 198X

	£	£
Fixed Assets		–
Working Capital		
Current Assets		
Stock	1,800	
Cash	13,300	
	15,100	
Less Current Liabilities		
Overdraft	5,000	
Net Current Assets		10,100
Total		10,100
Financed by		
Share Capital		10,000
Retained earnings (reserves)		100
		10,100

1. Stock costing £250 was sold for £400, received in cash.
2. Freehold land costing £15,000 was purchased by paying £1,500 cash and taking a 20-year mortgage for the balance.

3. A company car costing £3,000 was purchased, High Finance agreeing to pay the garage cash in 60 days.
4. Stock costing £3,000 was purchased, the supplier agreeing to payment within 30 days.
5. Stock costing £1,800 was sold for £2,700, the customer agreeing to pay within 120 days.
(All these transactions can be assumed to have happened over a period of a few days.)

2. The following is a list of items you would normally expect to find in a Profit and Loss Account. Unfortunately they are not in the right order. Re-arrange them in the correct order, and so arrive at the business's net profit after tax.

	£
Purchases during the period	90,000
Miscellaneous Expenses	1,900
Interest Expenses	3,000
Sales	174,000
Rent from subletting part of workshop	400
Provision for income tax	5,240
Opening Stock	110,000
Administration Expenses	21,000
Selling Expenses	7,000
Advertising Expenses	2,100
Closing Stock at end of the period	73,700

Chapter 3

Cash Flow and Funds Flow — Where we are going

One of the characteristics that most new or small businesses have in common is a tendency to change their size and shape quickly. In the early months and years customers are few, and each new customer (or a particularly big order) can mean a large percentage increase in sales. A large increase in sales in turn means an increase in raw materials and perhaps more wages and other expenses. Generally, these expenses have to be met before your customer pays up, not, however, before his order appears on your Profit and Loss Account as additional income, and perhaps profit. Remember that income is realised in the P and L Account when the 'goods' are despatched and the invoice raised. But until the money comes in, the business has to find cash to meet its bills. If it cannot find the cash to meet these day-to-day bills then it becomes 'illiquid' and very often goes bust.

Overtrading

Bankers have a name for it. They call it overtrading. Put simply it means taking on more business than you have the cash to finance. The following simple example will illustrate the problem.

A CASE STUDY IN OVERTRADING (AND HOW TO AVOID DOING IT)

The High Note Company is a new business, set up to retail music products, including sheet music, instruments and tapes/records. Customers will include schools, colleges and other institutions who will expect trade credit, and members of the public who will pay cash. The owner plans to put in £10,000 and he has high hopes of borrowing a further £10,000 from his bank. The premises being taken on are in good repair, but £12,500 will have to be spent on fixtures and fittings. This will leave £7,500 to meet immediate trading expenses, but customers' cash should come in quickly enough to meet day-to-day bills. The rent, rates and other basic expenses (telephone, heat, light, power and transport) should come to £27,600 over the full year. (This will include running repairs and renewals of fittings.) Apart from the owner, staff wages and book-keeping costs will be £12,000. It is also planned to spend £250 per month on advertising. The first six months are going to be the most crucial; however, High Note's owner is confident of sales of £60,000 in that period, and the average mark-up across the product range will be 50 per cent. On this basis the following Profit and Loss Account was prepared:

High Note
Projected P and L Account — six months April—September*

		£
Sales		60,000
Cost of Goods Sold		30,000
Gross Profit		30,000
Expenses†		
Rent, Rates etc	13,800	
Wages	6,000	
Advertising	1,500	21,300
Net Profit before Interest Charges and Tax		8,700

This appears to be a very respectable profit, certainly enough to support a £10,000 loan, and perhaps enough to support the owner. However, this is not the whole picture. Customers will not pay on the nail; suppliers will want cash as this is a new business; wage earners and the landlord will want immediate payment. So the cash position will look more like the table opposite.

The top of the cash flow forecast shows the cash coming into the business each month. While High Note had a sales income in the first six months of £60,000, only £48,000 cash came in. Some customers have yet to pay up. Also the owner's start-up capital comes in, in April, along with the loan capital.

The middle of the cash flow forecast shows the cash payments out of the business. Purchases of instruments, sheet music, books, records and tapes make up the largest element of this. £30,000's worth of purchases are needed to support sales of £60,000 (gross margin 50 per cent), and at least one month's stock has to be available in September to meet October's

---

* Note that as this is a six-month period, only half the expenses are included.

† Strictly speaking, we should either depreciate or write off the furniture and fixtures. In this simplified case, this has been omitted.

High Note
Six month Cash Flow Forecast

	April £	May £	June £	July £	Aug £	Sept £	Totals for Sales and Purchases only £
Cash Receipts in*							
Sales	4,000	5,000	5,000	7,000	12,000	15,000	48,000
Owner's Capital	10,000						
Loan Capital	10,000						
Total Cash in	24,000	5,000	5,000	7,000	12,000	15,000	
Cash Payments out							
Purchases	5,500	2,950	4,220	7,416	9,332	9,690	39,108
Rent, Rates etc	2,300	2,300	2,300	2,300	2,300	2,300	
Wages	1,000	1,000	1,000	1,000	1,000	1,000	
Advertising	250	250	250	250	250	250	
Fixtures and Fittings	12,500	–	–	–	–	–	
Total Cash out	21,550	6,500	7,770	10,966	12,882	13,240	
Cash Balances							
Monthly Cash Balance	2,450	(1,500)	(2,770)	(3,966)	(882)	|1,760	
Balance brought forward	–	2,450	950	(1,820)	(5,786)	(6,668)	
Balance to carry forward or Net Cash Flow	2,450	950	(1,820)	(5,786)	(6,668)	(4,908)	

demand. So £39,108 must be paid out to suppliers. Following this are all the other cash payments listed in the months they are to be paid.

The bottom of the cash flow forecast shows the cash balances. The monthly cash balance shows the surplus (or deficit in brackets) for each month; the balance brought forward shows the amount brought forward from the preceding month, and the balance to carry forward shows the cumulative cash position, or net cash flow as it is usually called.

For the first two months of trading, High Note has enough cash to meet its needs. But from June to August, as sales build up, the position gets progressively worse: by August the company needs £6,668 cash to meet current needs. By this stage most of the owner's time is probably being spent badger-

---

* Value added tax is paid and collected by all businesses with a turnover greater than £18,000 per annum. To keep this example simple, VAT has been ignored, but you should remember that you will probably have to show VAT separately. That is, Sales, and VAT on Sales separately, and quarterly cash payments to the Customs and Excise.

ing good customers to pay up early, very often driving them into the arms of competitors, pleading with suppliers for credit, or worse still, searching out inferior sources of supply. The business is now being constrained by a cash corset and the needs of the market place have become a low priority.

Forecasting cash needs

Fortunately, this cash flow statement is a projection and High Note has still time to prevent such problems. From the trend of the figures it looks as though the cash deficit will be wiped out by Christmas. If this is the case perhaps an overdraft could provide an answer. However, Christmas is probably a high sales period so the cash position might deteriorate again. As a general rule, if a business is alternating between periods of cash surplus and cash deficit, an overdraft is the answer. If there are no periods of cash surplus then the business is under-capitalised. In other words, either the owner must put in more cash or, if the profits warrant it, more outside money can be borrowed, long term.

While High Note was largely a fictional example, the experience for new and small businesses is an all too common one. It is vital to forecast cash flow month by month for the year ahead. It would be prudent to look ahead for a further year or so on a quarterly basis. If you are asking other people to invest in your business proposition, the cash flow forecast will be even more interesting than the projected profit. This forecast will reveal your chances of surviving long enough to collect your 'profits'.

Questions

Working through the following questions will help you to consolidate your understanding of cash flow and the other two important financial statements.

1. Work out High Note's closing Balance Sheet at the end of September. Use the information given in the example. Remember that they still have to collect £12,000 from customers; they are carrying forward £9,108 of stock, and they have 'acquired' an overdraft of £4,908.

2. Re-work the cash flow forecast for High Note, making the following revised assumptions: first, they receive £1,000 per

month more cash in from customers. Second, the furniture and fittings cost £2,000 less, ie, £10,500. Your answer should provide a pleasant surprise for High Note's owner and his bankers.

3. Check if you agree with the answer to question 2, then re-calculate the Profit and Loss Account for the six months' trading and the closing Balance Sheet. (Once again ignore depreciation of furniture and fixtures.)

Package of Accounts for Funds Flow Analysis at 31 December 1983 and 31 December 1984

		1983		1984
	£	£	£	£
Fixed Assets		37,340		60,340
Working Capital				
Current Assets				
Stock	19,840		29,300	
Debtors	49,460		77,600	
Cash	8,680		1,500	
	77,980		108,400	
Less Current Liabilities				
Bank Overdraft	10,000		12,000	
Creditors	48,000		58,280	
Tax	5,920		9,000	
	63,920		79,280	
Net Current Assets		14,060		29,120
Total Assets		51,400		89,460
Financed by				
Share Capital		20,000		20,000
Retained Earnings		11,400		33,460
Long-term Loan		20,000		36,000
(at 12%)		51,400		89,460

Profit and Loss Account 31 December 1983 – 31 December 1984

	£
Sales	672,060
Gross Profit	110,900
Expenses	75,520
Operating Profit	35,380
Loan Interest	4,320
Net Profit before Tax	31,060

Funds flow

The cash flow statement looks at the forecast movement of cash in and out of the business, but as we already know, cash is not the only money in the business. The term 'funds' is used to mean 'cash and credit', which is nearly but not quite the same as cash. From a historical point of view, a business would want to look back at the past sources and applications of funds to help predict future funding patterns.

The funds flow statement is prepared from the package of accounts. That is the opening and closing Balance Sheet, and the intervening Profit and Loss Account. Look at the example on page 41 which puts these Balance Sheets side by side, followed by a Profit and Loss Account.

Now by subtracting the opening Balance Sheet from the closing Balance Sheet and using the profit, from the Profit and Loss Account we can prepare the funds flow statement as follows:

Sources and Applications of Funds Statement

			£
Cash and liquid funds at start of year			(1,320)
(Cash + Overdraft = £8,680 + (£10,000))			

Sources of Funds		£	
From trading ie, last year's profit before tax		31,060	
From new long-term loan		16,000	47,060
			45,740

Applications (uses of funds)		£	
Purchase of Fixed Assets		23,000	
Tax paid		5,920	
Increases in Working Capital	£		
Stock (29,300–19,840)	9,460		
Debtors (77,600–49,460)	28,140		
Creditors* (58,280–48,000)	(10,280)	27,320	£
			56,240
Cash and liquid funds at year end			(10,500)
(Cash + Overdraft = £1,500 + (£12,000))			45,740

Questions

Now try and answer the following question on funds flow.

4. Look at the Parkwood and Company accounts on page 67. Calculate the funds flow statement using that information.

---

* Creditors are people you have borrowed money from, so that has to be subtracted.

Part 2 The Tools of Financial Analysis

Chapter 4
Business Controls

An understanding of financial reports is essential to anyone who wants to control a business, but simply knowing how these reports are constructed is not enough. To be effective, the businessman must be able to analyse and interpret that financial information.

It is highly likely that a business will want to borrow money either to get started or to expand. Bankers and other sources of finance will use specialised techniques to help them decide whether or not to invest. These techniques are the same as those used by the prudent businessman. Understanding them will help you to speak the same language as the bankers.

The starting point for any useful analysis is some appreciation of what should be happening in a given situation. If, for example, you fill your car up with petrol until it flows out, you expect the fuel gauge to read full. If it does not you would think the gauge suspect. (If you had left someone else to fill up the car you might have other doubts as well.) This would also be true for any other car you may come across.

Business objectives

There are universal methods of measuring what is happening in a business. All businesses have two fundamental objectives in common which allow us to see how well (or otherwise) they are doing.

MAKING A SATISFACTORY RETURN ON INVESTMENT

The first of these objectives is to make a satisfactory return (profit) on the money invested in the business.* It is hard to

---

* One of the most well known returns on investment is the building society deposit rate. In recent years this has ranged between 6 and 12 per cent, so for every £100 invested, depositors received between £6 and £12 return, each year. Their capital, in this example £100, remained intact and secure.

think of a sound argument against this aim. To be 'satisfactory' the return must meet four criteria:

First, it must give a fair return to shareholders bearing in mind the risk they are taking. If the venture is highly speculative and the profits are less than building society interest rates, your shareholders (yourself included) will not be happy.

Second, you must make enough profit to allow the company to grow. If a business wants to expand sales it will need more working capital and eventually more space or equipment. The safest and surest source of money for this is internally generated profits, retained in the business — reserves. You will remember from the Balance Sheet that a business has three sources of new money: share capital or the owner's money; loan capital, put up by banks etc; retained profits, generated by the business.

Third, the return must be good enough to attract new investors or lenders. If investors can get a greater return on their money in some other comparable business, then that is where they will put it.

Fourth, the return must provide enough reserves to keep the real capital intact. This means that you must recognise the impact inflation has on the business. A business retaining enough profits each year to meet a 5 per cent growth in assets is actually contracting by 5 per cent if inflation is running at 10 per cent.

To control the business we have to examine carefully the various factors that affect return on investment.* Shareholders' and other lenders' funds are invested in the capital, both fixed and working, of the business, so this must be the area we relate to profitability. The example opposite shows the factors that directly influence the return on capital employed (Capital Employed = Investment; remember the Balance Sheet must balance).

You can see that this is nothing more than a Profit and Loss Account on the left and the capital employed section of the Balance Sheet on the right. Any change that increases net profit (eg, more sales, lower expenses, less tax etc), but does not increase the amount of capital employed, will increase the ROCE percentage. Any decrease in capital employed (eg, lower stocks, fewer debtors etc), that does not lower profits, will also increase ROCE. Conversely, any change that increases capital

---

* Return on investment is calculated in a number of different ways. The methods most suitable for a small business are covered in Chapter 5.

Factors that affect the Return on Capital Employed (ROCE)

	£			£
Sales	100,000	Fixed Assets		12,500
– Cost of Sales	50,000			
= Gross Profit	50,000	Working Capital		
		Current Assets	23,100	
– Expenses	33,000	– Current Liabilities	6,690	
= Operating Profit	17,000			16,410
– Finance Charges and Tax	8090			
=		=		
Net Profit	8,910 ÷	Capital Employed		28,910
		= % Return on Capital Employed		30.82%

employed without increasing profits in proportion will reduce ROCE.

We shall look in detail at all the important factors that affect ROCE in Chapter 5.

MAINTAINING A SOUND FINANCIAL POSITION
As well as making a satisfactory return, investors, creditors and employees expect the business to be protected from unnecessary risks. Clearly, all businesses are exposed to market risks: competitors, new products and price changes are all part of a healthy commercial environment.

The sort of unnecessary risks that investors and lenders are particularly concerned about are high financial risks.

We have already seen how High Note (page 38) ran out of cash trying to make a very high return (87 per cent – £8,700 on £10,000 share capital). This was a financial risk decision, and whether taken, or stumbled into, by High Note's management, it exposed the business to the threat of liquidation.

Cash flow problems are not the only threat to a business's financial position. Heavy borrowings can bring a big interest burden to a small business. This may be acceptable when sales and profits are good, and when times are bad, shareholders can be asked to tighten their belts. Bankers, however, expect to be paid all the time. So business analysis and control are not just about profitability, but about survival and the practice of sound financial disciplines.

47

Ratios, the tools of analysis

All analysis of financial information requires comparisons. We have already seen that certain objectives are fundamental to all types of business. It is also true that there are three yardsticks against which business performance can be measured.

First, you can see how well you are meeting a personal goal. For example, you may want to double sales or add 25 per cent to profits. In a more formalised business this activity would be called budgeting, then comparisons would be made between actual results and the budget.

Second, you might want to see how well you are doing this year compared with last, comparing performance against an historical standard. This is the way in which growth in sales or profits is often measured. There are two main limitations to this sort of comparison. One rarely affects a small business and one affects all sizes of business.

If accounting methods change from year to year, perhaps in the way depreciation is dealt with, then you are not comparing like with like. Also the pounds in one year are not the same as the pounds in another, simply because inflation has changed them, so a 10 per cent growth in sales, when inflation is running at 15 per cent represents a real drop in sales volume.

Third, you may want to see how well you are doing compared with someone else's business, perhaps a competitor, or someone in a similar line of business elsewhere. This may provide useful pointers to where improvements can be made, or to new and more profitable business opportunities. For this type of analysis you need external information. Fortunately the UK has an unrivalled wealth of readily available financial data on companies and industries. The chief sources of this information are explained in Chapter 5.

The main way in which all these business yardsticks are established is through the use of ratios. A ratio is simply something expressed as a proportion of something else, and it is intended to give an appreciation of what has happened. For example, a percentage is a particular type of ratio, where events are always compared with a base of 100.

We have already seen earlier in this chapter the return on capital employed ratio, which was expressed as a percentage. In our everyday lives we apply ratios to tell us how well, or otherwise, something is performing. One measure of a car's performance is in miles per gallon. If the mpg rate drops, say, from 35 to 1, to 20 to 1, it tells us the car is long overdue for a service — or worse. Statisticians tell us the average number of children in a family is 1.8. That is a ratio of 1.8 children to one couple.

In the financial field the opportunity for calculating ratios is great, for useful ratios, not quite so great. Chapters 5 to 7 concentrate on explaining the key ratios for a small business. Most you can calculate yourself, some you may need your book-keeper or accountant to organise for you. All take a little time and may cost a little money, but they do tell you a lot about what is going on. Derek Bok, a president of Harvard University, summed this field up nicely in the following quotation, 'If you think knowledge is expensive, try ignorance.'

The main value of financial analysis using ratios is that it points to questions that need answers. A large difference between what actually happened and what standard was set suggests that something may be wrong. The tools of analysis (the ratios covered in the next three chapters) allow managers to choose from the hundreds of questions that might be asked, the handful that are really worth answering. In a small or expanding business where time is at a considerable premium, this quick pre-selection of key questions is vital.

In the examples given in the following chapters, year end Balance Sheets and annual Profit and Loss Accounts have been used to calculate ratios. It would be more usual and useful to use monthly accounts for internal control, but for the purposes of illustration, annual figures are satisfactory.

Some problems in using ratios

Finding the information to calculate business ratios is often not the major problem. Being sure of what the ratios are really telling you almost always is.

The most common problems lie in the four following areas. (It would be very useful to read this section again, after reading the next three chapters.)

WHICH WAY IS RIGHT?

There is a natural feeling with financial ratios to think that high figures are good ones, and an upward trend represents the right direction. This theory is, to some extent, encouraged by the personal feeling of wealth that having a lot of cash engenders.

Unfortunately, there is no general rule on which way is right for financial ratios. In some cases a high figure is good, in others a low figure is best. Indeed, there are even circumstances in which ratios of the same value are not as good as each other. Look at the two working capital statements below.

Difficult Comparisons

	1.		2.	
	£	£	£	£
Current Assets				
Stock	10,000		22,990	
Debtors	13,000		100	
Cash	100	23,100	10	23,100
Less Current Liabilities				
Overdraft	5,000		90	
Creditors	1,690	6,690	6,600	6,690
Working Capital		16,410		16,410
Current Ratio*		3.4:1		3.4:1

The amount of working capital in each example is the same, £16,410, as are the current assets and current liabilities, at £23,100 and £6,690 respectively. It follows that any ratio using these factors would also be the same. For example, the current ratios in these two examples are both identical, 3.4:1, but in the first case there is a reasonable chance that some cash will come in from debtors, certainly enough to meet the modest creditor position. In the second example there is no possibility of useful amounts of cash coming in from trading, with debtors at only £100, while creditors at the relatively substantial figure of £6,600 will pose a real threat to financial stability. So in this case the current ratios are identical, but the situations being compared are not. In fact, as a general rule, a higher working capital ratio is regarded as a move in the wrong direction. The more money a business has tied up in working capital, the more difficult it is to make a satisfactory return on capital employed, simply because the larger the denominator the lower the return on capital employed.

In some cases the right direction is more obvious. A high return on capital employed is usually better than a low one, but even this situation can be a danger signal, warning that higher risks are being taken. And not all high profit ratios are good: sometimes a higher profit margin can lead to reduced sales volume and so lead to a lower ROCE.

In general, business performance as measured by ratios is best

---

* The Current Ratio = Current Assets ÷ Current Liabilities. It is explained in greater detail in Chapter 6 on Control of Working Capital.

thought of as lying within a range, liquidity (current ratio), for example, staying between 1.5:1 and 2.5:1. A change in either direction represents a cause for concern.

ACCOUNTING FOR INFLATION
Financial ratios all use pounds as the basis for comparison — historical pounds at that. That would not be so bad if all these pounds were from the same date in the past, but that is not so. Comparing one year with another may not be very meaningful unless we account for the change in value of the pound.

One way of overcoming this problem is to 'adjust for inflation', perhaps using an index, such as that for consumer prices. Such indices usually take 100 as their base at some time in the past, for example, 1975. Then an index value for each subsequent year is produced showing the relative movement in the item being indexed.

The two tables below show how this could be done for High Note.

Comparing Unadjusted Ratios

Year	Sales	Sales Growth	Percentage Growth (ie, the ratio year on year)
	£	£	
1	100,000	–	–
2	130,000	30,000	30
3	145,000	15,000	11.5

These unadjusted figures show a substantial growth in sales in each of the past two years.

Now if High Note's owner used a consumer price index for the appropriate time period to adjust his figures, the years could be properly compared. Let us assume that the indices for years 1, 2 and 3 were 104, 120 and 135 respectively. Year 3 is the most recent set of figures, and therefore the one we want to use as the base for comparison.

So to convert the pounds from years 1 and 2 to current pounds, we use this sum:

$$\text{Current Pounds} = \frac{\text{Index for Current Year}}{\text{Index for Historic Year}} \times \text{Historic Pounds}$$

For year 1 sales now become 135/104 x £100,000 = £129,808
2 135/120 x £130,000 = £146,250
3* 135/135 x £145,000 = £145,000

* In other words, year 3 is virtually 'now'.

We can now construct an adjusted table, showing the real sales growth over the past three years.

Comparing Adjusted Ratios

Year	Adjusted Sales	Adjusted Sales Growth	Adjusted Growth Ratios
	£	£	%
1	129,808	–	–
2	146,250	16,442	12.7
3	145,000	-1,250	-0.9

The real situation is nothing like as rosy as we first thought. The sales growth in year 2 is barely a third of the original estimate. In year 3, High Note did not grow at all — in fact it contracted slightly.

The principle of this technique can be applied to any financial ratio. The appropriate index will, to some extent, depend on the nature of the business in question. Information on current British indices is published each week in *British Business,* a Department of Trade and Industry publication.

APPLES AND PEARS

There are particular problems in trying to compare one business's ratios with another. You would not expect a Mini to be able to cover a mile as quickly as a Jaguar. A small new business can achieve quite startling sales growth ratios in the early months and years. Expanding from £10,000 sales in the first six months to £50,000 in the second would not be unusual. To expect a mature business to achieve the same growth would be unrealistic. For ICI to grow from sales of £5bn to £25bn would imply wiping out every other chemical company in the world. So some care must be taken to make sure that like is being compared with like, and allowances made for differing circumstances in the businesses being compared (or if the same business, the trading/economic environment of the years being compared).

It is also important to check that one business's idea of an account category, say current assets, is the same as the one you want to compare it with. The concepts and principles used to prepare accounts leave some scope for differences, as Chapter 1 demonstrates.

SEASONAL FACTORS

Many of the ratios that we have looked at make use of information in the Balance Sheet. Balance Sheets are prepared at one moment in time, and may not represent the average situation. For example, seasonal factors can cause a business's sales to be particularly high once or twice a year. A Balance Sheet prepared just before one of these seasonal upturns might show very high stocks, bought in specially to meet this demand. Conversely, a look at the Balance Sheet just after the upturn might show very high cash and low stocks. If either of those stock figures were to be treated as an average it would give a false picture.

Sources of financial information

The three following chapters explain the key internal control ratios. The information you need to calculate these comes from your own accounts. For a variety of reasons you may want to know ratios for another company or even an industry as a whole. A number of organisations have been set up to help you find this information.

Some of the most useful sources in this field are listed below, together with an outline of their services. At least one of these, The Centre for Interfirm Comparisons, carries out its work both inside an individual business and in the industry sector in general. Many of these organisations' services extend to cover international markets. Much of their published information is freely available in the reference section of major public libraries. Examples of some of these services are given in Appendix 2.

The Centre for Interfirm Comparison Ltd, 8 West Stockwell Street, Colchester, Essex CO1 1HN; 0206 62274, and 25 Bloomsbury Square, London WC1A 2PJ; 01-637 8406. This is a non-profit making organisation, established in 1959 by the British Institute of Management and the British Productivity Council to meet the need for a neutral, expert body to conduct interfirm comparisons on a confidential basis, and to help managers to improve business performance. Participating firms feed a range of information into the centre, who in turn provide yardsticks against which they can compare systematically the performance of every important aspect of their business with other, similar firms. Together with the yardstick ratios come written reports on the findings and ideas for action, but only, of course, to the participating firms, and even then only on a 'comparative' basis so that no one company's data can ever be identified.

The uniqueness of this method rests in part on the data itself which goes far beyond anything supplied in companies' annual returns to Companies House or production monitor figures. Thousands of companies, large and small, have participated, and comparisons are made in over 100 industries, trades, services and professions both in the UK and abroad.

The centre publishes a number of free booklets that explain their activities, the ratios they use and why, and, more importantly, how you can use them to improve performance.

Credit Ratings Ltd, 51 City Road, London EC1Y 1AY; 01-251 6675. This company provides an ad hoc subscription service credit report. The cost varies from £15 to £12 for each report, which can normally be provided within 24 hours. Each credit report provides a company profile, financial performance figures for the past two years, and eight credit ratios (including an estimate of how long they normally take to pay their bills). These ratios are then compared with the average for that industry, and are followed by a short commentary bringing important factors to the reader's attention.

Companies Registration Office keeps records of all limited companies. For England and Wales these records are kept at Companies House, 55 City Road, London EC1; 01-253 9393, and for Scotland at the Registrar of Companies for Scotland, 102 George Street, Edinburgh EH2 3JD. For Northern Ireland the same service is available from the Department of Commerce, 437 Chichester Street, Belfast BT1 4PJ; 0232 34121.

The records kept include financial statements, accounts, directors' names and addresses, shareholders, and changes of name and structure. The information is available on microfiche at £1 per company, and can be photocopied at 10p per sheet. This service is available to personal callers only. There are a number of commercial organisations who will obtain this information for you. Two such organisations are: The Company Search Centre, 1-3 Leonard Street, London EC2A 4AQ; 01-251 2566; and Extel, 37-45 Paul Street, London EC2A 4PB; 01-253 3400, telex 262687. The charges for this service are about £3 to £3.50 for a microfiche of each company, or for a photocopy of the report and accounts, around £8.

Extel Quoted Service cards are published each year by the Exchange Telegraph Co Ltd. Cards for each of the 3,000 UK companies quoted on the Stock Exchange contain the following information: name and business of the company together with details of subsidiaries and associates; the date on which the company was registered (formed), along with any change of name or status (eg, private to public); directors — their positions (chairman, managing director, etc) and their shareholdings, as well as the names of the company secretary, bankers, auditors and solicitors. Ten years' profit and loss accounts and at least three years' balance sheets are given, together with sources and applications of funds statements. The highest and lowest share prices over the ten year period are also given, as well as the chairman's latest statement on the company position.

A news card is published three or four times a year, giving details of dividends declared, board changes, acquisitions, liquidations, loans raised and other elements of operating information. A selection of these cards is held in many reference libraries. Individual cards can be bought for £1.95 from Extel Statistical Services Ltd at the above address or from the Manchester Office; 061-236 5802.

Extel Unquoted Service provides a similar service for some 2,000 ordinary companies. These cards cost £5.85 each, as considerably more work has to be done to get at this information, and the call for it is less.

Financial Times Index, introduced in 1981, provides a monthly and yearly index to the references to some 35,000 companies. Instead of thumbing through back issues, you can locate the abstract of each story by using the corporate index, the general index covering products and industries, or the personality section covering key people. This series costs £240 per annum, and is available from Financial Times Information Ltd, Minster House, Arthur Street, London EC4R 9AX. The index is also available on microfiche, floppy disc and magnetic tape.

ICC Business Ratios produce 150 business sector reports analysing the performance of some 12,000 leading UK companies over a three-year period. For each sector (for example, window maufacturers, retail chemists, the toy industry or computer equipment) key performance ratios are shown for each company in the sector and an average for the sector as a whole. You can therefore use this information to compare your performance, actual or projected, against an industry standard. There are 19 key ratios, and they cover profitability, liquidity, asset utilisation, gearing, productivity and exports. Growth rates are monitored, including sales, total assets, capital employed, average wages and exports. It is thus possible to see quickly which company is growing the fastest in your sector, and to compare your growth against the best, the worst or the average. Reports are priced at about £100 each, and further details are available from The Business Ratio Manager, ICC Business Ratios, 23 City Road, London EC1Y 1AA; 01-638 2946.

Jordan's Business Information Service, Jordan House, 47 Brunswick Place, London N1 6EE; 01-253 3030. They also have offices in Bristol, Cardiff, Edinburgh and the Isle of Man. The Company Search Department can get you information on any UK company in Companies House, and their rapid reply service can guarantee despatch within a few hours. Alternatively, if you really are in a hurry, they have a telex and telephone service. They also produce a range of annual business surveys covering some 80 industries, priced between £8 and £85.

Jordan's new companies service could be particularly useful for a small company looking for sales leads. Over 5,000 new companies are incorporated each month, and Jordans report on about half. They eliminate the companies with convenience directors and registered offices (each of which offers no contact point), leaving several thousand 'genuine' new potential customers each month. Naturally, these companies could be anywhere in the UK, so in order to make the service more useful to small businesses, they produce a county-by-county service, with London split into eight. These selected services cost from £60 to £600 per annum. The whole UK service could cost around £4,000, and London alone around £2,000. At just over 13p a 'lead', this could prove a cost-effective way to expand sales.

Questions

1. What are the two fundamental objectives that every business has in common?

2. Look back to the example of factors that can affect the return on capital employed on page 47. Assume that the gross profit will remain at a constant £50,000, whatever changes you decide to make. Recommend four changes that would increase ROCE.

3. What yardsticks could you use to measure your business's performance?

4. High Note's sales figures for the first three years have been confirmed as £100,000, £130,000 and £160,000 respectively. You also know that the consumer index for each year was 106, 124 and 140. Calculate the unadjusted sales growth ratios. Compare them with the ratios you get once you have accounted for inflation.

Chapter 5
Measures of Profitability

There are two main ways to measure a business's profitability. They are both important, but they reveal different things about the performance and perhaps even the strategy of the business. To know and understand what is happening you need information in both areas: return on capital employed and profit margins.

Return on capital employed (ROCE)

The financial resources employed in a business are called capital. We have already seen that capital can come into a business from a number of different sources. These sources have one thing in common: they all want a return — a percentage interest — on the money they invest.

There are a number of ways in which return on capital can be measured, but for a small business two are particularly important.

The ROCE ratio is calculated by expressing the profit before long-term loan interest and tax as a proportion of the total capital employed. So if you look at the High Note Profit and Loss Account on page 63 you can see that for year 1, the profit before tax is £14,850. To this we have to add the loan interest of £1,250. If we did not do this we would be double counting our cost of loan capital by expecting a return on a loan which had already paid interest. This makes the profit figure £16,100. We also ignore tax charges, not because they are unimportant or insignificant, but simply because the level of tax is largely outside the control of the business, and it is the business's performance we are trying to measure.

Now look at the balance sheet. The capital employed is the sum of the owner's capital, the profit retained and the long-term loan, in this case £28,910 (£10,000 + £8,910 + £10,000). So the ROCE ratio for the first year is:

$\dfrac{£16,100}{£28,910} = 0.56$ which expressed as a percentage = 56%

The great strength of this ratio lies in the overall view it takes of the financial health of the whole business. If you look at the same ratio for the second year, you will see a small change. The ratio gives no clue as to why this has happened — it simply provides the starting point for an analysis of business performance, and an overall yardstick with which to compare absolute performance.

A banker might look to this ratio to see if the business could support more long-term borrowing (not in isolation, of course).

RETURN ON SHAREHOLDERS' CAPITAL (ROSC)
The second way a small business would calculate a return on capital, is by looking at the profit available for shareholders. This is not the money actually paid out, for example, as dividends, but is a measure of the increase in 'worth' of the funds invested by shareholders.

In this case the net profit after tax is divided by the owner's capital plus the retained profits (these, although not distributed, belong to the shareholders).

So in our example this would be the sum:

$$\frac{£\ 8,910}{£18,910} = 0.47 \text{ which expressed as a percentage} = 47\%$$

And for the second year this ratio would be 41 per cent.

If someone was considering investing in shares in this business, then this ratio would be of particular interest to them.

Once again the difference in the ratios is clear, but the reasons are not. This is only the starting point for a more detailed analysis.

Gearing and its effect on ROSC

All businesses have access to two fundamentally different sorts of money. Equity, or owner's capital, including retained earnings, is money that is not a risk to the business. If no profits are made then the owner and other shareholders simply do not get dividends. They may not be pleased, but they cannot usually sue.*

Debt capital is money borrowed by the business from outside sources; it puts the business at financial risk and is also risky for

* See preference shares, page 210.

the lenders. In return for taking that risk they expect an interest payment every year, irrespective of the performance of the business.

High gearing is the name given when a business has a high proportion of outside money to inside money. High gearing has considerable attractions to a business that wants to make high returns on shareholders' capital, as the example below shows.

The effect of gearing on ROSC

	No Gearing	Average Gearing	High Gearing	Very High Gearing
	–	1:1	2:1	3:1
Capital Structure	£	£	£	£
Share Capital	60,000	30,000	20,000	15,000
Loan Capital (at 12%)	–	30,000	40,000	45,000
Total Capital	60,000	60,000	60,000	60,000
Profits				
Operating Profit	10,000	10,000	10,000	10,000
Less Interest on Loan	None	3,600	4,800	5,400
Net Profit	10,000	6,400	5,200	4,600
Return on Share Capital $=$	$\frac{10,000}{60,000}$	$\frac{6,400}{30,000}$	$\frac{5,200}{20,000}$	$\frac{4,600}{15,000}$
$=$	16.6%	21.3%	26%	30.7%
Times Interest Earned $=$	N/A	$\frac{10,000}{3,600}$	$\frac{10,000}{4,800}$	$\frac{10,000}{5,400}$
$=$	N/A	2.8X	2.1X	1.8X

In this example the business is assumed to need £60,000 capital to generate £10,000 operating profits. Four different capital structures are considered. They range from all share capital (no gearing) at one end, to nearly all loan capital at the other. The loan capital has to be 'serviced', that is, interest of 12 per cent has to be paid. The loan itself can be relatively indefinite, simply being replaced by another one at market interest rates when the first loan expires.

Following the tables through, you can see that ROSC grows from 16.6 to 30.7 per cent by virtue of the changed gearing. If the interest on the loan were lower, the ROSC would be even more improved by high gearing, and the higher the interest the lower the relative improvement in ROSC. So in times of low interest, businesses tend to go for increased borrowings rather than raising more equity, that is money from shareholders.

At first sight this looks like a perpetual profit growth machine. Naturally owners would rather have someone else 'lend' them the money for their business than put it in themselves, if they could increase the return on their investment. The problem comes if the business does not produce £10,000 operating profits. Very often, in a small business, a drop in sales of 20 per cent means profits are halved. If profits were halved in this example, it could not meet the interest payments on its loan. That would make the business insolvent, and so not in a 'sound financial position', in other words, failing to meet one of the two primary business objectives.

Bankers tend to favour 1:1 gearing as the maximum for a small business, although they have been known to go much higher. (A glance at the Laker accounts will show just how far the equation can be taken, with £200 million plus of loans to a £1 million or so equity.)

As well as looking at the gearing, lenders will study the business's capacity to pay interest. They do this by using another ratio called 'times interest earned'.

This is calculated by dividing the operating profit by the loan interest. It shows how many times the loan interest is covered, and gives the lender some idea of the safety margin. The ratio for this example is given at the end of the tables on page 60. Once again rules are hard to make, but much less than 3X interest earned is unlikely to give lenders confidence.

Profit margins

Any analysis of a business must consider the current level of sales activity. If you look at High Note's P and L Accounts (page 63), you will see that materials consumed in sales have jumped from £30,000 to £43,000, a rise of 43 per cent. However, a quick look at the change in sales activity will show that the situation is nothing like so dramatic. Materials as a proportion of sales have risen from 30 to 33 per cent (30,000/100,000 = 30% and 43,000/130,000 = 33%). Obviously the more you sell the more you must make.

To understand why there have been changes in the level of return on capital employed, we have to relate both profit and capital to sales activity. The ROCE equation can be expanded to look like this:

$$\frac{\text{Profit}}{\text{Capital}} = \frac{\text{Profit}}{\text{Sales}} \times \frac{\text{Sales}}{\text{Capital}}$$

61

This gives us two separate strands to examine, the profit strand and the capital strand. The first of these is usually called profit margins. The capital strand will be looked at in the next two chapters.

When we examine profit margins, all costs, expenses and the different types of profit are expressed as a percentage of sales. This ratio makes comparisons both possible and realistic.

An analysis of High Note's Profit and Loss Account will show the following changes:

Area	Change	Some possible causes
Material Cost of Sales	Up from 30% to 33%	(a) Higher prices paid (b) Change in product mix (c) Increased waste
Labour Cost of Sales	Down from 20% to 19%	(a) Reduction in wage rates (b) Increase in work rate (c) Change in product mix
Gross Profit	Down from 50% to 48%	(a) 3 per cent increase in materials (b) 1 per cent increase in labour = net 2 per cent decline in gross margin
Operating or Trading Profit	Up to 18.5% from 17%	A 3½ per cent improvement in expense ratios offset by a 2 per cent decline in gross margin = net 1½ per cent improvement in trading profit.
Net Profit before Tax	Up to 16.8% from 14.8%	Interest charges down from 2.1 per cent of sales to 1.6 per cent. Means another ½ per cent increase in net profit + 1½ per cent net increase in trading profit = 2 per cent.

Had we simply looked at the net profit margin, we would have seen a satisfactory increase, from 8.9 to 10.1 per cent. It was only by looking at each area in turn, the components of gross profit, operating or trading profit and net profit, that a useful analysis can be made. High Note's owner now has a small number of specific questions to ask in the search for reasons for changes in performance.

To summarise, the ratios of profitability that allow attention to be focused on specific areas are:

GROSS PROFIT PERCENTAGE
This is deducting the cost of sales from the sales, and expressing

the result as a percentage of sales.

In the High Note example for year 1 this is £100,000 (Sales) – £50,000 (Cost of Sales) = £50,000 (Gross Profit); then £50,000 (Gross Profit) ÷ £100,000 (Sales) = 50 per cent.

This ratio gives an indication of relative manufacturing efficiency.

OPERATING OR TRADING PROFIT PERCENTAGE
This is calculated by deducting expenses from the gross profit, to arrive at the operating profit. This figure is then divided by sales and expressed as a percentage. For High Note in year 1, this is £50,000 (Gross Profit) – £33,000 (Expenses) = £17,000 (Operating Profit); then £17,000 (Operating Profit) ÷ £100,000 (Sales) = 17 per cent.

NET PROFIT BEFORE TAX PERCENTAGE
In this case finance charges are deducted from operating profits to arrive at net profit before tax. This is then expressed as a percentage of sales.

For High Note, in year 1, this is £17,000 (Trading Profit) – £2,150 (Interest Charge) = £14,850 (Net Profit before Tax) = 14.85 per cent.

High Note's Financial Statements
Profit and Loss Account for Years 1 and 2

	£	£	%	£	£	%
Sales		100,000	100		130,000	100
Cost of Sales						
Materials	30,000		30	43,000		33
Labour	20,000	50,000	20	25,000	68,000	19
Gross Profit		50,000	50		62.000	48
Expenses						
Rent, Rates etc	18,000			20,000		
Wages	12,000			13,000		
Advertising	3,000			3,000		
Expenses	–	33,000		2,000	38,000	
Operating or Trading Profit		17,000	17		24,000	18.5
Deduct Interest on:						
Overdraft	900					
Loan	1,250	2,150		1,250	2,050	
Net Profit before Tax		14,850	14.8		21,950	16.8
Tax Paid		5,940			8,750	
Net Profit after Tax		8,910	8.9		13,200	10.1

Balance Sheet for Year Ends 1 and 2

Fixed Assets	£	£	£	£	£	£
Furniture and Fixtures			12,500			28,110
Working Capital						
Current Assets						
Stock	10,000			12,000		
Debtors	13,000			13,000		
Cash	100	23,100		500	25,500	
Less Current Liabilities						
Overdraft	5,000			6,000		
Creditors	1,690	6,690		5,500	11,500	
Net Current Assets			16,410			14,000
Capital Employed			28,910			42,110
Financed by						
Owner's Capital	10,000			18,910		
Profit Retained	8,910		18,910	13,200		32,110
Long-term Loan			10,000			10,000
Total			28,910			42,110

Taxation

The more successful a small business is, the greater its exposure to tax liabilities. Its exact tax position will depend on the legal nature of the business. A limited company will be subject to corporation tax, and while profits are less than £100,000 the tax rate is 38 per cent. Once profits exceed £500,000 the full rate of 52 per cent corporation tax applies. This means that a business could retain only 48p in every pound of profit earned. If the business is not a limited company its proprietor will be subject to income tax under Schedule D Case I or II and subject to rates between 30 and 75 per cent.

It follows that simply monitoring pre-tax ratios, which in themselves are satisfactory measures of trading performance only, is not enough. The owner/manager is concerned with the net profit after tax. This, after all, is the money available to help the business to grow, or to meet unforeseen problems.

Managing the tax position is one area where timely professional advice is essential. This is made even more important because tax rules change with each year's Finance Act (the Act that ratifies the Budget). Good advice can both help to reduce the overall tax bill and so increase the 'worth' of profits to the business, and it can help improve cash flow by influencing the timing of tax payments. The examples below of Business A and Business B will serve to highlight the importance of this area.

TAX AND CASH FLOW

Deciding when your business started trading is rarely a clear-cut decision. Often business expenses were incurred months and even years before the first cash came in. Left to their own devices, most people prepare their first accounts for a 12-month period, based either on the calendar or tax year. They mistakenly think that administrative tidiness or convenience are the only factors to consider. That is not so. There is an opportunity to influence the timing of cash flow in the business's favour. This sort of advantage can often mean the difference between success and failure in the first year. Look at the two cases below.

Business A decides on 31 March 1983 as the end of its first financial year. Half of the tax on the profits is due on 1 January 1984 and the balance on 1 July 1984, so tax is paid an average of 12 months after the profits have been made. (31 March 1983 to 1 January 1984 = 9 months; 31 March 1983 to 1 July 1984 = 15 months; (9 + 15) ÷ 2 = 12 months.)

Business B, however, decides to have 30 April 1983 as the end of its first financial year, as this is now after the end of the Inland Revenue's tax year, which ended on 5 April 1983, so tax is not due until 1985. Half is paid on 1 January 1985 and the balance on 1 July 1985. This means an average of 23 months elapses before tax is paid, giving an *extra 11 months' interest-free credit.*

This cash flow benefit is created by the simple expedient of choosing the best first year end for a particular business.

This example is something of an over-simplification and other factors will come into play. It will not, for example, apply to new limited companies who all have to pay tax a flat nine months after their year end, whatever that date is, but it does serve to illustrate the potential benefits to be gained by using professional advice.

REDUCING THE TAX BILL

Clearly, no business plans to make losses long term but tax losses can be attractive under certain circumstances. A tax loss can occur when trading profits are 'spent' before the end of the year in question. The key question is what to spend the profits on. Obviously, whatever is bought must be of benefit to the business and the owners. The example below assumes that the owner's marginal tax rate is 40 per cent. (That is the tax band that the next sum of future income will be taxed at.)

Business A makes a trading profit of £7,500 which is declared, and tax of £3,000 is paid to the Inland Revenue. The business-man retains £4,500 of the valuable resource 'cash' (£7,500 – £3,000).

Business B also makes a trading profit of £7,500, but before the year end the owner makes the following purchases:

(a) £1,300 into an approved self-employed pension scheme.
(b) A small microcomputer which costs £5,000 and will reduce dependence on an outside bureau.

Taxable profits then become £7,500 – (£1,300 + £5,000) = £1,200. Tax paid on this will be £480, leaving £720 cash.

So Business B ends up having desirable assets of 'cash' (£720), a pension (£1,300) and a computer (£5,000); a total of £7,020. Business B has £2,520s' worth of assets more than Business A at the year end (£7,020 – £4,500). This has been provided by Business B paying £2,520 less tax than Business A. These are only two examples of how wrong tax decisions can be made.

The Hambro Tax Guide, produced each year, provides a clear, comprehensive and up-to-date coverage of the business tax field.

Question

1. From the Parkwood accounts set out opposite calculate the following ratios for each year.

(a) Return on total capital employed;
(b) Return on shareholders' capital (after tax);
(c) Gearing;
(d) Times interest earned;
(e) Gross profit;
(f) Operating profit;
(g) Net profit after tax.

Parkwood & Co
Balance Sheet at 20 January 1983 and 1984 respectively

	1983		1984
	£	£	£	£
Fixed Assets		18,670		30,170
Working Capital				
Current Assets				
Stock	9,920		14,650	
Debtors	24,730		38,800	
Cash	4,340		750	
	38,990		54,200	
Less Current Liabilities				
Bank Overdraft	5,000		6,000	
Creditors	24,000		29,140	
Tax	2,960		4,500	
	31,960		39,640	
Net Current Assets		7,030		14,560
Total Assets		25,700		44,730
Financed by				
Share Capital		10,000		10,000
Retained Earnings		5,700		16,730
Long-term loan		10,000		18,000
(at 12%)		25,700		44,730

Profit and Loss Account

	1983	1984
	£	£
Sales	249,340	336,030
Cost of Goods Sold	209,450	280,580
Gross Profit	39,890	55,450
Expenses		
Sales and Marketing	10,000	15,000
Administration	10,000	20,000
General	6,668	2,760
Total Expenses	26,668	37,760
Operating Profit	13,222	17,690
Loan Interest	1,200	2,160
Net Profit before Tax	12,022	15,530
Tax due on profits	4,809	4,500
Net Profit after Tax	7,213	11,030

Chapter 6

Control of Working Capital (or Liquidity)

The capital strand of the return on capital employed (ROCE) calculation has two main branches of its own.

$$\frac{\text{Sales}}{\text{Capital}} \; (\text{ROCE}) = \frac{\text{Sales}}{\text{Fixed Assets and Working Capital}}$$

The more dynamic of these is working capital, the day-to-day money used to finance the working of the business. It is important to monitor the relationship between sales and the various elements of working capital, to see how efficiently that capital is being used. But as the working capital is the difference between current assets and current liabilities, it is also important to monitor their relationship, both in total and in their component parts.

This area is very often referred to as liquidity, or the business's ability to meet its current liabilities as they fall due. The most important ratios in this area are:

The current ratio

A business's ability to meet its immediate liabilities can be estimated by relating its current assets to current liabilities. If for any reason current liabilities cannot be met, then the business is being exposed to an unnecessary level of financial risk. Suppliers may stop supplying or could even petition for bankruptcy if they are kept waiting too long for payments.

In our accounts for High Note (on page 64), the first year's picture on the Balance Sheet shows £23,100 current assets to £6,690 current liabilities.

$$\text{The Current Ratio} = \frac{\text{Current Assets}}{\text{Current Liabilities}}$$

$$\text{Therefore High Note's current ratio} = \frac{23,100}{6,690} = 3.4$$

This shows current liabilities to be covered 3.4 times, and the ratio is usually expressed in the form 3.4:1.

In the second year this has come down to 2.2:1.

At first glance this figure may look worse than the first year's position. Certainly current liabilities have grown faster than current assets, but up to a point this is a desirable state of affairs, because it means the business is having to find less money to finance working capital.

There is really only one rule about how high (or low) the current ratio should be. It should be as close to 1:1 as the safe conduct of the business will allow. This will not be the same for every type of business.

A shop buying in finished goods on credit and selling them for cash could run safely at 1.3:1. A manufacturer, with raw material to store and customers to finance, may need over 2:1. This is because the period between paying cash out for raw materials and receiving cash in from customers is longer in a manufacturing business than in a retail business.

It is a bit like the oil dip-stick on a car. There is a band within which the oil level should be. Levels above or below that band pose different problems. So for most businesses, less than 1.2:1 would probably be cutting things a bit fine. Over 1.8:1 would mean too much cash was being tied up in such items as stocks and debtors.

An unnecessarily high amount of working capital makes it harder for a business to make a good ROCE because it makes the bottom half of the sum bigger.* Too low a working capital, below 1:1 for example, exposes the business to unacceptable financial risks, eg, foreclosure by banks or creditors.

The quick ratio or acid test

The quick ratio is really a belt and braces figure. In this, only assets that can be realised quickly, such as debtors and cash in hand, are related to current liabilities.

$$\text{The Quick Ratio} = \frac{\text{Debtors} + \text{Cash}}{\text{Current Liabilities}}$$

For our example, looking at year one only, we would exclude

---

* Remember ROCE = Profit ÷ Total Capital Employed, and Total Capital = Fixed Assets + Working Capital.

the £10,000 stock because, before it can be realised, we would need to find customers to sell to and collect in the cash. All this might take several months. High Note's quick ratio would be 13,100 (cash + debtors) ÷ 6,690 (current liabilities): a perhaps too respectable 1.9:1. In the second year this has dropped to 1.2:1 (13,500 ÷ 11,500).

Once again general rules are very difficult to make, but a ratio of 0.8:1 would be acceptable for most types of business.

Credit control

Any small business selling on credit knows just how quickly customers can eat into their cash. This is particularly true if the customers are big companies. Surprisingly enough bad debts (those which are never paid) are rarely as serious a problem as slow payers. Many companies think nothing of taking three months' credit, and it is important to remember that even if your terms are 30 days it will be nearer 45 days *on average* before you are paid. This to some extent depends on how frequently invoices are sent out. Assuming they do not go out each day — and perhaps more importantly, your customer *does* batch his bills for payment monthly — then that is how things will work out.

There are two techniques for monitoring debtors. The first is to prepare a schedule by 'age' of debtor. The table below gives some idea of how this might be done.

High Note's Debtors Schedule — End of Year 1

	2 months (or less) £	3 months £	4 months £	Over 4 months £	Total £
Brown & Co	1,000				
Jenkins & Son	1,000				
Andersons		3,000			
Smithers		2,500			
Thomkinsons			500		
Henry's			2,500		
Smart Inc				2,500	
	2,000	5,500	3,000	2,500	13,000

This method has the great merit of focusing attention clearly on specific problem accounts. It may seem like hard work, but once you have got the system going it will pay dividends.

The second technique for monitoring debtors is using the ratio *average collection period*.

This ratio is calculated by expressing debtors as a proportion of credit sales, and then relating that to the days in the period in question.

$$\text{Average Collection Period} = \frac{\text{Debtors}}{\text{Sales}} \times 365$$

Let us suppose that all High Note's sales are on credit and the periods in question are both 365-day years (ie, no leap years). Then in year 1 the average collection period would be:

$$\frac{£13,000 \text{ Debtors}}{£100,000 \text{ Sales}} \times 365 \text{ (days in period)} = 47 \text{ days}$$

In year 2 the average collection period is:

$$\frac{£13,000 \text{ Debtors}}{£130,000 \text{ Sales}} \times 365 \text{ (days in period)} = 36 \text{ days}$$

So in the second year High Note are collecting their cash from debtors 11 days sooner than in the first year. This is obviously a better position to be in, making their relative amount of debtors lower than in year 1. It is not making the absolute amount of debtors lower, and this illustrates another great strength of using ratios to monitor performance. High Note's sales have grown by 30 per cent from £100,000 to £130,000, and their debtors have remained at £13,000.

At first glance then, their debtors are the same, neither better nor worse. But when you relate those debtors to the increased levels of sales, as this ratio does, then you can see that the position has improved.

This is a good control ratio, which has the great merit of being quickly translatable into a figure any businessman can understand, showing how much it is costing to give credit.

If, for example, High Note is paying 12 per cent for an overdraft, then giving £13,000 credit for 36 days will cost £153.86 $\frac{(12\% \times £13,000 \times 36)}{365}$.

AVERAGE DAYS' CREDIT TAKEN

Of course the credit world is not all one sided. Once a small business has established itself, it too will be taking credit. You can usually rely on your suppliers to keep you informed on your indebtedness — but only on an individual basis. It would be prudent to calculate how many days' credit, on average, are being taken from suppliers: a very similar sum to average collection period. The ratio is as follows:

$$\text{Average Collection Period} = \frac{\text{Creditors}}{\text{Purchases}} \times 365$$

For High Note, in year 1, this sum would be:

$$\frac{£ \ 1,690 \ \text{Creditors}}{*£30,000 \ \text{Purchases}} \times 365 \text{ (days in period)} = 21 \text{ days}$$

In year 2 this ratio would be:

$$\frac{£ \ 5,500 \ \text{Creditors}}{£43,000 \ \text{Purchases}} \times 365 \text{ (days in period)} = 47 \text{ days}$$

The difference in these two ratios probably reflect High Note's greater creditworthiness in year 2. The longer the credit period you can take from your suppliers the better, provided that you still meet their terms of trade. They may, however, put you to the bottom of the list when supplies get scarce, or give you up altogether when they find a 'better' customer.

MORE CREDITOR CONTROLS
There are two other useful techniques to help the owner manager keep track of these events. One is simply to relate days' credit given to days' credit taken. If they balance out then you are about even in the credit game.

In year 1, High Note gave 47 days' credit to their customers and took only 21 days from their suppliers, so they were a loser. In the second year they got ahead, giving only 36 days while taking 47.

The other technique is to 'age' your creditors in exactly the same way as the debtors (see page 70). In this way it is possible to see at a glance which suppliers have been owed what sums of money, and for how long.

Stock control

Any manufacturing, subcontracting or assembling business will have to buy in raw materials and work on them to produce

---

* In this example it is assumed that all materials have been purchased in the period in question.

finished goods. They will have to keep track of three sorts of stock: raw materials, work in progress, and finished goods.

A retailing business will probably only be concerned with finished goods, and a service business may have no stocks at all.

If we assume that all High Note's stock is in finished goods, then the control ratio we can use is as follows:

$$\text{Days' finished goods stock} = \frac{\text{Finished Goods Stock}}{\text{Cost of Sales*}} \times \text{Days in period}$$

For High Note in year 1 this would be:

$$\frac{10,000}{50,000} \times 365 = 73 \text{ days}$$

In year 2 the ratio would be 64 days.

It is impossible to make any general rules about stock levels. Obviously, a business has to carry enough stock to meet customers' demand, and a retail business must have it on display or on hand. However, if High Note's supplier can always deliver within 14 days it would be unnecessary to carry 73 days' stock.

The same basic equation can be applied to both raw material and work-in-progress stock, but to reach raw material stock you should substitute raw materials consumed for cost of sales. Once again the strength of this ratio is that a business can quickly calculate how much it is costing to carry a given level of stock, in just the same way as customer credit costs were calculated earlier.

Cash control

The residual element in the control of working capital is cash, or if there is no cash left, the size of overdraft needed in a particular period.

Usually the amount of cash available to a small business is finite and specific, also the size of overdraft it can take, so stock levels, creditor and debtor policies, and other working capital elements are decided with these limits in mind. This information

---

* Cost of sales is used because it accurately reflects the amount of stock. The sales figure includes other items such as a profit margin. If you are looking at an external company it is probable that the only figure available will be that for sales. In this case it can be used as an approximation.

is assembled in the cash flow forecast, which was examined in greater detail in Chapter 3.

Circulation of working capital

The primary ratio for controlling working capital is usually considered to be the current ratio. This, however, is of more interest to outside bodies, such as bankers and suppliers wanting to see how safe their money is. The manager of a business is more interested in how well the money tied up in working capital is being used.

Look at High Note's Balance Sheets for the last two years. You can see that net current assets, another name for working capital, have shrunk from £16,410 to £14,000. Not too dramatic. Now let us look at these figures in relation to the level of business activity in each year.

$$\text{Circulation of working capital} = \frac{\text{Sales}}{\text{Working Capital}}$$

For year 1 this is $\frac{100,000}{16,410} = 6X$, and year 2 $\frac{130,000}{14,000} = 9X$.

The X is shorthand for 'times' — a convention when using this ratio.

So we can see that not only has High Note got less money tied up in working capital in the second year, it has also used it more efficiently. In other words, it has circulated it faster. Each pound of working capital now produces £9 of sales, as opposed to only £6 last year. And as each pound of sales makes profit, the higher the sales the higher the profit.

Averaging ratios

Ratios which involve the use of stock, debtors or creditors can be more accurately calculated by using the average of the opening and closing position. Seasonal factors or sales growth (contraction) will almost always make a single figure unrepresentative.

Look back to the High Note accounts on page 63. Here you can see an example where sales have grown by 30 per cent from £100,000 in the first year to £130,000 in the second. Obviously, neither the opening stock figure of £10,000, nor the closing stock of £12,000, is truly representative of what has happened in the intervening year. It seems much more likely that the average of the opening and closing stock figures is the best figure to use in calculating the stock control ratios shown on page 73. So in this example, £11,000 (10,000 + 12,000 ÷ 2) would be the figure to use.

Questions

1. What do you understand by the term 'overtrading'?

2. Using the Parkwood accounts on page 67, calculate these ratios for both years.
   (a) The current ratio;
   (b) The quick ratio;
   (c) The average collection period (assuming all sales are on credit);
   (d) Average days' stock held (assuming all stock is finished goods);
   (e) Circulation of working capital.

3. Comment on the key changes in the ratios.

Chapter 7
Controlling Fixed Assets

A major problem that all new or expanding businesses face is exactly how much to have, of such items as equipment, storage capacity and work space. New 'fixed assets' tend to be acquired in large chunks and are sometimes more opportunistic than market related in nature.

In any event, however, and for whatever reason acquired, once in the business it is important to make sure the asset is being effectively used. Controlling fixed assets splits down into two areas: looking at how effectively existing fixed assets are being used, and how to plan for new capital investments.

The fixed asset pyramid

Generally, the best way to measure how well existing fixed assets are being used is to see how many pounds' worth of sales each pound of fixed assets is generating.

The overall ratio is that of Sales ÷ Fixed Assets which gives a measure of this use of the fixed assets.

Look back to the High Note accounts on page 63. The use of fixed asset ratio in that example is:

$$\text{Year 1} \quad \frac{100,000}{12,500} = 8\text{X}.^* \qquad\qquad \text{Year 2} \quad \frac{130,000}{28,110} = 4.6\text{X}.$$

This means that each pound invested in fixed assets has generated £8s' worth of sales in year 1 and only £4.60 in year 2.

This 'inefficient' use of fixed assets has consumed all the benefit High Note gained from its improved use of working capital — and a little more. In fact this is the main reason why the return on capital employed (ROCE) has declined in year 2. This may be a short-term problem which will be cured when expected new sales levels are reached: not at all unusual if, for

---

* X is a convention for times.

example, a new piece of machinery was bought late in the second year.

Providing the rules outlined later in this chapter on planning capital investments are followed, this problem will correct itself. Otherwise a more detailed analysis may be needed.

Looking at the overall fixed asset picture is rather like looking at the circulation of working capital ratio only as a means of monitoring working capital. There we looked at stock control, debtors and creditors as well. Fixed assets use is looked at both in total and in its component parts. A pyramid of ratios stretches out below this prime ratio.

The fixed asset pyramid will look something like this, although the nature of the assets of a particular business may suggest others be included.

The Fixed Asset Pyramid

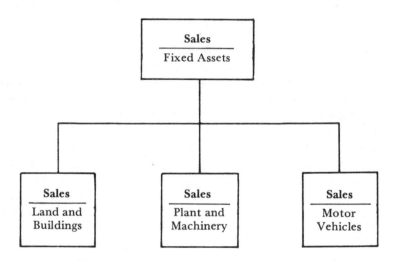

For example, a shop will also be interested in sales per square foot of selling space.

MORE DETAIL STILL

More sophisticated businesses also monitor the output of individual pieces of equipment. They look at 'down time' (how long the equipment is out of commission), repair and maintenance costs, and the value of its output. If your business warrants it you can do this by simply expanding the pyramid as follows:

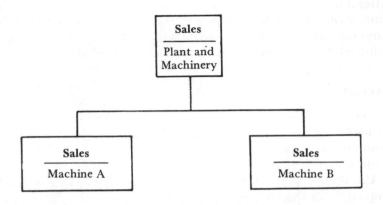

Planning new capital investment

Most businesses discover quite early on that the equipment, machinery, space etc that they started up with is not adequate for their future needs. That does not necessarily make them bad businessmen; it just shows how difficult it is to predict the future shape of any business. Perhaps they prudently chose second-hand items, or they were extremely conservative in their sales forecasts, and now simply cannot meet the demand. In any event decisions have to be taken on new investments. Should existing equipment be replaced? Should more space be acquired?

If the answers to both these questions is yes, then decisions have to be made on which equipment or space should be chosen.

It is very rare that one piece of equipment is the only absolutely correct one for the job. Suppliers compete, and most products have significant differences. They may cost more, but last longer, or cost less, but be more expensive to run.

Work space in offices and shops also comes in different shapes, sizes and locations. All these capital decisions have two things in common. They usually involve (a) spending or committing a lump sum now, to get (b) a stream of benefits in the future.

Anyone buying a new piece of equipment expects it to be used to help make more products that will in turn produce cash and profits. The same argument is true if equipment is being replaced. The equipment that produces the best return should be chosen. But how will it be chosen? What tools are available to help make a sound financial choice?

Clearly it is important to try and get these decisions right. After all, these types of assets tend to be around for a long time. Also, their resale value declines rapidly in the early years. Anyone who has bought a new car will not need further emphasis on this point.

Average return on capital employed (ARCE)

We know that one of the two primary objectives of a business is to make a satisfactory return on the capital employed in the business. Clearly .any new capital investment will have to achieve that same objective.

Until now we have only looked at the return on capital employed for an individual year. This would not be enough to see if a new investment proposal was worthwhile. Imagine your own reaction if someone asked you for £1,000 and explained only how they could return £200 at the end of the first year. You would expect them to come up with a complete proposal, one that covered the return of all the money you had lent — plus interest.

The same is true of any capital investment proposal. We have 'lent' the project, whatever it may be, a sum of capital. We expect a return on that capital over the working life of the assets bought. The ARCE method sets out to do just that. It measures the average profit over the life of a project and compares that with the capital employed.

Let us take an example to illustrate the method. A company is considering buying a new lathe for £5,000. The working life of the lathe will be five years, by which time it will be worthless. Net profit from the output of the lathe will come in as follows:

The ARCE Method

Year	Net Profit (after charging 100% depreciation)*
	£
1	500
2	1,000
3	2,000
4	2,000
5	175
Total 5 years	5,675

* For further clarification on depreciation see page 206.

Over the five years the capital invested in the lathe will produce an average return of £1,135 (5,675 ÷ 5) each year. As the capital concerned is £5,000 and the average return is £1,135, then the average return on the capital employed is 22.7 per cent or (1,135 ÷ 5,000) x 100.

This figure is simple to calculate and is of some help. For example, if on average the business buying the lathe is making a return of 30 per cent on capital employed, then buying the lathe will dilute the ROCE of the business as a whole.

The table below shows what happens to ROCE when the present business and the new project are 'merged' together to form the new business.

Limitations of ARCE 1

Present Business	+		New Project	= New Business
		£	£	£
Average Net Profit	6,000		1,135	7,135
Capital Employed	20,000		5,000	25,000
ROCE	30%		22.7%	24.5%

While this information is of some use as a tool for helping with capital investment decisions generally, ARCE has two severe limitations.

Let us suppose that the company has decided to buy a lathe — but there are two on offer. The first we have already examined. Profits from this lathe will build up gradually over the years and tail off sharply in the final year. The second lathe has rather different characteristics. It swings into action immediately, achieves high profits and tails off over the last three years.

Limitations of ARCE 2

Year	Net Profit from 2nd Lathe (after charging 100 per cent depreciation)	1st Lathe Net Profit
	£	£
1	2,650	500
2	2,650	1,000
3	125	2,000
4	125	2,000
5	125	175
Totals 5 years	5,675	5,675

As the overall total profits are the same, over the five years this investment will also produce an ARCE of 22.7 per cent. And yet, if all other factors were equal and only the figures on these pages had to be considered, most businessmen would prefer the second lathe project. The reason they would give is that they get their profit in quicker. By the second year that lathe had paid for itself, while the first did not 'break even' until well into year 4.

This would be a 'gut reaction' and it would probably be right. That does not mean that 'gut reactions' are better than financial techniques; it just means we have got the wrong technique. We need a technique that takes account of when the money comes in — clearly timing matters.

This leads into average rate of return's other major failing. It uses profit as one of the measures, although a business may have to wait months and even years for that profit to be realised as cash.

The other measure it uses is the cash spent on a capital investment, so like is not being compared with like: profit on the top of the equation and cash on the bottom. Two projects could generate identical profits, but if one generated those profits in immediate cash, the ARCE technique would not recognise it. But a businessman's 'gut reaction' would once again choose the project that brought in the cash soonest. And once again he'd be right.

Payback period

A more popular technique for evaluating capital investment decisions is the payback period method.

Payback attempts to overcome the fundamental weaknesses of the ARCE method. It compares the cash cost of the initial investment with the annual net cash inflows (or savings) that are generated by the investment. This goes beyond simply calculating profit as shown in the Profit and Loss Account, which is governed by the realisation concept. The timing of the cash movements is calculated. That is, for example, when debtors will actually pay up, and when suppliers will have to be paid. By using cash in both elements it is comparing like with like.

Payback also attempts to deal with the timing issue by measuring the time taken for the initial cost to be recovered.

The following example will illustrate the method:

The Payback Method

	£
Initial cost of project	10,000
Annual net cash inflows	
Year 1	2,000
2	4,000
3	4,000
4	2,000
5	1,000

The payback period is three years. That is when the £10,000 initial cash cost has been matched by the annual net cash inflows of £2,000, £4,000 and £4,000 of the first three years. Now we have a method that uses cash and takes some account of time.

Unfortunately it leaves us with a result that is difficult to compare directly with the profit performance of the rest of the business. If the business is currently making a 25 per cent return on capital employed, and a project has a payback period of three years, will the project enhance or reduce overall profitability? Without further calculation this question cannot be answered — and even then the answer will not necessarily be correct. Look again at the preceding example. The payback method looks only at the period taken to repay the initial investment. The following years are completely ignored, and yet the net cash inflows in those years are a benefit to the business, and their size matters.

This weakness is brought sharply into focus when competing projects are being compared.

Let us suppose your task is to choose between Projects A and B purely on financial criteria.

Limitations of Payback

	Project A £	Project B £
Initial cost of project	10,000	10,000
Annual net cash inflows		
Year 1	2,000	2,000
2	4,000	4,000
3	4,000	4,000
4	500	4,000
5	250	2,000
6	250	1,000
Total cash inflow	11,000	17,000
Payback period	3 years	3 years

The payback period for each proposal is three years, which signals that each project is equally acceptable on financial grounds. Clearly this is nonsense. It seems highly probable that Project B, which generates an extra £6,000 cash, is a better bet.

Payback has some merits, not least of which is its simplicity. It is often used as a cut-off criterion in the first stages of an evaluation. In other words, a business decides that it will not look at any project with a payback period greater than, say, four years. This provides a common starting point from which a more exacting comparison can be made. Beyond that use the method's weaknesses make it a poor tool to use in investment decisions in a small business.

Big businesses do not expect to get all their capital investment decisions right. Small businesses have to, as their very survival depends on it.

Discounted cash flow

Neither the ARCE nor payback methods for evaluating capital investment projects are wholly satisfactory. They provide neither a sound technique for deciding whether or not to invest, nor a technique to help choose between competing projects. They fail for the reasons already described, but they also fail for a more fundamental reason.

The businessman's 'gut feeling' that timing is important is perhaps more true than he thinks. No one is going to invest a pound today, unless they expect to get back more than a pound at some future date. The level of that reward, if you like, is related in some way to the riskiness of the investment. But whatever the level of risk, no one wants less money back as that would involve making a loss.

The factor that alters the value of an investment over time is the interest rate. The longer the time period or the higher the interest rate the larger the final sum returned is. This relationship between the initial sum invested and the sum finally returned is familiarly known as compound interest.

The *compound interest equation* that calculates the precise figure for any interest rate or time period is:

$$\text{Future Value} = £P \times (1 + r)^n$$

In this equation P = the initial sum invested, or principal; r = the interest rate expressed in decimals, and n = the time period in years.

So if we invest £100 for three years at 10 per cent we can expect a future value of:

$$£100 \times (1 + 0.1)^3$$
$$= £100 \times (1.1)^3$$
$$= £100 \times (1.1 \times 1.1 \times 1.1)$$
$$= £100 \times 1.331$$
$$= £133.10.$$

For the doubters, the sum can be worked out in longhand.

Compound Interest Calculation

	Start	Year 1	Year 2	Year 3
	£	£	£	£
Balance brought forward	100.00	100.00	110.00	121.00
Interest at 10%	–	10.00	11.00	12.10
Value of investment	100.00	110.00	121.00	133.10
				Finish

You could consider the situation to be similar to looking through a telescope: looking forward in time through the compound interest equation magnifies the value of an investment.

But what happens when you look through the other end of a telescope? Images appear to shrink. To some extent this is similar to the problem a businessman faces when making up his mind about capital investment decisions. He knows he is not prepared to pay £1 now to get £1 back in the future. That would be bad business. What he has to calculate is exactly how much less than £1 he would pay to receive £1 back in, say, one year's time.

The thinking might go something like this. 'For this kind of investment I have to make 10 per cent profit, so I need to know what figure less 10 per cent will equal £1, and that is what I will pay now.' This is rather like moving to the other end of the telescope and looking backwards.

This problem is exactly the inverse of compounding and is called discounting. To calculate the appropriate discount factor we simply stand the compound interest equation on its head.

Discounting Calculations

$$\frac{1}{(1 + r)^n} = \frac{1}{(1 + 0.1)^1} = \frac{1}{1.1} = 0.909$$

So we would recommend that only £0.909 is paid today for £1 to be received in a year's time.

You can test the equation yourself by adding 10 per cent to £0.909. It should total £1.00.

Now we have an equation that lets us allow for the time value of money. (This is nothing whatever to do with the effects of inflation. Those effects are important and are covered later in this chapter.) Let us look at the ways to put the concept to use.

Present value

Just as the future value of an investment can be calculated using compounding, the present value of cash coming in during the years ahead can be calculated using discounting.

We have already seen the heart of the present value equation. In full, using the same symbols as for compound interest, it is:

Present Value Equation

$$\text{Present Value} = £P \times \frac{1}{(1 + r)^n}$$

The basic requirement of any present value calculation is that you have some idea of what percentage profit you want from an investment. That is not usually a very difficult problem. If you have to borrow the money at 12 per cent, pay tax on the profits and take risks as well, it is not too hard to focus on an acceptable range of interest rates.

Alternatively, the yardsticks of current returns, competitors' or industry returns, or even a personal objective, can all be used to help arrive at an acceptable cut-off interest rate for discounting. Below this cut-off rate, a project is simply not acceptable.

Look at the following example. The proposition is that you should invest £50,000 now to make £80,000 over the next five years: a clear profit of £30,000, apparently a satisfactory situation. The cash will come in and out as follows:

Cash Flow of Investment

Year	Cash out	Cash in	Net Cash Flow
	£	£	£
0	50,000	–	(50,000)
1	5,000	15,000	10,000
2	5,000	15,000	10,000
3	12,500	37,500	25,000
4	12,500	37,500	25,000
5	5,000	15,000	10,000
			30,000

This is based on a £50,000 investment now, followed by some cash expenses and cash income in the future. In other words, a typical business buying in materials, adding value and selling mainly on monthly terms. The fourth column shows the net cash flow for each year of the project's life. Cash in exceeds cash out by £30,000 – in other words the profit.

However, we know that the net cash flow received in future years is not worth as much as present pounds. Remember, no businessman will pay £1 now to receive only £1 back in the future. Our problem is to discount all the future cash flows back to present values, in exactly the same manner as we did on page 84.

Once again we could use our present value equation, but that would be rather time consuming. Fortunately there are tables that do all the sums for us, and this facility is becoming increasingly available on calculators. A set of these tables is shown on pages 100-103.

All we have to decide on now is a discount rate. Well, if we know we can have a risk-free investment of 12 per cent, it may not seem worthwhile taking a risk unless we can make 17 per cent, a modest enough figure for a risk project.

Using the discount tables we can select the appropriate year and interest rate, to arrive at the present value factor.

Present Value of Cash Flow of Investment

Year	Net Cash Flow	Present Value Factor at 17%	Net Present Value
	£		£
0	(50,000)	1.000	(50,000)
1	10,000	0.855	8,550
2	10,000	0.731	7,310
3	25,000	0.624	15,600
4	25,000	0.534	13,350
5	10,000	0.456	4,560
			(630)

Take the present value factor for each year and multiply it by the net cash flow. This gives the net present value of the cash that this investment generates. In this case it comes to £49,370 (8,550 + 7,310 + 15,600 + 13,350 + 4,560), which is £630 less than the £50,000 we put in. So if you had expected to make 17 per cent return on your investment, you would have been disappointed.

Interestingly enough both the ARCE and payback methods would probably have encouraged you to go ahead. ARCE would have come up with average profits of £16,000 per annum, which represents a 32 per cent return on capital employed, and the payback period is 3 years and 2½ months — not long at all. But the fatal flaw in both those methods is revealed clearly by the present value concept. The timing of the cash flow over the working life of the investment is crucial, and that must form the central part of any judgement on whether to invest or not.

The profitability index

Present value is clearly a superior capital investment appraisal method, overcoming the weaknesses of the other two techniques. But in its present form it only provides the answer to our first question. Should we invest or not? Having decided on the level of return (interest) we want, and calculated the net cash flow, we simply discount to arrive at the net present value. If this is greater than zero, then the project is acceptable.

Suppose, like our problem with the lathes, the question is not simply whether to invest or not, but also to choose between alternatives, then would the present value method work? This fairly extreme example will highlight the difficulty of using the present value method alone to solve both types of problem.

Comparing Projects using the Present Value Method

	Project A			Project B		
Year	Net Cash Flow	Present Value Factor at 10%	Net Present Value	Net Cash Flow	Present Value Factor at 10%	Net Present Value
	£		£	£		£
0	(7,646)	1.000	(7,646)	(95,720)	1.000	(95,720)
1	3,000	0.909	2,727	30,000	0.909	27,270
2	4,000	0.826	3,304	40,000	0.826	33,040
3	5,000	0.751	3,755	50,000	0.751	37,550
	Present Value		9,786	Present Value		97,860
	Net Present Value		2,140	Net Present Value		2,140

Here we have two possible projects to invest in. One calls for capital of £7,646 and the other for £95,720. Leaving aside the problem of finding the money, which is the better investment proposition? If we are happy with making a 10 per cent return on our investment, then both projects are acceptable. Both end up with a net present value of £2,140, so that cannot be the deciding factor. Yet it is clear that A is a better bet than B, simply because the relationship between the size of the investment and the present value of the cash flow is 'better'.

The way these elements are related is through the profitability index, which is set out below:

The Profitability Index

$$\text{Profitability Index} = \frac{\text{Present Value of Earnings}}{\text{Cost of Investment}}$$

In this example the index for Project A is 128 per cent (9,786 ÷ 7,646), and for B 102 per cent (97,860 ÷ 95,720). The profitability index clearly signals that Project A is the better choice

In fact, any comparison of projects that do not have identical initial investments and lifetimes can only be properly made using the profitability index.

To summarise then, the first step is to see if the various possible projects are acceptable by discounting their net cash flows at the cut-off interest rate. If a choice has to be made between the acceptable projects, calculate each one's profitability index, and then rank them as follows:

Project Ranking by Profitability Index

Project	Profitability Index
	%
A	135
B	127
C	117
D	104
E	101

It is not possible to have a profitability index lower than 100 per cent. That would imply a negative net present value, which in turn would eliminate the proposal at the first stage of the evaluation process.

Internal rate of return

One important piece of information has not been provided by either the net present value or the profitability index. A capital investment proposal may have a satisfactory net present value, that is a positive one, at our cut-off interest rate. It may also come out ahead of other choices in the profitability index ranking, but we still do not know exactly what rate of return we can expect to get.

This is important information for three main reasons. First, it allows us to compare new investment proposals with the rest of the business, something that neither present value nor the profitability index will do. Second, it gives us a yardstick understood by people outside the business. For example, bankers or other potential investors will understand a proposal for funds with a straightforward percentage as the end result. They will not be so sure of a figure such as £1,000 net present value. This could be misunderstood for the total profit, and be rejected. Finally, under most circumstances, the internal rate of return, as this is known, is a satisfactory method of comparing projects. (In any doubtful situations the profitability index will be the deciding factor.)

We do know, however, that the rate of return must be greater than the cut-off interest rate, provided, of course, that the net present value is positive.

This is how Project A's net present value was calculated in the profitability index example:

Calculating the Internal Rate of Return 1

Year	Net Cash Flow	Present Value Factor at 10%	Net Present Value
	£		£
0	(7,646)	1.000	(7,646)
1	3,000	0.909	2,727
2	4,000	0.826	3,304
3	5,000	0.751	3,755
		Present Value	9,786
		Net Present Value	2,140

We know that Project A is expected to make a rate of return higher than 10 per cent simply because the net present value is positive. If we increase the present value factor to, say 20 per cent by arbitrarily raising our cut-off level, we can see whether it meets that test.

Calculating the Internal Rate of Return 2

Year	Net Cash Flow	Present Value Factor at 20%	Net Present Value
	£		£
0	(7,646)	1.000	(7,646)
1	3,000	0.833	2,499
2	4,000	0.694	2,776
3	5,000	0.579	2,895
		Present Value	8,170
		Net Present Value	524

We can see that the project still shows a positive net present value at our new cut-off rate of 20 per cent. However, the figure is much smaller and suggests we are getting close to the 'internal rate of return'. That is the discount rate which, when applied to the net cash flow, results in a zero net present value. We could go on experimenting to reach that rate, but this would be time consuming, and not very rewarding, for reasons explained at the end of the chapter.

There is a simple technique known as interpolating, which we can use providing we have one positive and one negative net present value figure.

This is how interpolation works: let us select a discount rate that we are reasonably certain will lead to a negative net present value, for example 25 per cent.

Calculating the Internal Rate of Return 3

Year	Net Cash Flow	Present Value Factor at 25%	Net Present Value
	£		£
0	(7,646)	1.000	(7,646)
1	3,000	0.800	2,400
2	4,000	0.640	2,560
3	5,000	0.512	2,560
		Present Value	7,520
		Net Present Value	(126)

Now we know that the internal rate of return must lie between 20 and 25 per cent. That is because the project had a positive net present value at 20 per cent and a negative one at 25 per cent. Using the interpolation equation we can arrive at a good approximation of the discount rate.

Interpolating Equation

The Internal = Lowest + [Positive Cash Flow / Range of Cash Flow x Difference between High and Low Rates] %
Rate of Trial
Return (IRR) Rate

For this example the equation would be:

$$IRR = 20 + \left[\frac{524}{524 + 126} \times (25\text{-}20) \right]\%$$

$$= 20 + 4.03\% = 24.03\%* = 24\%.$$

* It is normal practice to only use whole numbers when calculating rates of return.

Had we used the net present value figure from the 10 per cent discount calculation, we would have arrived at a different IRR. The reason is that to give an accurate IRR figure, both net present value figures used in the interpolation equation must be fairly small.

You will have an opportunity to prove both that the equation works, and that it is more accurate with low figures, at the end of the chapter.

Risk and sensitivity analysis

Discounted cash flow (DCF) gives us a sound tool for deciding whether an investment proposal is acceptable or not. It also helps us to choose between competing projects. DCF can perform one more important task: it can be used to examine the circumstances that could make a project *unacceptable*.

Look back at the table on page 89. If the cut-off interest rate is 20 per cent this project is acceptable. The net cash flow has been calculated on a series of assumptions about sales levels, days' credit taken and given, expenses etc. But what if any one of those assumptions is wrong? For example, supposing debtors pay up much more slowly and the resultant cash flow takes longer to build up — but of course lasts longer, with some people not paying until year 4?

The following example shows how the cash flow will look if these new 'assumptions' occur.

Sensitivity Analysis

Year	First Estimate of Net Cash Flow	New Estimate of Net Cash Flow	Present Value Factor at 20%	Net Present Value
	£	£		£
0	(7,646)	(7,646)	1.000	(7,646)
1	3,000	2,000	0.833	1,666
2	4,000	3,000	0.694	2,082
3	5,000	4,000	0.579	2,316
4		3,000	0.482	1,446
Total Positive Cash Flow	12,000	12,000	Present Value	7,510
			Net Present Value	(136)

Under these circumstances the investment would not be acceptable, so now we know how 'sensitive' the project is to customers paying up promptly. We have to assess what the risk is of these new circumstances occurring.

The same technique can be applied to any of the assumptions built into the cash flow forecast, and a good, or robust, investment proposal is one that can withstand a range of 'what if' type tests.

Dealing with inflation

A common assumption is that varying the discounted cash flow cut-off point is a good way to deal with inflation. For example, if you felt that 20 per cent was a good rate|of return last year, and inflation is set to be 6 per cent next year, then 26 per cent should be the new cut-off rate.

Although attractively simple, the logic is wrong. Inflation is already dealt with in the assumptions built into the cash flow forecast (or it certainly should be). For example, the sum covering payments for materials is based on three assumptions: the volume of materials needed, how much they will cost, and when they will be paid for. The middle assumption here is where inflation is allowed for.

Discounted cash flow in working capital decisions

So far we have treated DCF as though it were exclusively for looking at investments in fixed assets. Any investment in fixed assets almost inevitably has an effect on working capital levels. DCF techniques have to be able to accommodate both fixed and working capital factors in investment decisions. Working through the following case study will show how DCF is used under these circumstances.

Launching a new product: a capital budgeting case study

Your marketing director is actively considering the launch of a new product. The following information on likely revenues and expenses has been obtained to help in the decision.

PRODUCTION COSTS
The new product will require new equipment costing £250,000 and alterations to existing buildings and plant layout costing £120,000.

SALES FORECASTS AND GROSS MARGINS
The long range plan (LRP) for the new product expects sales to

grow to £1.2m by the fifth year, with gross marketing margin running at 60 per cent.

Year	Sales Forecast (Cash)	Cash Generated by New Product
	£	£
1	200,000	120,000
2	400,000	240,000
3	800,000	480,000
4	1,000,000	600,000
5	1,200,000	720,000

The sales of this new product are not expected to eat into sales of existing products.

MARKETING AND SALES EXPENSES
You expect advertising and promotional expenditure to be heaviest in the first two years, tailing off to a relatively low figure later.

Promotional Expenditure

Year	£
1	150,000
2	200,000
3	100,000
4	70,000
5	50,000

Additionally, eight new sales people will be recruited to promote the product, four at the start of year 2 and the remainder at the start of year 4. Each salesperson costs the company £18,700 per annum (that includes car etc).

DEBTORS AND STOCKS
These are expected to build up over the five years to a total of £220,000, about 20 per cent of sales. At the end of each year, the following amounts of extra cash will be required to finance debtors and stocks:

Year	£
1	40,000
2	40,000
3	80,000
4	40,000
5	20,000
Total investment by year 5 =	220,000

COMPANY PROFIT REQUIREMENT

The company is unlikely to sanction a proposal generating less than 25 per cent on a DCF basis.

CASE STUDY ASSIGNMENT QUESTIONS

1. Work out the net cash flow for each year from 0-5 inclusive.

2. Calculate the net present value (NPV) at the 25 per cent discount rate.

3. What is the internal rate of return (IRR) of the project?

Use the worksheet provided. If you get stuck, look at the solution, which will show the logic and answer.

Launching a New Product — Worksheet

1. Annual Cash Flows
2. Cash Flow Discounted at 25%

Year		Cash Out £	Cash In £	Net Cash Flow £	Discount Rate 25%	Discounted Cash Flow £	Discount at 20%	Discounted Cash Flow £
0	Production				1.000		1.000	
1	Promotion							
	Debtors and Stock				0.800		0.833	
2	Promotion							
	Salesmen							
	Debtors and Stock				0.640		0.694	
3	Promotion							
	Salesmen							
	Debtors and Stock				0.512		0.579	
4	Promotion							
	Salesmen							
	Debtors and Stock				0.410		0.482	
5	Promotion							
	Salesmen							
	Debtors and Stock				0.328		0.402	

3. The Internal Rate of Return

True Rate = [   ] % = [   ]

Launching a New Product – Solution

1. Annual Cash Flows
2. Cash Flow Discounted at 25%

Year		Cash Out £	Cash In £	Net Cash Flow £	Discount Rate 25%	Discounted Cash Flow £	Discount at 20%	Discounted Cash Flow £
0	Production	370,000	0	(370,000)	1.000	(370,000)	1.000	(370,000)
1	Promotion	150,000						
	Debtors and Stock	40,000						
		190,000	120,000	(70,000)	0.800	(56,000)	0.833	(58,310)
2	Promotion	200,000						
	Salesmen	74,800						
	Debtors and Stock	40,000						
		314,800	240,000	(74,800)	0.640	(47,872)	0.694	(51,911)
3	Promotion	100,000						
	Salesmen	74,800						
	Debtors and Stock	80,000						
		254,800	480,000	225,200	0.512	115,302	0.579	130,390
4	Promotion	70,000						
	Salesmen	149,600						
	Debtors and Stock	40,000						
		259,600	600,000	340,400	0.410	139,564	0.482	164,073
5	Promotion	50,000						
	Salesmen	149,600						
	Debtors and Stock	20,000						
		219,600	720,000	500,400	0.328	164,131	0.402	201,161
						(54,875)		15,403

3. The Internal Rate of Return

$$\text{True Rate} = 20 + \left[\frac{15,403}{70,278} \times 5 \right] \% = 21.10\%$$

So don't invest if you want to make 25 per cent.

Some general factors in investment decisions

Some considerable space has been devoted to the subject of new investment appraisal. It is an area where many small businesses get into fatal problems very early on. People starting up rarely have a proper framework for deciding how much money to invest in a business idea. They are usually more concerned with how to raise the money. A critical look using discounted cash flow would probably change their minds, both about how much to spend on starting up and on expansion.

However, in the end, any investment appraisal is only as good as the information that is used to build up the cash flow forecast. Much of the benefit in using DCF is that it forces 'investors' to think through the whole decision thoroughly.

The bulk of the work in investment appraisal is concerned with:

1. Assessment of market size, market share, market growth and selling price.
2. Estimating and phasing the initial cost of the investment; working life of facilities; working capital requirements.
3. Assessment of plant output rate.
4. Ensuring that the provision of additional services and ancillaries has not been overlooked.
5. Estimating operating costs.
6. Estimating the rate of taxation.
7. Estimating the residual value of the asset.

The relatively simple task is that of using sound investment appraisal techniques.

A general purpose DCF worksheet is provided on page 99 for use with your own projects, and the following questions.

Questions

1. Test the interpolated IRR rate of 24 per cent on page 90 to prove it is correct.

2. Use 10 per cent as the lowest trial rate in the interpolation equation on pages 89 and 90 to show that the nearer the net present values are to zero, the more accurate the interpolation.

3. You have to choose between the following two machines. Each has an expected life of five years and will result in net cash flows (savings) as follows:

	Machine A £	Machine B £
Cost	12,500	15,000
Net Cash Flow		
Year 1	2,000	3,000
2	4,000	6,000
3	5,000	5,000
4	2,500	3,000
5	2,000	2,000
Residual Value	1,500	2,500

To help you make your choice, calculate:

(a) The net present value of each machine at the 10 and 15 per cent discount rates.

(b) Their respective internal rates of return.

(c) Their profitability indices at the 10 per cent discount factor.

What is your choice?

General Purpose DCF Working Sheet

Cash flow discounted at:

Time in Years from Today	Cash Outflow	Cash Inflow	Net Cash Flow	% Discount Factor	Present Value	% Discount Factor	Present Value	% Discount Factor	Present Value	% Discount Factor	Present Value
	£	£	£								
0											
1											
2											
3											
4											
5											
6											
7											
8											
9											
10											
11											
12											
13											
14											
15											
Net present value											

Interpolating to deduce true rate of return

$$\text{True Rate} = \text{Lowest Trial Rate} + \left[\frac{\text{Positive Cash Flow} \times \text{Difference between high and low rates}}{\text{Range of Cash Flow}} \right] \%$$

Discount Tables

The present value of 1

Year	Percentage									
	1	2	3	4	5	6	7	8	9	10
1	0.990099	0.980392	0.970874	0.961538	0.952381	0.943396	0.934579	0.925926	0.917431	0.909091
2	0.980296	0.961169	0.942596	0.925556	0.907029	0.889996	0.873439	0.857339	0.841680	0.826446
3	0.970590	0.942322	0.915142	0.888996	0.863838	0.839619	0.816298	0.799832	0.772183	0.751315
4	0.960980	0.923845	0.888487	0.854804	0.822702	0.792094	0.762895	0.735030	0.708425	0.683013
5	0.951466	0.905731	0.862609	0.821927	0.783526	0.747258	0.712986	0.680583	0.649931	0.620921
6	0.942045	0.887971	0.837484	0.790315	0.746215	0.704961	0.666342	0.630170	0.596267	0.564474
7	0.932718	0.870560	0.813092	0.755918	0.710681	0.665057	0.622750	0.583490	0.547034	0.513158
8	0.923483	0.853490	0.789409	0.730690	0.676839	0.627412	0.582009	0.540269	0.501866	0.466507
9	0.914340	0.836755	0.766417	0.702587	0.644609	0.591898	0.543934	0.500249	0.460428	0.424098
10	0.905287	0.820348	0.744094	0.675564	0.613913	0.558395	0.508349	0.463193	0.422411	0.385543
11	0.896324	0.804263	0.722421	0.649581	0.584679	0.526788	0.475093	0.428883	0.387533	0.350494
12	0.887449	0.788493	0.701380	0.624597	0.556837	0.496969	0.444012	0.397114	0.355535	0.318631
13	0.878663	0.773033	0.680951	0.600574	0.530321	0.468839	0.414964	0.367698	0.326179	0.289664
14	0.869963	0.757875	0.661118	0.577475	0.505068	0.442301	0.387817	0.340461	0.299246	0.263331
15	0.861349	0.743015	0.641862	0.555265	0.481017	0.417265	0.362446	0.315242	0.274538	0.239392
16	0.852821	0.728446	0.623167	0.533908	0.458112	0.393646	0.338735	0.291890	0.251870	0.217629
17	0.844377	0.174163	0.605016	0.513373	0.436297	0.371364	0.316574	0.270269	0.231073	0.197845
18	0.836017	0.700159	0.587395	0.493628	0.415521	0.350344	0.295864	0.250249	0.211994	0.179859
19	0.827740	0.686431	0.570286	0.474642	0.395734	0.330513	0.276508	0.231712	0.194490	0.163508
20	0.819544	0.672971	0.553676	0.456387	0.376889	0.311805	0.258419	0.214548	0.178431	0.148644

Percentage

Year	11	12	13	14	15	16	17	18	19	20
1	0.900901	0.892857	0.884956	0.877193	0.869565	0.862069	0.854701	0.847458	0.840336	0.833333
2	0.811622	0.797194	0.783147	0.769468	0.756144	0.743163	0.730514	0.718184	0.706165	0.694444
3	0.731191	0.711780	0.693050	0.674972	0.657516	0.640658	0.624371	0.608631	0.593416	0.578704
4	0.658731	0.635518	0.613319	0.592080	0.571753	0.552291	0.533650	0.515789	0.498669	0.482253
5	0.593451	0.567427	0.542760	0.519369	0.497177	0.476113	0.456111	0.437109	0.419049	0.401878
6	0.534641	0.506631	0.480319	0.455587	0.432328	0.410442	0.389839	0.370432	0.352142	0.334898
7	0.481658	0.452349	0.425061	0.399637	0.375937	0.353830	0.333195	0.313925	0.295918	0.279082
8	0.433926	0.403883	0.376160	0.350559	0.326902	0.305025	0.284782	0.266038	0.248671	0.232568
9	0.390925	0.360610	0.332885	0.307508	0.284262	0.262953	0.243404	0.225456	0.208967	0.193807
10	0.352184	0.321973	0.294588	0.269744	0.247185	0.226684	0.208037	0.191064	0.175602	0.161506
11	0.317283	0.287476	0.260698	0.236617	0.214943	0.195417	0.177810	0.161919	0.147565	0.134588
12	0.285841	0.256675	0.230706	0.207559	0.186907	0.168463	0.151974	0.137220	0.124004	0.112157
13	0.257514	0.229174	0.204165	0.182069	0.162528	0.145227	0.129892	0.116288	0.104205	0.093464
14	0.231995	0.204620	0.180677	0.159710	0.141329	0.125195	0.111019	0.098549	0.087567	0.077887
15	0.209004	0.182696	0.159891	0.140096	0.122894	0.107927	0.094888	0.083516	0.073586	0.064905
16	0.188292	0.163122	0.141496	0.122892	0.106865	0.093041	0.081101	0.070776	0.061837	0.054088
17	0.169663	0.145644	0.125218	0.107800	0.092926	0.080207	0.069317	0.059980	0.051964	0.045073
18	0.152822	0.130040	0.110812	0.094561	0.080805	0.069144	0.059245	0.050830	0.043667	0.037561
19	0.137678	0.116107	0.098064	0.082948	0.070265	0.059607	0.050637	0.043077	0.036695	0.031301
20	0.124043	0.103667	0.086782	0.072762	0.061100	0.051385	0.043280	0.036506	0.030836	0.026084

Year	Percentage									
	21	22	23	24	25	26	27	28	29	30
1	0.826446	0.819672	0.813008	0.806452	0.800000	0.793651	0.787402	0.781250	0.775194	0.769231
2	0.683013	0.671862	0.660982	0.650364	0.640000	0.629882	0.620001	0.610352	0.600925	0.591716
3	0.564474	0.550707	0.537384	0.524487	0.512000	0.499906	0.488190	0.476837	0.465834	0.455166
4	0.466507	0.451399	0.436897	0.422974	0.409600	0.396751	0.384402	0.372529	0.361111	0.350128
5	0.385543	0.369999	0.355201	0.341108	0.327680	0.314882	0.302678	0.291038	0.279931	0.269329
6	0.318631	0.303278	0.288781	0.275087	0.262144	0.249906	0.238329	0.227374	0.217001	0.207176
7	0.263331	0.248589	0.234782	0.221844	0.209715	0.198338	0.187661	0.177636	0.168218	0.159366
8	0.217629	0.203761	0.190879	0.178907	0.167772	0.157411	0.147765	0.138778	0.130401	0.122589
9	0.179859	0.167017	0.155187	0.144280	0.134218	0.124930	0.116350	0.108420	0.101086	0.094300
10	0.148644	0.136899	0.126168	0.116354	0.107374	0.099150	0.091614	0.084703	0.078362	0.072538
11	0.122846	0.112213	0.102576	0.093834	0.085899	0.078691	0.072137	0.066174	0.060745	0.055799
12	0.101526	0.091978	0.083395	0.075673	0.068719	0.062453	0.056801	0.051699	0.047089	0.042922
13	0.083905	0.075391	0.067801	0.061026	0.054976	0.049566	0.044725	0.040390	0.036503	0.033017
14	0.069343	0.061796	0.055122	0.049215	0.043980	0.039338	0.035217	0.031554	0.028297	0.025398
15	0.057309	0.050653	0.044815	0.039689	0.035184	0.031221	0.027730	0.024652	0.021936	0.019537
16	0.047362	0.041519	0.036435	0.032008	0.028147	0.024778	0.021834	0.019259	0.017005	0.015028
17	0.039143	0.034032	0.029622	0.025813	0.022518	0.019665	0.017192	0.015046	0.013182	0.011560
18	0.032349	0.027895	0.024083	0.020817	0.018014	0.015607	0.013537	0.011755	0.010218	0.008892
19	0.026735	0.022865	0.019580	0.016788	0.014412	0.012387	0.010659	0.009184	0.007921	0.006840
20	0.022095	0.018741	0.015918	0.013538	0.011529	0.009831	0.008393	0.007175	0.006141	0.005262

Year	Percentage									
	31	32	33	34	35	36	37	38	39	40
1	0.763359	0.757576	0.751880	0.746269	0.740741	0.735294	0.729927	0.724638	0.719424	0.714286
2	0.582717	0.573921	0.565323	0.556917	0.548697	0.540657	0.532793	0.525100	0.517572	0.510204
3	0.444822	0.434789	0.425055	0.415610	0.406442	0.397542	0.388900	0.380507	0.372354	0.364431
4	0.339559	0.329385	0.319590	0.310156	0.301068	0.292310	0.283869	0.275730	0.267880	0.260309
5	0.259205	0.249534	0.240293	0.231460	0.223014	0.214934	0.207204	0.199804	0.192720	0.185934
6	0.197866	0.189041	0.180672	0.172731	0.165195	0.158040	0.151243	0.144786	0.138647	0.132810
7	0.151043	0.143213	0.135843	0.128904	0.122367	0.116206	0.110397	0.104917	0.099746	0.094865
8	0.115300	0.108495	0.102138	0.096197	0.090642	0.085445	0.080582	0.076027	0.071760	0.067760
9	0.088015	0.082193	0.076795	0.071789	0.067142	0.062828	0.058819	0.055092	0.051626	0.048400
10	0.067187	0.062267	0.057741	0.053574	0.049735	0.046197	0.042933	0.039922	0.037141	0.034572
11	0.051288	0.047172	0.043414	0.039980	0.036841	0.033968	0.031338	0.028929	0.026720	0.024694
12	0.039151	0.035737	0.032642	0.029836	0.027289	0.024977	0.022875	0.020963	0.019223	0.017639
13	0.029886	0.027073	0.024543	0.022266	0.020214	0.018365	0.016697	0.015190	0.013830	0.012599
14	0.022814	0.020510	0.018453	0.016616	0.014974	0.013504	0.012187	0.011008	0.009949	0.008999
15	0.017415	0.015538	0.013875	0.012400	0.011092	0.009929	0.008896	0.007977	0.007158	0.006428
16	0.013294	0.011771	0.010432	0.009254	0.008216	0.007301	0.006493	0.005780	0.005149	0.004591
17	0.010148	0.008918	0.007844	0.006906	0.006086	0.005368	0.004740	0.004188	0.003705	0.003280
18	0.007747	0.006756	0.005898	0.005154	0.004508	0.003947	0.003460	0.003035	0.002665	0.002343
19	0.005914	0.005118	0.004434	0.003846	0.003339	0.002902	0.002525	0.002199	0.001917	0.001673
20	0.004514	0.003877	0.003334	0.002870	0.002474	0.002134	0.001843	0.001594	0.001379	0.001195

Chapter 8
Costs, Volume, Pricing and Profit Decisions

In the preceding chapters we have seen how business controls can be developed. These can be used to monitor performance against the fundamental objectives of profitability, and the business's capacity to survive. So far we have taken certain decisions for granted and ignored how to cost the product or service we are marketing, and indeed, how to set the selling price. These decisions are clearly very important if you want to be sure of making a profit.

Adding up the costs

At first glance the problem is simple. You just add up all the costs and charge a bit more. The more you charge above your costs, provided the customers will keep on buying, the more profit you make.

Unfortunately as soon as you start to do the sums the problem gets a little more complex. For a start, not all costs have the same characteristics. Some costs, for example, do not change however much you sell. If you are running a shop, the rent and rates are relatively constant figures, completely independent of the volume of your sales. On the other hand, the cost of the products sold from the shop is completely dependent on volume. The more you sell the more it costs you to buy in stock.

You can't really add up those two types of costs until you have made an assumption about volume — how much you plan to sell.

	£
Rent and rates for shop	2,500
Cost of 1,000 units of volume of product	1,000
Total Costs	3,500

Look at the simple example above. Until we decide to buy, and hopefully sell, 1,000 units of our product, we cannot total the costs.

With the volume hypothesised we can arrive at a cost per unit of product of:

Total Costs ÷ Number of Units
= £3,500   ÷ 1,000   = £3.50

Now provided we sell out all the above at £3.50 we shall always be profitable. But will we? Suppose we do not sell all the 1,000 units, what then? With a selling price of £4.50 we could, in theory, make a profit of £1,000 if we sell all 1,000 units. That is a total sales revenue of £4,500, minus total costs of £3,500. But if we only sell 500 units, our total revenue drops to £2,250 and we actually lose £1,250* (total revenue £2,250 – total costs £3,500). So at one level of sales a selling price of £4.50 is satisfactory, and at another it is a disaster.

This very simple example shows that all those decisions are intertwined. Costs, sales volume, selling prices and profits are all linked together. A decision taken in any one of these areas has an impact on the other areas.

To understand the relationship between these factors, we need a picture or model of how they link up. Before we can build up this model, we need some more information on each of the component parts of cost.

The components of cost

Understanding the behaviour of costs as the trading patterns in a business change is an area of vital importance to decision makers. It is this 'dynamic' nature in every business that makes good costing decisions the key to survival. The last example showed that if the situation was static and predictable, a profit was certain, but if any one component in the equation was not a certainty (in that example it was volume), then the situation was quite different.

To see how costs behave under changing conditions we first have to identify the different type of cost.

Fixed costs

Fixed costs are costs which happen, by and large, whatever the level of activity. For example, the cost of buying a car is the

---

* The loss may not be as dramatic as that because we may still have the product available to sell later, but if it is fresh vegetables, for example, we will not. In any event, stored products attract new costs, such as warehousing and finance charges.

same whether it is driven 100 miles a year or 20,000 miles. The same is also true of the road tax, the insurance and any extras, such as a radio.

In a business, as well as the cost of buying cars, there are other fixed costs such as plant, equipment, typewriters, desks, and telephone answering machines. But certain less tangible items can also be fixed costs, for example, rent, rates, insurances etc, which are usually set quite independent of how successful or otherwise a business is.

Costs such as most of those mentioned above are fixed irrespective of the time scale under consideration. Other costs, such as those of employing people, while theoretically variable in the short term, in practice are fixed. In other words, if sales demand goes down and a business needs fewer people, the costs cannot be shed for several weeks (notice, holiday pay, redundancy etc). Also, if the people involved are highly skilled or expensive to recruit and train (or in some other way particularly valuable) and the downturn looks a short one, it may not be cost effective to reduce those short run costs in line with falling demand. So viewed over a period of weeks and months, labour is a fixed cost. Over a longer period it may not be fixed.

We could draw a simple chart showing how fixed costs behave as the 'dynamic' volume, changes. The first phase of our cost model is shown opposite (top).

This shows a static level of fixed costs over a particular range of output. To return to a previous example, this could show the fixed cost, rent and rates for a shop, to be constant over a wide range of sales levels.

Once the shop owner has reached a satisfactory sales and profit level in one shop, he may decide to rent another one, in which case his fixed costs will 'step' up. This can be shown in the variation on the fixed cost model opposite.

Variable costs

These are costs that change in line with output. Raw materials for production, packaging materials, bonus, piece rates, sales commission and postage are some examples. The important characteristic of a variable cost is that it rises or falls in direct proportion to any growth or decline in output volumes.

Cost Model 1

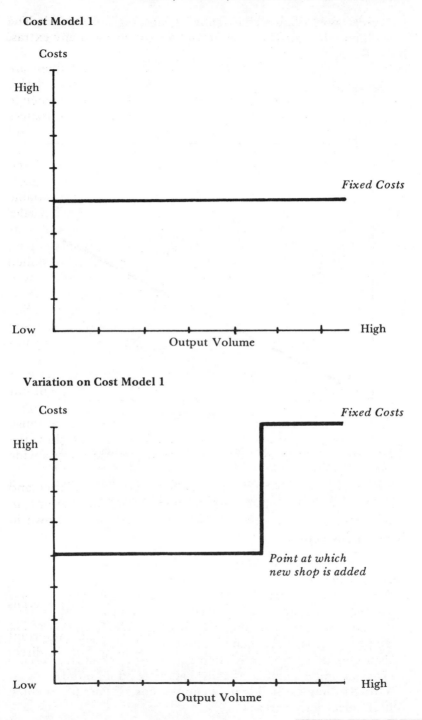

Variation on Cost Model 1

We can now draw a chart showing how variable costs behave as volume changes. The second phase of our cost model will look like this:

Cost Model 2

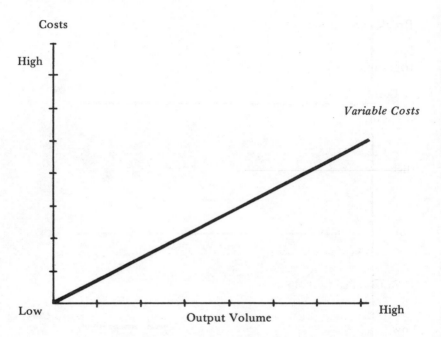

There is a popular misconception that defines fixed costs as those costs that are predictable, and variable costs as those that are subject to changing at any moment. The definitions already given are the only valid ones for costing purposes.

Semi-variable costs

Unfortunately not all costs fit easily into either the fixed or variable categories.

Some costs have both a fixed and a variable element. For example, a telephone has a quarterly rental cost which is fixed, and a cost per unit consumed which is variable. In this particular example low consumers can be seriously penalised. If only a few calls are made each month, their total cost per call (fixed rental + cost per unit ÷ number of calls) can be several pounds.

Other examples of this dual component cost are photocopier rentals, electricity and gas.

These semi-variable costs must be split into their fixed and variable elements. For most small businesses this will be a fairly simple process,* nevertheless it is essential to do it accurately or else much of the purpose and benefits of this method of cost analysis will be wasted.

Break-even point

Now we can bring both these phases of the costing model together to show the total costs, and how they behave.

Cost Model 3

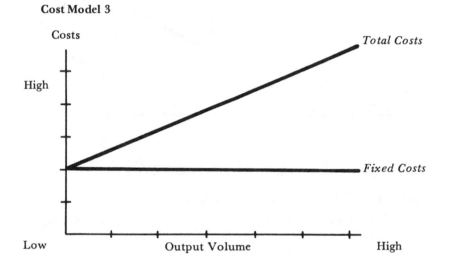

By starting the variable costs from the plateau of the fixed costs, we can produce a line showing the total costs. Taking vertical and horizontal lines from any point in the total cost line will give the total costs for any chosen output volume. This is

---

* A technique known as the method of least squares can be used in more complex cases. For example, if you know the total semi-variable costs for each of the past few months, and the output for each of these months, it is possible using this method to estimate the fixed and variable elements of the costs. The method requires you to 'solve' the following quadratic equations, to find the values of *a* and *b*.

(i) $\Sigma xy = a \Sigma x + b \Sigma x^2$

(ii) $\Sigma y = na + b \Sigma x$

Where x = number of units produced each month; y = costs per month; a = total fixed cost per month; b = variable costs per unit; n = number of pairs of x and y values; Σ = total.

If you understand this equation the problem is simple to solve. If not, it is probably best to talk it over with your accountant.

109

an essential feature of the costing model that lets us see how costs change with different output volumes: in other words, accommodating the dynamic nature of a business.

It is to be hoped we are not simply producing things and creating costs. We are also selling things and creating income. So a further line can be added to the model to show sales revenue as it comes in. To help bring the model to life let's add some figures, for illustration purposes only.

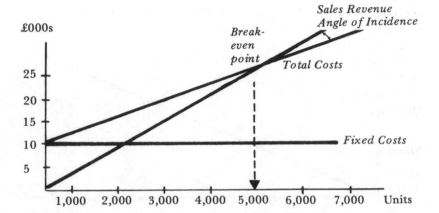

This illustration shows the break-even point (BEP). Perhaps the most important single calculation in the whole costing exercise is to find the point at which real profits start to be made.

The point where the sales revenue line crosses the total costs line is the break-even point. It is only after that point has been reached that a business can start to make profits. We can work this out by drawing a graph, such as the example above, or by using a simple formula. The advantage of using the formula as well is that you can experiment by changing the values of some of the elements in the model quickly.

The equation for BEP is:

$$\text{BEP} = \frac{\text{Fixed Costs}}{\text{Unit Selling Price} - \text{Variable Costs per Unit}}$$

This is quite logical. Before you can reach profits you must pay for the variable costs. This is done by deducting those costs from the unit selling price. What is left (usually called the unit contribution) is available to meet the fixed costs. Once enough units have been sold to meet these fixed costs, the BEP has been reached.

Let's try the sum out, given the following information shown on the break-even chart:

Fixed Costs = £10,000
Selling Price = £5 per unit
Variable Cost = £3 per unit

$$\text{So the BEP} = \frac{£10,000}{£5 - £3} = \frac{£10,000}{£2} = 5,000 \text{ units}$$

Now we can see that 5,000 units must be sold at £5 each before we can start to make a profit. We can also see that if 7,000 is our maximum output we have only 2,000 units available to make our required profit target.

Obviously, the more units we have available for sale (ie, the maximum output that can realistically be sold) after our break-even point, the better. This relationship between total sales and the break-even point is called the margin of safety.

Margin of safety

This is usually expressed as a percentage and can be calculated as follows:

	£	
Total Sales	35,000	(7,000 units x £5 selling price)
Minus Break-even point	25,000	(5,000 units x £5 selling price)
Margin of safety	10,000	
Margin of safety as a Percentage of Sales	29%	(10,000 ÷ 35,000)

Clearly the lower this percentage, the lower the business's capacity for generating profits. A low margin of safety might signal the need to rethink fixed costs, selling price or the maximum output of the business.

The angle formed at the BEP between the sales revenue line and the total cost line is called the angle of incidence. The size of the angle shows the rate at which profit is made after the break-even point. A large angle means a high rate of profit per unit sold after BEP.

Costing to meet profit objectives

By adding in the final element, desired profits, we can have a comprehensive model to help us with costing and pricing

111

decisions.

Supposing in the previous example we knew that we had to make £10,000 profits to achieve a satisfactory return on the capital invested in the business, we could amend our BEP formula to take account of this objective:

$$\text{BEPP (Break-even Profit Point)} = \frac{\text{Fixed Costs} + \text{Profit Objective}}{\text{Unit Selling Price} - \text{Variable Costs per Unit}}$$

Putting some figures from our last example into this equation, and choosing £10,000 as our profit objective, we can see how it works.

$$\text{BEPP} = \frac{£10,000 + £10,000}{£5 - £3} = \frac{20,000}{2} = 10,000 \text{ units}$$

Unfortunately, without further investment in fixed costs, the maximum output in our example is only 7,000 units, so unless we change something the profit objective will not be met.

The great strength of this model is that each element can be changed in turn, on an experimental basis, to arrive at a satisfactory and achievable result.

Let us return to this example. We could start our experimenting by seeing what the selling price would have to be to meet our profit objective. In this case we leave the selling price as the unknown, but we have to decide the BEP in advance (you cannot solve a single equation with more than one unknown). It would not be unreasonable to say that we would be prepared to sell our total output to meet the profit objective.

So the equation now works out as follows:

$$7,000 = \frac{20,000}{£ \text{ Unit Selling Price} - £3}$$

Moving the unknown over to the left-hand side of the equation we get:

$$£ \text{ Unit Selling Price} = £3 + \frac{20,000}{7,000} = £3 + 2.86 = £5.86$$

We now know that with a maximum capacity of 7,000 units and a profit objective of £10,000, we have to sell at £5.86 per unit. Now if the market will stand that price then this is a satisfactory result. If it will not, then we are back to experimenting with the other variables. We must find ways of decreasing the fixed or variable costs, or increasing the output of the plant, by an amount sufficient to meet our profit objective.

Costing for special orders

Every small business is laid open to the temptation of taking a particularly big order at a 'cut-throat' price. However attractive the proposition may look at first glance, certain conditions must be met before the order can be safely accepted.

Let us look at an example — a slight variation on the last one. Your company has a maximum output of 10,000 units, without any major investment in fixed costs. At present you are just not prepared to invest more money until the business has proved itself. The background information is:

Maximum output	10,000 units
Output to meet profit objective	7,000 units
Selling Price	£5.86
Fixed Costs	£10,000
Unit Variable Cost	£3.00
Profitability objective	£10,000

The break-even chart will look like this:

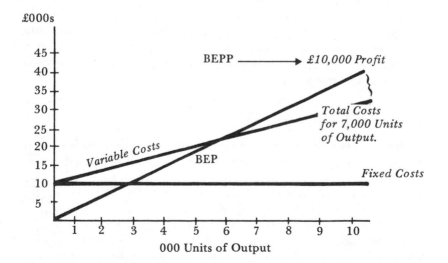

You are fairly confident that you can sell 7,000 units at £5.86 each, but that still leaves 3,000 units unsold — should you decide to produce them. Out of the blue an enquiry comes in for about 3,000 units, but you are given a strong hint that

113

nothing less than a 33 per cent discount will clinch the deal. What should you do?

Using the costing information assembled so far, you can show the present breakdown of costs and arrive at your selling price.

Unit Cost Breakdown

	£	
Variable costs	3.00	
Contribution to fixed costs	1.43	(£10,000 fixed costs ÷ 7,000 units)
Contribution to meet profitability objective	1.43	(£10,000 profitability objective ÷ 7,000 units)
Selling price	5.86	

As all fixed costs are met on the 7,000 units sold (or to be sold), the remaining units can be sold at a price that covers both variable costs and the profitability contribution, so you can negotiate at the same level of profitability, down to £4.43, just under 25 per cent off the current selling price. However, any selling price above the £3.00 variable cost will generate extra profits, but these sales will be at the expense of your profit margin. A lower profit margin in itself is not necessarily a bad thing if it results in a higher return on capital employed, but first you must do the sums (see Chapter 5).

There is a great danger with negotiating orders at marginal costs, as these costs are called, in that you do not achieve your break-even point soon enough and the deal results in a loss. (Look back to the first example in this chapter to see how missed sales targets affect profitability.)

Costing for business start-up

Paradoxically, one of the main reasons small businesses fail in the early stages is that too much start-up capital is used to buy fixed assets. While clearly some equipment is essential at the start, other purchases could be postponed. This may mean that 'desirable' and labour saving devices have to be borrowed or hired for a specific period. Obviously, not as nice as having them to hand all the time but if, for example, photocopiers, electronic typewriters, word processors, micros and even delivery vans are brought into the business, they become part of the fixed costs. The higher the fixed cost plateau, the longer it usually takes to reach break-even and then profitability. And time is not usually on the side of the small, new business. It has to become profitable relatively quickly or it will simply run out of money and die.

Look at these two hypothetical new small businesses. They are both making and selling identical products at the same price, £10. They plan to sell 10,000 units each in the first year. The owner of Company A plans to get fully equipped at the start. His fixed costs will be £40,000, double that of Company B. This is largely because, as well as his own car, he has bought such things as a delivery van, new equipment and a photocopier. Much of this will not be fully used for some time, but will save some money now. This extra expenditure will result in a lower unit variable cost than Company B can achieve, a typical capital intensive result. Company B's owner, on the other hand, proposes to start up on a shoestring. Only £20,000 will go into fixed costs, but of course, his unit variable cost will be higher, at £4.50. The variable cost is higher because, for example, he has to pay an outside carrier to deliver, while A uses his own van and pays only for petrol.

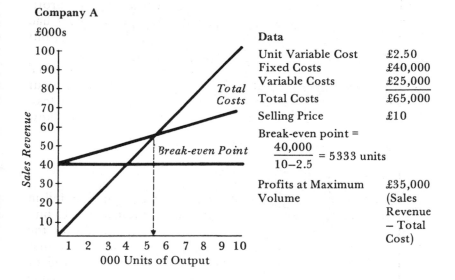

Company A

Data

Unit Variable Cost	£2.50
Fixed Costs	£40,000
Variable Costs	£25,000
Total Costs	£65,000
Selling Price	£10

Break-even point =

$$\frac{40,000}{10-2.5} = 5\,333 \text{ units}$$

Profits at Maximum Volume	£35,000 (Sales Revenue – Total Cost)

The break-even chart for Company B is on page 116. From the data on each company you can see that total costs for 10,000 units are the same, so total possible profits, *if* 10,000 units are sold are also the same. The key difference is that Company B starts making profits after 3,636 units have been sold. Company A has to wait until 5,333 units have been sold.

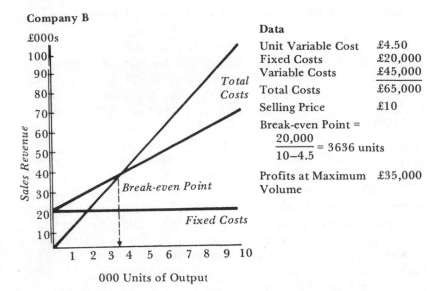

Company B

£000s

Sales Revenue

Total Costs

Break-even Point

Fixed Costs

000 Units of Output

Data

Unit Variable Cost	£4.50
Fixed Costs	£20,000
Variable Costs	£45,000
Total Costs	£65,000
Selling Price	£10

Break-even Point =

$$\frac{20,000}{10-4.5} = 3636 \text{ units}$$

Profits at Maximum Volume   £35,000

Now another pair of reasons why small businesses fail very early on are connected with the market place. They are frequently over-optimistic on how much they can sell. They also under-estimate how long it takes for sales to build up. So for these reasons, and spending too much start-up capital on fixed assets, great care should be taken to keep start-up fixed costs to the minimum.*

Costing to eliminate unprofitable products

Not all the business's products will always be profitable. Settling down to allocate 'real' fixed costs to products can be something of an eye opener to owner-managers. Look at the example opposite. The business manufactures three products. Product C is bulky, complicated and a comparatively slow seller. It uses all the same sort of equipment, storage space and sales effort as products A and B, only more so. When fixed costs are allocated across the range, it draws the greatest share.

---

* There are all sorts of 'persuasive' arguments to go for a capital intensive cost structure. In periods of high growth, the greater margin on sales will produce a higher ROCE, but high fixed costs will *always* expose a new or small business to higher risks. A small business has enough risks to face, with a survival rate of less than 20 per cent in its first few years, without adding to them.

Product Profitability 1

	A	B	C	Total
	£	£	£	£
Sales	30,000	50,000	20,000	100,000
Variable Costs	20,000	30,000	10,000	60,000
Allocated Fixed Costs	4,500	9,000	11,500	25,000
Total Costs	24,500	39,000	21,500	85,000
Operating Profit	5,500	11,000	(1,500)	15,000

This proves something of a shock. Product C is losing money, so it has to be eliminated, which will produce the following situation:

Product Profitability 2

	A	B	Total
	£	£	£
Sales	30,000	50,000	80,000
Variable Costs	20,000	30,000	50,000
New Allocated Fixed Costs	8,333	16,667	25,000
Total Costs	28,333	46,667	75,000
Operating Profit	1,667	3,333	5,000

Fixed costs will not change so the £25,000 has to be re-allocated across the remaining two products. This will result in profits dropping from £15,000 to £5,000; therefore our conventional product costing system has given the wrong signals. We have lost all the 'contribution' that Product C made to fixed costs, and any product that makes a contribution will increase overall profits. Because fixed costs cannot be ignored, it makes more sense to monitor contribution levels and to allocate costs in proportion to them.

Looking back to the first table we can see that the products made the following contributions (Contribution = Sales − Variable Costs):

Allocating Fixed Costs by Contribution Level

	Contribution		Fixed Cost Allocated
	£	%	£
Product A	10,000	25	6,250
B	20,000	50	12,500
C	10,000	25	6,250
Total	40,000	100	25,000

Now we can re-cast the product Profit and Loss Account using this marginal costing basis.

117

Marginal Costing Product P and L Account

	A	%	B	%	C	%	Total
	£		£		£		£
Sales	30,000		50,000		20,000		100,000
Marginal Costs	20,000		30,000		10,000		60,000
Contribution	10,000	33	20,000	40	10,000	50	40,000
Fixed Costs	6,250		12,500		6,250		25,000
Product Profit	3,750	13	7,500	15	3,750	19	15,000

Not only should we not eliminate Product C, but because in contribution terms it is our most profitable product, we should probably try to sell more.

Questions

1. Calculate the margin of safety for Companies A and B in the example given on pages 115 and 116.

2. You are planning to start up a domestic burglar alarm business. You will be buying in the product and marketing it yourself. The main marketing effort will be a salesperson working on salary plus commission, and an advertising campaign. The financial facts are as follows:

Item	£
Car, annual leasing charge	1,500
Sales Commission, per unit	5
Salesperson's basic salary	5,000
Office/Show room rent, rates, HLP*	3,500
Unit buy-in price	30
Other fixed costs	4,500
Unit installation cost	10
Advertising campaign + literature	2,000
Sundry variable costs, per unit	5
Unit selling price	100

(a) Calculate the break-even point.

(b) You decide you must have £10,000 per annum to live off. Now what unit sales do you have to achieve?

(c) You decide it is unrealistic to expect to sell more than 400 units in the first year. What must your selling price be both to break even and make the £10,000 you need to live off?

(d) You decide to take on an installation engineer at £6,000

---

* Heat, light and power.

a year together with another car on lease at £1,000 a year. At the same time you increase the salesperson's salary to £8,000 and cancel the commission. Now what are your answers to questions (a), (b) and (c)?

Chapter 9
Budgets and Plans

Everyone has made a budget or plan at some time. In our
personal lives we are always trying to match the scarce resource
'pay', with the ever expanding range of necessities and luxuries
in the market place, a battle we all too often lose, with
mortgage costs, car running expenses, food and children's
clothes taking more cash out than we can put in. Usually the
domestic budget is confined to a periodic attempt to list and
total likely future bills. These are then split into essential and
non-essential items. The 'essentials' total is then deducted from
expected pay (or income) and if anything is left over we can
plan how to spend it.

Temporary shortages of cash are made up by taking out an
overdraft, the judicious use of a credit card, or talking to a rich
aunt.

Every year we review how well we have kept within our
budget and moan about the unexpected expenses that always
knock us off course. The usual result is that next year's pay rise
just about clears the overdraft in time to start again.

Budgeting for a business

A business has to do much the same type of budgeting and
planning, although much more thoroughly if it wants to survive
and prosper. A business's environment is much more complex
than an individual's. For example, most people have only one
main source of income, and the amount of money they are
likely to get in any one year is fairly easy to predict accurately.
Even the smallest business has dozens or even hundreds of
potential sources of income — customers — but forecasting how
much they will spend is not so easy. Some small businesses start
off with their plans in the owner's head or on the back of the
proverbial envelope. Most of these end up going broke in the
first year. (There are simply not enough 'rich aunts' to go
round.)

The central problem is that to make a profit a business must take risks. A small new business must take many more risks than an established or larger one, with each risk having more important consequences if things go wrong. For example, an established firm with a thousand customers can 'afford' to lose a few to the competition. A firm with a dozen customers cannot really afford to lose any.

There is no way to eliminate all risks in business. Successful entrepreneurship is all about anticipating the sort of risks that have to be taken, and understanding how they will affect the business. This knowledge is then used as the basis of a plan or budget. Putting this information together usually means gathering facts and opinions on the market place; interpreting their probable impact on your business; deciding what you want to happen; and finally deciding how you intend to make things happen; in other words, developing your strategy.

The small business that starts its life with a well thought through plan has great advantages over the 'seat of the pants' type of business. For a start, the plan or budget acts as a means of communicating your intentions to three vitally important audiences: the entrepreneur, the staff and the providers of finance. It is the entrepreneur's own 'dry run' before real money is put into the business and possibly lost. He can experiment with various sales levels, profit margins and growth rates to arrive at a realistic picture of how he would like his business to develop, before committing himself to a particular course of action. We looked at a variation of this approach in Chapter 8 when we examined the relationship between cost/volume/profit and prices. This process will give him an invaluable insight into the mechanics of his business and help him to prepare for problems before they happen.

Also, other people working in the business will be in a better position to pull together if they know where the business is going. They can then become committed to common goals and strategies.

Bankers or shareholders outside the business will be more likely to be supportive if they see that the owner/manager knows what he wants to happen, and how to make it come about. For example, they will not be surprised by calls for cash to finance sales growth, or capital expenditure if they have seen the plans in advance.

Finally, most people who start up in business are fairly competitive. The budget acts as a standard against which they can measure their own business performance. This is particularly important for a new business in its first trading period, with no history to go on. In other words you cannot really try to do better than last year, if there wasn't one, so the only guide available is a realistic and achievable plan.

Time-scale and detail

Any attempt at planning invariably begs the question, 'How far ahead should I plan?' The answer, 'As far ahead as you can usefully see,' is not particularly helpful but it is the one most frequently given. Here are a few guidelines that may help bring the planning horizon into view.

Outsiders, such as bankers may have a standard period over which they expect you to plan, if you want to borrow money from them. Usually this is at least three years, and for a new business preparing its first plan, three years is probably at the horizon itself.

The payback period, discussed in Chapter 7 is another useful concept. If it is going to take you four or five years to recover your original investment and make a satisfactory profit, then that is how far you may want to plan.

The rate of technological change is yet another yardstick used in deciding how far ahead to plan. If your business is high-tech, or substantially influenced by changes in technology, then that factor must influence your choice of planning horizon. Companies in the early stages of the computer business who looked only three years ahead would have missed all the crucial technological trends, and as technological trends are vital factors influencing the success of any business in this field, the planning time horizon must accommodate them.

The amount of detail with which you plan may also help make a long planning horizon more feasible. For example, every business should plan its first year in considerable detail. As well as a description of what the business is going to do, these plans should be summarised into month-by-month cash flow projection;* a comprehensive quarterly Profit and Loss Account; and a full opening and closing position Balance Sheet. This first year plan is usually called the budget.

---

* In a cash business such as a shop you may need to project cash flow on a weekly basis.

Future years could be planned in rather less detail, giving only quarterly cash flow projection, for example. If the planning horizon is very long, plans for the final years could be confined to statements about market (and technological) trends, anticipated market share and profit margins. The detail of these plans is covered more comprehensively later in this chapter.

One final point before we look at how the budget and plans are prepared. There is a tendency to think of the budgeting process as a purely financial exercise, rather theoretical and remote from the day-to-day activity of the business. This is a serious misconception, usually fostered in larger companies, where the planners and the doers lead separate existences. People who have spent time in a large organisation have to recognise that in a small business the decision maker has to prepare his own plans. This is a cornerstone philosophy of good planning. No one likes to have someone else's plans foisted upon him, a useful point to remember if a small business has a number of decision takers working in it.

In the end the budgets and plans are expressed in financial terms: cash flow forecasts, Profit and Loss Accounts and Balance Sheets. But the process of preparing the budget is firmly rooted in the real business world.

Objectives

'To the man who does not know where he is going — any road will take him there.' Every plan needs to start with a clear objective if it is to succeed. At the simplest level, for example, imagine you are planning a journey. Before you can consider whether to fly, drive, walk or take a train, you have to know your destination. You also have to know when you want to arrive and how much baggage etc you need with you. In other words, a clear objective. 'I want to be in Edinburgh on Thursday not later than 11 am with no more than an overnight bag.' This is a clear unambiguous objective and only now can you plan the route and the means of transport in the most effective manner.

A business also needs clear objectives to be stated before the budgeting and planning process can get under way. It needs both market and financial objectives to cover the range of its activities.

MARKET OBJECTIVES

Sometimes referred to as the business mission or purpose, market objectives go beyond a simple statement of what product(s) you are going to sell. This mission should define precisely the market you are entering and in a way that helps you to understand the needs you are trying to satisfy. To some extent products come and go, but markets go on for ever — at least the needs that the products aim to satisfy do. A simple reflection on the way in which people satisfy the need to travel will illustrate the transient nature of products. While the need to travel has grown rapidly over the past 50 years, with more people travelling more often, 'products' such as the railways and ocean liners have declined. New 'products', the motor car, the coach and the aeroplane have absorbed all the extra demand and more. (It goes without saying that this market must be compatible with your own skills and resources. A fundamental mismatch in this area would be fatal.)

For example, you may be skilled at designing and making clothes. The market place could be vast. You could concentrate on high fashion, one-off dresses, perhaps produce a range of inexpensive clothes for young girls, or you could make and market baby clothes. Each of these markets is different, and until you define your 'mission' you cannot start to plan. The following statement is the mission of one small business: 'We will design, make and market clothes for mothers-to-be that make them feel they can still be fashionably dressed.' This meets the two criteria every mission must meet.

First, it is narrow enough to give direction and guidance to everyone in the business. This concentration is the key to business success, because it is only by focusing on specific needs that a small business can differentiate itself from its larger competitors. Nothing kills off new business faster than trying to do too many different things too quickly. But the mission narrows down the task in clear steps: we are concentrating on women; this is further reduced to women at a certain stage in their lives — ie, pregnancy; this is finally reduced to those pregnant women who are fashion conscious. This is a clearly recognised need which specific products can be produced to satisfy. This is also a well defined market that we can come to grips with.

Second, the example mission opens up a large enough market to allow the business to grow and realise its potential.

Interestingly enough one of the highest incidences of failure in small businesses is in the building trade. The very nature of this field seems to mitigate against being able to concentrate on any specific type of work, or customer need. One successful new small builder defined his mission in the following sentence. 'We are going to concentrate on domestic house repair and renovation work, and as well as doing a good job we will meet the customers' two key needs: a quotation that is accurate and starting and completion dates that are met.' When told this mission, most small builders laugh. They say it cannot be done, but then most go broke.

At the end of the day, there has to be something unique about your business idea or yourself that makes people want to buy from you. That uniqueness may be confined to the fact that you are the only photocopying shop in the area, but that is enough to make you stand out (provided of course that the area has potential customers).

Also, within the market objective area you need some idea of how big you want the business to be. Your share of the market, in other words. It certainly is not easy to forecast sales, especially before you have even started trading, but if you do not set a goal at the start and you just wait to see how things develop, then one of two problems will occur. Either you will not sell enough to cover your fixed costs and you will lose money and perhaps go out of business. Or you will sell too much and run out of cash, in other words overtrade (see Chapter 3 on cash flow).

Obviously, before you can set a market share and sales objective you need to know the size of your market. We shall consider how to find that out in the next section of this chapter. Later on, when the business has been trading for a few years, it may be possible to use that sales history and experience to forecast ahead. If there are few customers then you can build up likely sales on a customer by customer basis. If there are many, then some simple mathematical technique, perhaps computer based, could be used.

But to a large extent the 'size' you want your business to be is more a judgement than a forecast, a judgement tempered by the resources you have available to achieve those objectives and, of course, some idea of what is reasonable and achievable and what is not. You will find the range of discretion over a size objective seriously constrained by the financial objectives chosen.

Profit objectives

The profit objective of every business must be to make a satisfactory return on the capital employed. We saw in Chapter 4 on business controls, that unless the return on capital employed ratio was at a certain level, a business would find it very difficult to attract outside funds. A bank manager would be fairly cool to a request for a long-term loan well below market rates. By definition 'market rates' means he could lend the money elsewhere at a rate satisfactory to him.

Another yardstick might be how much profit other people make in this type of business (see sources of financial information, page 53), or even how much you could make if you invested elsewhere.

As well as making a satisfactory ROCE, the business and its profits have to grow, otherwise it will not earn enough to replace equipment or launch new products, both costly exercises. And without working equipment and a fresh product range to match the competition a business is effectively dead or dying.

So the main objectives of a new business with say £50,000 start-up capital, that wanted to double sales in four years, grow a little faster than the market, make a healthy and growing ROCE, and increase slightly its profit margin, might be summarised as follows:

Business Objectives

	Start-up Budget	Planning Period	4 years On
Sales	£80,000	Details	£160,000
Profit Margin	12.5%	Omitted	13.5%
Profit	£10,000		£21,600
Capital Employed	£50,000		£86,400
ROCE	20%		25%
Market Share	5%		7%

Without a well defined mission and clearly stated objectives a business leaves its success to chance and improvisation. (Chance leads most small businesses to fail in their first three years.)

Once we have set these primary objectives, the purpose of the budget and plans is to make sure we can achieve them. Stating the objectives provides a clear guide to future action. For example, it is obvious from the primary profit objectives on ROCE and profit margins that an extra £36,400 (£86,400 −

£50,000) of capital is needed to finance the desired sales growth over the period of the plan.

There is a school of thought that says you have to build up the plans from the market and resource appreciation, steps both described below. Then an objective can be deduced as the sum of the achievable tasks. But this exposes you to the question, 'What if this sum is not satisfactory?' It could also leave opportunity untapped. Neither of these is a very satisfactory position, so the objective's first approach, and then market appreciation, must be adopted.

Market appreciation

All businesses live or die by virtue of their success or otherwise in the market place. People very often talk of a particular market or business sector as being profitable, but without much idea of why. Years of research into the factors that influence a market's relative profitability have produced the following conclusion. 'The more intense the competition the lower the return on capital employed.' While that does not come as a great surprise in itself, it does provide some valuable pointers on how to analyse the market place. It follows that any budget or plan must be based on a sound appreciation of the competitive forces at work in a market, otherwise the primary profit objective may simply not be attainable.

For someone who has not yet started up a business, this process can act as a filter to eliminate the undesirable. For those already trading it can provide guidance on areas upon which to concentrate and on likely problem areas.

The chart overleaf shows a way to look at these competitive forces as a whole.

Before you can start to plan in any detail you need answers to the following questions:

Where is my market? The starting point in any market appreciation has to be a definition of the scope of the market you are aiming for. A small general shop may only serve the needs of a few dozen streets. A specialist restaurant may have to call on a catchment area of 10 or 20 miles. While trends and behaviour in the wider market are helpful facts to know, your main activity is within your own area.

You may eventually decide to sell to several different markets. For example, a retail business can serve a local area through its shop and a national area by mail order. A small

Competitive Forces in a Market

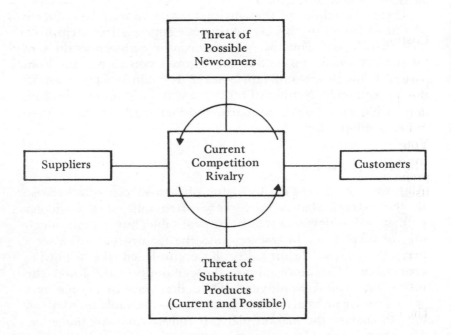

manufacturing business can branch out into exporting. People all too often flounder in their market research by describing their markets too broadly; for example, the motor industry, when they really mean car sales in Perth, or health foods, when they mean wholemeal bread in one small village.

Who are the customers, potential and actual? Some products are aimed at the general public, others at particular trades or professions, males or females only, or perhaps large institutions and government departments. Some products cut across all these customer groups.

Focusing on the particular people who could buy the product gives a better idea of how many are likely to buy. Equally important, it will help you understand why they should buy from you. This really is the key to the whole business and its growth.

One entrepreneur started up a drinks vending machine business. Finding a vending machine that was reliable and easy to operate and maintain was the first task he tackled. This took two months. Next he searched for suitable ingredients ending up with a very acceptable and economic range of hot and cold drinks. He then found a finance company to lease machines to his customers. All this vital background work took nearly four months and eventually he hit the road selling. He quickly found that his potential customers were new or smallish businesses without a vending machine already, most of which were unacceptable to the leasing company because they had no financial track record. Or he had to find a large company that was on the point of changing its equipment for one reason or another. The nature of his potential customers meant he had to call cold. (An advertising campaign using leaflets would take a long time to produce sales and he had already spent half his working capital). He had to make something like 80 cold calls to get two interviews and it took 10 interviews to get three quotations in. Only one of those would result in an order. He ran out of cash before he could get a significant number of customers, as well as having a nervous breakdown from cold calling, a task he did not enjoy. Bringing his potential customers sharply into focus at the start and taking account of them in his business plan may have avoided this disaster.

How big is the market? You need to know this to see whether or not your sales objectives are reasonable and attainable. If there are only 1,000 possible customers for your product in the geographical market you have chosen, and five well established competitors, then expecting to sell to 500 of them in year 1 is not on.

Is the market growing or contracting? In a growth market there are often opportunities for new companies to come in, or for small businesses to expand. In a contracting market existing competitors slog it out leaving little room for new entrants or expansion. You should find out in which direction the market is moving and at what speed. The state of the general economy may not have much bearing on the market you are in. For example, the number of video rental outlets reached their zenith in a period of economic decline in the UK.

Who are the competition and what are their strengths and weaknesses? Most products have competitors. To some extent this is reassuring because you know in advance that you are likely to achieve some sales, but you have to identify who they are and how they can affect your business. You have to know everything about them: their product range, prices, discount structure, delivery arrangements, specifications, minimum order quantities, terms of trade etc.

You also have to look at two less visible types of competitor. First, those who have not arrived on the scene yet. You have to consider what conditions would attract new businesses into the market. For example, businesses that require very little start-up capital, or add little value to goods, are always vulnerable to new competitors opening up. On the other hand, a business that can protect its ideas with patents, or achieve high volume sales quickly, is less exposed.

Second, under certain circumstances customers can be persuaded to buy a quite different or substitute product from the one you are offering, and still satisfy their same needs. In other words, you have a secondary layer of competition.

Who are the suppliers? Most businesses buy in and process raw materials of one sort or another. They add value, sell out, and make a profit. If you have only a handful of possible suppliers then they have the initiative and can set the terms of trade. For a new small business the problem is very often one of finding someone to supply in small enough volume. Nevertheless it is a key strategic task to find at least two sources of supply for all vital products, and to negotiate the best possible deal. Otherwise the products themselves will be uncompetitive.

Forecasting sales

One of our primary market objectives is how much we would like to sell — or need to sell to achieve profit objectives. For a new business this and market share may be the only guidelines as to what sales volume could be achieved. However, a business with a sales history has another clue — the sales trend.

The chart opposite shows the quarterly sales results of a hypothetical business that has been trading for the past two years. Sales have grown from about 50 units per quarter up to just over 250 in the eight quarters.

It is possible either mathematically or by eye to fit a trend line through these points. Continuing this trend line over the planning period shows what sales are likely to be, if the past can be accepted as a good guide to the future.

Now we can superimpose our sales objective on to a chart showing the sales trend. This will show the gap between where the business is going by virtue of its own momentum, and where we should like sales to be.

Apart from continuing our present efforts to achieve sales and sales growth, our objectives call for extra results to fill the sales

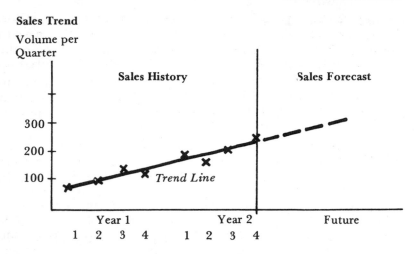

gap, so within our sales operating plan specific tasks to achieve this growth have to be identified.

It is beyond the scope of this book to give more than an outline of the task involved in a market appreciation suitable for preparing a business plan. While most financial matters are common to all types of enterprise, most marketing matters are unique to a particular business. A section on sources of market information is given in Chapter 10 (page 147) which should provide answers to marketing questions, and a better understanding of the issues involved.

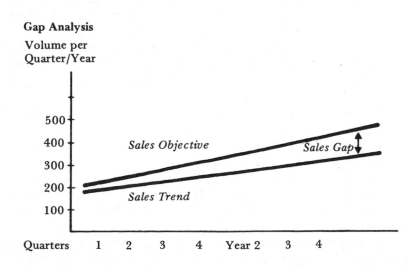

131

Resources appreciation

The market appreciation is a look outside the business to see the opportunities and threats to the business and its products. A business reacts to these by mobilising its resources to take advantage of the opportunities and to neutralise the threats.

Business resources can be loosely grouped under four main headings: people, facilities, information and finance.

PEOPLE

People, and in particular those who are vital to the success or failure of the business. Before you begin to identify specific people it is probably more important to highlight the sorts of skills and knowledge you want them to have. So the process could be summarised as a series of questions with the answers giving some guidance for future action.

Auditing your own knowledge and skills is an obvious starting point. By identifying gaps in these you can decide whom you need. The worksheet on page 133 will help to get ideas flowing.

You can then search out the people or agencies that you need to help achieve your objectives.

FACILITIES AUDIT

Facilities, such as office, workshop space, storage, machinery etc, are another key source. The worksheet below can summarise the position here.

1. What fixtures, fittings, premises etc do you have or need? List.

Need	Have	Can borrow	Must find

2. What production equipment etc do you have or need? List.

Need (including some idea of output that can be achieved)	Have	Can borrow	Must find

3. Other key facilities.

PERSONAL SKILLS RESOURCE AUDIT

How good are you at:

	Satisfactory	Inadequate	Person/ Help available	If not, what will you do?
MARKETING				
Market research				
Salesmanship				
Publicity/Advertising				
Product development				
Distribution				
Others (list)				
PRODUCTION				
Technical matters				
Buying				
Planning production				
Quality control				
Stock control				
Others (list)				
PEOPLE				
Selecting people				
Leading people				
Motivating people				
Team work				
Listening to people				
Giving clear instructions				
Others (list)				
FINANCE AND ADMINISTRATION				
Forming a company or partnership				
Finding premises				
Book-keeping, tax and VAT				
Raising money				
Budgeting and managing money				
Collecting in money				
Writing letters				
Forward planning				
Dealing with regulations				
Others (list)				

You may find you already have resources you do not need. Either put them to use or dispose of them if they cannot be pressed into service soon. They will only increase the fixed asset base of the business, tie up capital unnecessarily and make it harder to achieve your ROCE objective. (Look back at Chapter 5 to refresh your memory.)

INFORMATION AUDIT

Information, other than pure market information, is also an important and frequently neglected resource area. Carry out an information audit.

1. What book-keeping system have you planned? Who will run it and will it give you the control you need?

2. Are there any possible legal problems related to:
   Your product or service
   Your premises
   Present or future employees
   Yourself (ie, conditions in a past service contract may prevent
      you from working in a certain field)
   Patents etc

FINANCIAL RESOURCE AUDIT

Financial resources are clearly an important consideration in any planning process. They are nearly always the major constraint in any plans for a new business, whether starting up or expanding. A financial resources audit looks for answers to three questions. How much money have you got that you are prepared to commit to your business? How much do you need? Where will you get the balance from?

1. Obviously the first place to start is to find out exactly how much you have to invest in the business. You may not have much in ready cash, but you may have valuable assets that can be converted into cash, or other borrowing. The difference between your assets and liabilities is your 'net worth'. This is the maximum security that you can offer for any money borrowed, and hopefully, the calculations below will yield a pleasant surprise.

Your Net Worth

Liabilities	£	*Assets*	£
Overdraft		Cash in hand and in banks	
Mortgage		Building society, National	
Other loans		Savings or other deposits	
Hire purchase		Stocks and shares	
Tax due,		Current redemption value	
including		of insurance policies	
capital gains		Value of home	
Credit cards		Any other property	
due		Motor car(s) etc	
Garage, local		Jewellery, paintings and	
shop accounts		other marketable valuables	
due		Any money due to you	
Any other		Value of your existing	
financial		business	
obligations			
Total Liabilities		Total Assets	

Net Worth = Total Assets – Total Liabilities

2. The sum you need to achieve your plan is calculated as follows:

   (a) First year start-up costs: £
   Fixed Capital (tools, equipment, premises etc)
   Working Capital (materials, opening stocks,
      wages, rent, your living expenses etc)

   Total Start-up Costs

   (b) Additional capital to finance growth. (In the table of business objectives on page 126, item 4, the additional capital required is £36,400.)

   (c) Total capital required over planning period is the total of (a) and (b).

3. The capital you need to find is the difference between 1 and 2. Chapter 12 explains the sources of capital for starting up a business and financing its expansion.

Key strategies and operating plans

So far in the budgeting and planning process we have set our business objectives, looked at market opportunities and examined our own resources. The next step is to decide what resources to commit to what market and business tasks.

Key strategies are the areas of action that are vital to the success of the business. The market strategies define exactly what products/services you plan to offer to which specific customer group(s). The financial strategies explain the sources of funds and the profitability expected.

An operating plan must be made for each area of the business. For example, sales, advertising, production, equipment purchasing, raw material supplies, premises, deliveries etc. The operating plan must state the specific task to be achieved and when; what will be done, by whom and by what date. It should also monitor results. If appropriate each task should also have an expense budget estimate against it. Your plans are complete when you have set enough tasks to achieve your primary business objectives. These plans must not be complicated, but they must be written down. They provide the backbone to the business, and the statement for others (bankers, shareholders etc) to see that you know your business direction.

An example of an operating plan is shown in the table on page 137.

People launching small businesses or trying to expand never cease to be amazed at how long their plans take to come to fruition. The much quoted rule is to estimate a time scale, double it, then double it again for good measure. The problem is that most of them simply do not think through their plans step by step, in the manner prescribed for an operating plan. Small businesses simply do not have the cash resources to allow for extensive time scales.

CONTINGENCY PLANS

Any plan is built on a number of assumptions. Many of these assumptions are outside the planners' control, and some are keys to the success of the venture. Look back at the earlier example of a personal objective to get to Edinburgh by a certain time (page 123). Suppose, after reviewing all the market opportunities (ie trains, planes, hire cars, cars, buses etc) and assessing our resources (ie, money, our own car etc), we decide to go by train. Unfortunately, when we get to the station we find the train has been cancelled.

A key assumption in our plan is that the train will run — but this is clearly outside our control. If by going for the train, we miss the opportunity to fly, and it is then too late to go by car or bus, we have no contingency plans. No means of achieving our objective. Now obviously in this example we could postpone going to Edinburgh, or perhaps arrive later after telephoning to explain.

Operating Plan 198X

Planning Area	Task/Objective	Cost Budget	Time Scale	Action Required	Date	By Whom	Results of Task on Costs
Premises	Find 2,000 sq. ft. of warehouse space within five miles of workshop	£800	April–July (must be in and working by 1 August)	1. Look at area. 2. Contact estate agents a, b, c. 3. Search papers. 4. Visit possible sites. 5. Review leases. 6. Sign up. 7. Take over premises.	6/5 6/5 10/5 10/6 20/6 1/7 20/7	GFK GFK GFK GFK TRD TRD GKF	
Raw material suppliers	Find two competitive suppliers of raw material 'x'	Petty cash	April–June	1. Search trade journals. 2. Write for specification and quotes. 3. Chase up replies. 4. Visit four best possibles. 5. Place trial orders. 6. Select two best. 7. Place orders.	6/5 10/5 15/5 20/5 25/5 15/6 25/6	TJ TJ TJ TJ TRD TRD TJ	

But there are business situations where our objectives must be met on time, and viable contingency plans have to be prepared to make sure this happens.

For example, if a piece of production equipment breaks down, do you know where you can hire or borrow a spare quickly? Small businesses cannot afford to be out of commission for long, so contingency arrangements for all sensitive areas are essential.

Chapter 10

The Financial Picture

Only now is it possible to construct a detailed financial picture of the business's budget and plans. This is an estimate of how the business will appear in money terms if the budget is achieved. The financial reports that summarise the effects of the operating plans are: the budgeted profit and loss; the cash flow budget; and the opening and closing balance sheets. The mechanics of preparing these financial statements have been covered in earlier chapters.

The budget

There are two further rules to be applied to the budget version of these reports, which are explained in the outline below.

Budgeted P and L Account

	This Month			Year to Date		
	Budget £	Actual £	Budget Variance %	Budget £	Actual £	Budget Variance %
Sales						
Cost of Sales						
Gross Profit						
Less Expenses						
Administration						
Selling						
Marketing						
Distribution						
TOTAL						
Operating Profit						

Summary of main reasons for important variances and proposed remedial action.

1. _____
2. _____
3. _____

This example shows the sales and expenses budget broken down month by month. It is useful to divide objectives up into manageable units, rather than just leaving it until the year end to find things have gone wrong. Columns are left to report actual performance and to compare this with the budget. It is also useful to report on the year to date, which lets you see how important a particular variance is. The section at the bottom of the budget is for comments on variances and planned future action.

Do not forget at the end of the day that the business has not only to achieve its sales and profit objectives, it must also maintain a sound financial position, so working capital and debts/equity ratios (see Chapter 5) have to be carefully examined.

Budget variance analysis

One important problem can come up when variances from budget are being examined. Look at the following example, which is a small part of a sales budget:

	Budget £	Actual £	Budget Variance Value £	%
Sales	100,000	125,000	25,000	25
Cost of Sales	40,000	50,000	(10,000)	(25)
Gross Profit	60,000	75,000	15,000	25
Less Expenses				
Selling	20,000	25,000	(5,000)	(25)
Distribution	10,000	12,500	(2,500)|	(25)
Marketing	5,000	5,000	–	–
Administration	5,000	5,000	–	–
Total	40,000	47,500	(7,500)	(18.75)
Operating Profit	20,000	27,500	7,500	37.5

The results compared with budget, in this example, show that while sales, gross profit and net profit have high positive variances, two of the expense budgets have large adverse variances, as has cost of sales.

Normally we would expect to take corrective action to deal with adverse variances. But in this case we know that selling and distribution costs will rise directly in proportion with sales (perhaps the sales force is on commission only). So the budget variance is giving out misleading signals. Despite adverse variances being thrown up, nothing is wrong.

It may be useful to express both the budget and the actual results as percentages of their respective sales figures. This allows the level of activity in the business to be taken into account as well as the actual results.

Building in Percentages

	Budget £	Ratio %	Actual £	Ratio %	Budget Variance Value £	%	Ratio Variances
Sales	100,000	100	125,000	100	25,000	25	—
Cost of Sales	40,000	40	50,000	40	(10,000)	(25)	—
Gross Profit	60,000	60	75,000	60	15,000	25	—
Less Expenses							
Selling	20,000	20	25,000	20	(5,000)	(25)	—
Distribution	10,000	10	12,500	10	(2,500)	(25)	—
Marketing	5,000	5	5,000	5	—	—	—
Administration	5,000	5	5,000	5	—	—	—
TOTAL	40,000	40	47,500	40	(7,500)	(18.75)	—
Operating Profit	20,000	20	27,500	20	7,500	37.5	—

You have to be careful interpreting these percentages. An absolute rise or fall in sales or expenses may still be a 'problem', even if the ratios signal no variance. Sales shortfalls have to be made up and higher than budgeted sales have to be financed.

Flexing the sales budget

Once the annual sales volume and value figures have been set there still remains the problem of spreading them over the year.

The cash flow forecast and the budgeted P and L have to be hinged around a particular sales figure for each month. We saw in the last section the major effect that different monthly sales can have on the business's performance, both its profitability and cash flow. It is too easy to breathe a sigh of relief and just divide the annual figure by 12. This would not reflect the way we expect things to happen. In practice some periods of the year are always better than others. Even when the sales trend is generally upwards, there is an underlying seasonal pattern to every business's sales performance.

If you are preparing your first budget and plan and have no sales history to go on, then you will have to make an educated guess. You will almost certainly be able to divide the year into very slow, slow, okay, good and very good months. The pattern can be deduced by asking around other similar businesses – or potential suppliers. They will have some idea of your industry's seasonal pattern, as it will influence their own sales.

The process of spreading the annual budget over each month (or period) of the year is usually referred to as 'flexing'. If a relatively small number of customers are involved it is possible to build up a plan customer by customer, though it is doubtful if you can estimate sales to them each month, or exactly when they will buy. If you have a large number of customers then an account-by-account approach is impractical. More sophisticated businesses use mathematical forecasting techniques to calculate the underlying and seasonality factors. In a small business you have to use a rough and ready 'rule of thumb' process.

Look at the example below. The left hand column shows that we sold 108,000 units last year. Each month's actual sales are given, ranging from 9,000 units in May to 16,000 units the following April.

Month	Last Year's Sales	Sales as Proportion of Average Monthly Sales	Sales Operating Plan Average Monthly Sales	Flexed Sales Using Last Year's Proportion
May	9,000	1.00	12,000	12,000
Jun	9,000	1.00	12,000	12,000
Jul	8,900	0.99	12,000	11,880
Aug	6,900	0.77	12,000	9,240
Sep	6,900	0.77	12,000	9,240
Oct	6,500	0.72	12,000	8,640
Nov	5,300	0.59	12,000	7,080
Dec	5,800	0.64	12,000	7,680
Jan	7,000	0.78	12,000	9,360
Feb	11,700	1.30	12,000	15,600
Mar	15,000	1.67	12,000	20,000
Apr	16,000	1.78	12,000	21,300
Total Sales	108,000		144,000	144,000
Average Monthly Sales	9,000		12,000	12,000

Now we can calculate the difference in proportion that each month's sales are from the average monthly sales. This can be done by dividing actual sales by average monthly sales. For example, for last August this proportion is 6,900 ÷ 9,000 = 0.77. So despite the fact that sales generally appear to be growing, seasonal factors, such as the weather or holidays, have caused sales in August to be lower than in July or February, for example.

The sales budget calls for a growth of 33½ per cent from 108,000 units to 144,000, so average monthly sales will rise from 9,000 to 12,000. Each month's sales will not be 'average', just like last year. The chances are that they will be influenced by the same seasonal factors as before.

Using the proportions already worked out we can predict what the budgeted sales should be for each month. In May, for example, the factor is 1.00 and the average sales are 12,000, so the flexed sales are 1.00 x 12,000 = 12,000. In August the factor is 0.77, so flexed sales are 0.77 x 12,000 = 9,240.

You will end up with a unit sales figure for each month/ period of the plan that is reasonable bearing in mind your growth objective and past seasonal experiences. This is a very rough and ready method but if you did not flex your budget and simply took an average — or average growth — you would spend the whole year either running out of cash or running out of stock.

Presenting business plans to financiers

Owners/managers sometimes think that having to present their plans to outside people such as their bank manager is a nuisance to be avoided. It is possible to have some sympathy with this point of view, but if your business needs cash then there is no alternative. On the positive side, having to present a plan does make sure it is prepared in the first place, and prepared to a standard that you can defend or justify. If you need outside money then a 'banker' will need to look carefully at both the proposal and the proposer.

The proposer's experience, ability, drive, integrity and resilience in times of trouble, will all be areas subject to examination. So you, the proposer, must be prepared to make your presentation with sufficient information and style to let these qualities be seen.

The proposal itself, even if made in person, should be supported with comprehensive back-up documentation. This should be sent in advance, after an appointment to 'present' has been made. This will give the 'banker' a chance to prepare himself and so be ready to give a quick decision. The information need not contain as much detail as your own business plans. Rather you want to produce a summary, but one that demonstrates that a thorough approach has been taken.

The information presented should include as much of the following data as possible. Obviously a start-up proposal will not have any trading history so that cannot be included, but then more emphasis must be placed on showing the management's competence and the business idea's viability.

Back-up documentation should include:

1. A description of the business, its history and past achievements. Include details of all products/services and perhaps literature.
2. Details of the experience, education and background of the directors and key managers. This should include other directorships and business interests.
3. If applicable, show the management structure, giving details of the responsibilities of each director/manager.
4. Give a list and details of other shareholders. If they are prestigious or with good business experience, emphasise any other help they may be able to give you.
5. Provide audited accounts as far back as possible, and current management accounts.
6. For a start-up proposal, give details of the type of financial controls to be used, and who will provide them.
7. An appraisal of the present and future markets for your products, with details of major competitors.
8. A detailed statement on the current order book, showing number and type of customers. Compare this with the past year or so.
9. What finance is now required? How is it to be used? By what means will it be repaid?
10. Provide projections for the years ahead. This is a summary of your current budget and three-year plan, containing a P and L Account for each year; a cash flow forecast month by month for first year and then quarterly for three years; opening and closing Balance Sheets for each year.

Keep the documentation as brief, succinct and simple as possible, but do not miss out anything important. Read it through asking yourself four questions as you do. Is it clear, concise, complete and correct? Also explain technical terms, and if possible bring along the end product or at least a picture.

Appendix 4 shows an example of a 1982 business plan. It is included as a guide to what can be produced simply, effectively and quickly by one person. It has the great merit of having achieved the desired results.

Using computers for budgeting and planning

Budgeting and planning are fields in which the computer can really prove useful. There are a number of packages available that can take the routine 'number crunching' out of this activity.

Three interlinked business planning programmes much in use are Visicalc, Visitrend and Visiplot. Visicalc lets you change one or more items of data and see the impact of that change on the whole calculation. So, for example, you could enter a budgeted Profit and Loss Account and define certain relationships on the following lines:

Visicalc Business Planning Program

Sales	1000		
Materials	300	—	30% of sales
GP	700	—	Sales — Materials
Wages	350	—	250 + 10% of sales
NHI	49	—	14% of Wages
Pension	21	—	6% of Pension
Rent	75		
Rates	50		
Power	15	—	5% of Materials
Other	25		
Total Expenses	585		
Net Profit	115		

The left-hand column shows the first attempt at your budget. The right-hand column shows the 'formula' that is in use, so materials are 30 per cent of sales, wages are £250 + 10 per cent of sales, etc. Now you can feed in any change, say, increasing sales by 10 per cent, and rapidly get a computer print out (or put the information on a screen) showing the revised profit and loss account. This can save hours of tedious calculation — but it is no substitute for decision making.

Visitrend and Visiplot allow you to plot future trends in sales and costs etc, and show that information in graphs or bar charts.

The whole field is extremely dynamic, but one organisation has been specifically set up to keep business men up to date, Microsystems Centres, described below. There is also a report by the Economist Intelligence Unit on computer-based Financial Planning Models. It is written for non-specialists and reviews the various techniques on the market. The address is 27 St James's Place, London, SW1A 1HT; 01-493 6711.

Microsystems Centres (MSC): a federation is being established, supported by the government and the National Computing Centre. These centres provide an independent, authoritative, practical and individual source of assistance, advice and information for anyone who is considering using a micro-computer in business. Small and new businesses will find the range of services particularly helpful. The services of each centre will include:

Training. The centres' flexible training programmes are aimed at specific needs, from clerical staff through to financial advisers. They run self-instruction and taught courses at most times including weekends, evenings and lunchtimes.

Consultancy and advice are available to help you choose the right computer; to analyse and select from available software; or to commission specific or modified software. This consultancy extends from the feasibility study designed to find out if a computer will help to solve your business problem, through to acceptance tests on installing any system you may decide to buy. The centres do not sell hardware or software, so the advice given is independent, and the cost for this consultancy advice is around £50 per hour.

Demonstrations by the trained staff can be given of a range of microcomputer systems on permanent display at centres. Information is available from the centres' comprehensively stocked book shops, which carry a range of books, magazines and articles on most aspects of the subject.

Centres are already open or will open shortly at the addresses given below and one will also be opening in Birmingham.

The London Centre is: *Microsystems Centre,* 11 New Fetter Lane, London EC4A 1PU; 01-353 0013. Contact: Colin Harris.

Avon Microsystems Centre Ltd, Bank of England Chambers, Wine Street, Bristol, BS1 2DN; 0272 277774.

Coventry Microsystems Centre, Henley College of Further Education, Henley Road, Bell Green, Coventry CV2 1ED; 0203 611021.

East Midlands Microsystems Centre, Trent Polytechnic, Burton Street, Nottingham NC1 4BU; 0602-48248.

Edinburgh: Waverley Microsystems Centre, INMAP, 21 Lansdowne Crescent, Edinburgh EH12 5EH; 031-225 3141.

Hertfordshire Microsystems Centre, De Havilland College, Elstree Way, Borehamwood, Hertfordshire WD6 1JE; 01-953 6024.

Milton Keynes Microsystems Centre, Information Technology Exchange, Midsummer House, 429 Midsummer Boulevard, Saxon Gate West, Central Milton Keynes MK9 2HE; 0908 668866.

South Yorkshire Microsystems Centre, Sheffield City Polytechnic, Dyson House, Suffolk Road, Sheffield S1 1WR; 0741 73862.

Greater Manchester Microsystems Centre, Salford University Industrial Centre Ltd, Salbec House, 100 Broughton Road, Salford M6 6GS; 061-736 5843.

Merseyside Microsystems Centre, Merseyside Innovation Centre, 131 Mount Pleasant, Liverpool L3 5TF; 051-708 0123.

South Wales Microsystems Centre, Computer Centre, Polytechnic of Wales, Pontypridd, Mid Glamorgan CF37 1DL; 0443 405133.

Strathclyde Microsystems Centre, Paisley College of Technology, 72 George Street, Paisley, Renfrewshire PA1 2LF; 041-887 1241 ext 379.

Tyne and Wear Microsystems Centre, Coach Lane Campus, Newcastle upon Tyne Polytechnic, Newcastle upon Tyne NE7 7XA; 0632 700504.

Ulster Microsystems Centre, Ulster Polytechnic, Shore Road, Newtonabbey, Co. Antrim BT37 OQB; 0231 65131.

West Yorkshire Microsystems Centre, Queenswood House, Beckett Park, Leeds LS6 3Q5; 0532 759741.

The Federation will have the addresses as they come on stream. The address is: *Federation of Microcentres,* The National Computing Centre Ltd, Oxford Road, Manchester M1 7ED; 061-228 6333, telex 668962. Contact: John Turnbull, Federation Manager.

Sources of market and business planning information

In some cases the answers to a market question simply do not exist, for example, if you want to know how many people pass a particular shop front each day, and what sort of people they are. This is important information to help assess probable sales, but it is unlikely that anyone else will be interested enough to have researched and published it. But many of the questions posed earlier in the chapter are common to a lot of businesses, and the answers have been assembled.

Some of the more important publications and information services are listed below. An example of information from one of these publications is given in Appendix 3. If you cannot find the information then information services exist to help you to do so. These are described at the end of the chapter.

MARKET INFORMATION

The A-Z of UK Marketing Data, published by Euromonitor Publications Ltd, 18 Doughty Street, London WC1N 2PN, provides basic market data for several hundred UK markets from adhesives to zip fasteners, by product area, market size, production, imports, exports, the main brands, their market share and a market forecast. A good glimpse at a wide range of markets.

Annual Abstract of Statistics, published by the Central Statistical Office, is the basic source of all UK statistics. Figures are given for each of the preceding 10 years, so trends can be recognised.

ASLIB Directory, Volume I. Information sources in science, technology and commerce, edited by Ellen M. Coldlin, 5th edition, 1982. A valuable reference tool if you need to track down information over a wide range of subjects. This edition has over 3,000 entries from a large number of sources, professional, amateur, big and small. A major factor in including sources was their willingness to make the information available.

BBC Data Enquiry Service, Room 3, The Langham, The British Broadcasting Corporation, Portland Place, London W1A 1AA. This is a personal information service drawing on the worldwide resources of the BBC. It is an inexpensive and speedy way of checking facts and drawing on a statistical data bank which covers people, products, countries and events. The service could tell you the price of a pint of milk in 1951 or the current state of the Dutch economy. Ad hoc enquiries can cost as little as £5, or an annual subscription £100.

British Rate and Data, updated monthly. Whatever market you are interested in, it is almost certain to have a specialised paper or journal which will be an important source of market data. BRAD lists all newspapers and periodicals in the UK and Eire, and gives their frequency and circulation volume, price, their executives' names, advertising rates and readership classification. There is also information on company acquisitions, liquidity and insolvencies.

Business Monitors are the medium through which the government publishes the business statistics it collects from over 20,000 UK firms. They are the primary, and very often the only source of detailed information on the sectors they cover. The *Monitors* can help businessmen by indicating trends and tracing the progress of 4,000 individual products, manufactured by firms in 160 industries. *Monitors* can also be used to rate your business performance against that of your industry and measure the efficiency of different parts of your business.

The *Monitors* are published in three main series. The *Production Monitors* are published monthly, quarterly and annually. The quarterly is probably the most useful, with comprehensive yet timely information. The *Service and Distributor Monitors* cover the retail market, the instalment credit business, the motor trade, catering and allied trades and the computer service industry, among others. Finally, there are *Miscellaneous Monitors* covering such topics as shipping, insurance, import/export ratios for industry, acquisitions and mergers of industrial and commercial companies, cinemas and tourism.

The *Annual Census of Production Monitors* cover virtually every sector of industry, and include data on total purchases, total sales, stocks, work in progress, capital expenditure, employment, wages and salaries. They include analyses of costs and output, of establishments by size, of full- and part-time employees by sex, and of employment, net capital expenditure and net output by region.

You can use the information — particularly that from the size analysis table — to establish such ratios as gross output per head, net output per head, net to gross output, and wages and salaries to net output. With these as a base, you can compare the performance of your own business with the average for firms of similar size and for that with your particular industry as a whole. For example, you can discover your share of the market, and compare employment figures, increases in sales and so on.

Most of the libraries listed later in this section will have a selection of the *Business Monitor* series. Individual monitors can be bought from HMSO Books, PO Box 569, London SE1 9NH. They are all individually priced.

Guide to Official Statistics is the main guide to all government produced statistics, including ad hoc reports. It is published by HMSO at £18.50. However, a brief, free guide is available from the Press and Information Service, Central Statistical Office, Great George Street, London SW1 3AQ.

Key Note Publications. Publishers of the same name at 28-42 Banner Street, London EC1Y 8QE; 01-253 3006, produce concise briefs on various sectors of the UK economy.

Each Key Note contains a detailed examination of the structure of an industry, its distribution network and its major companies; an in-depth analysis of the market, covering products by volume and value, market shares, foreign trade and an appraisal of trends within the market; a review of recent developments in the industry, highlighting new product development, corporate development and legislation; a financial analysis of named major companies, providing data and ratios over a three-year period together with a corporate appraisal and economic overview; forecasts on the future prospects for the industry, including estimates from Key Note's own database and authoritative trade sources. There is a very useful appendix detailing further sources of information — recent press articles, other reports and journals.

Over 100 market sectors are covered, including such areas as adhesives, after-dinner drinks, bicycles, butchers, commercial leasing, health foods, road haulage, public houses, travel agents and women's magazines. Each Key Note costs £35, falling to £17 for users of their voucher system.

Kelly's Manufacturers & Merchants Directory, published by IPC Business Press, 40 Bowling Green Lane, London EC1R ONE has an alphabetical list of manufacturers, merchants, wholesalers and firms, together with their trade descriptions, addresses, telephone and telex numbers. In addition, entries are listed by trade classification. A section lists British importers under the goods they import. Exporters are listed by the products they export and the continent and countries in which they sell. The directory covers 90,000 UK firms classified under 10,000 trade, product or service headings.

Kelly's Regional Directory of British Industry is published in eight volumes each October. It provides an exhaustive, town-by-town guide to industry and the products and services offered. This really is most useful if you want to confine your interests to one particular area, perhaps as an aid to a concentrated sales blitz.

Kelly's Post Office London Directory provides business listings by street, so a company's immediate neighbours can be identified. It is useful for finding concentrations of a particular type of business, or for finding gaps in the provisions of a particular type of business.

Key British Enterprises, published by Dun and Bradstreet Ltd, 26-32 Clifton Street, London EC2P 2LY; 01-247 4377, contains information on 20,000 UK companies that between them are responsible for 90 per cent of industrial expenditure. KBE is very useful for identifying sales prospects or confirming addresses, monitoring competitors and customers or finding new suppliers. As well as giving the names, addresses, telephone and telex numbers of the main office of each company, it gives branch addresses, products indexed by SIC (Standard Industrial Classification) code, sales turnover (UK and overseas), directors' names and responsibilities, shareholders, capital structure, trade names, and number of employees.

KBE is in two volumes, alphabetical and geographical. By using the directory you can quickly establish the size of business you are dealing with and what other products or services they offer. It is very often important to know the size of a firm if, for example, your products are confined to certain types of business. A book-keeping service is unlikely to interest a large company with several hundred employees; they would have their own accounts department. Conversely, a very small company may not need a public relations consultant.

Kompass is published in association with the Confederation of British Industry in two volumes: Volume I is indexed by product or service to help find suppliers, indicating whether they are manufacturers, wholesalers or distributors. It can be very useful indeed on certain occasions to be able to bypass a wholesaler and get to the manufacturer direct. Volume II gives basic company information on the 30,000 suppliers identified from Volume I. It includes the address, telephone and telex numbers, bankers, directors, office hours and the number of employees.

Office of Population, Census and Surveys produce demographic statistics for each county in England and Wales from the 1981 census. These provide data not only on total population in each area, but also on occupation, economic groups, etc. Similar reports for Scottish and Northern Ireland regions are also available. There is a reference library at OPCS, St Catherine House, 10 Kingsway, London WC2B 6JP; 01-242 0262. More information and answers to general enquiries on these reports are also available from this number on extensions 2009/2013.

Overseas Trade Statistics, published by the Department of Industry and Trade, provide a monthly statement of UK imports and exports by volume and value for each product group and individual country.

The Bill Entry Services, operated by HM Customs and Excise, Portcullis House, 17 Victoria Avenue, Southend-on-Sea SS2 6AL (0702 49421 ext 310), will provide more detailed information at a fee.

Published Data on European Industrial Markets, published by Industrial Aids Ltd, 14 Buckingham Palace Road, London SW1W OQP; 01-828 5036.

Part I lists over 1,900 market research reports available for purchase at prices from as low as £10 up to several thousand pounds. Although the directory is entitled 'industrial', the interpretation is fairly wide. It covers consumer goods as markets for industrial products, and financial and economic planning studies, where they are considered of possible interest to industry. This could be a relatively inexpensive way of finding out about a distant market place.

Part II is a guide to other sources of information on European industrial markets, including international statistical and individual country sources.

Reports Index, Business Surveys Ltd, PO Box 21, Dorking, Surrey RH5 4EE; 0306-87857. This is an index to reports in every field published and available for sale. Its sources include government publications, HMSO and others, market research organisers, educational establishments, EEC, industrial and financial companies. Again, at £94 per annum, the cost is modest.

The Retail Directory, published by Newman, 48 Portland Street, London W1; 01-439 0335, gives details of all UK department stores and private shops. It lists the names of executives and merchandise buyers as well as addresses and telephone numbers, early closing days, etc. It also covers multiple shops, co-operative societies, supermarkets and many other retail outlets. If you plan to sell to shops, this is a useful starting point, with around 1,305 department stores and large shops and 4,821 multiple shop firms and variety stores listed in 1,346 pages. If you are already selling retail, this directory could help you expand your prospects list quickly. The directory also identifies high turnover outlets for main product ranges. There is a useful survey, showing retail activities on each major shopping street in the country. It gives the name and nature of the retail businesses in each street.

A separate volume contains shop surveys for the Greater London area, with 27,830 shops listed by name, street number and trade. The head offices of 1,130 multiples are given, as are 233 surveys showing what sort of shops are in any area. This can be used for giving sales people useful contacts within their territory.

Sell's Directory, Sell's Publications Ltd, Sell's House, 39 East Street, Epsom, Surrey KT17 1BQ, and the Institute of Purchasing Management. It lists 65,000 firms alphabetically, with name, trade, address, telephone number and telex numbers. Using a classified cross-reference system, it covers 25,000 products and services. There is a guide to several thousand trade names cross-referenced back to each company. The remaining sections include a contractors' section, advertising firms seeking contract work, and a business information section. If you only know the trade name and want to find out who makes the product, then this directory will help you. You can then use it to find competitive sources of supply of similar products or services.

Finding the information

Now that you have an idea of the considerable mass of data that is available about companies, their products and markets, the next problem that remains is to track it down. Fortunately, many of the directories and publications are kept in reference sections of major libraries up and down the country. If you know exactly what information you want, then your problem is confined to finding a library or information service that has that information.

Specialist libraries

Apart from your local library there are hundreds of specialist libraries concentrated in government departments, major industrial companies, trade organisations, research centres and academic institutes. Two useful publications that will help you find out about these are listed below.

ASLIB Economic and Business Information Group Membership Directory, published by the group and available from the London Business School Library, Sussex Place, Regent's Park, London NW1 4SA; 01-262 5050. It provides a list of over 300 specialist business libraries throughout the country, and gives a very useful guide to their area of specialist interest.

Guide to Government Departments and Other Libraries. The 25th edition, published in 1982, is the latest, and it is available from the Science Reference Library, 25 Southampton Buildings, Chancery Lane, London WC2A 1AW, price £9. As the title indicates, this book concentrates on libraries in government departments and agencies, and particularly avoids duplicating the ground covered by the ASLIB Directory. The entries are arranged by subject, supplemented by an alphabetical index of the libraries, their locations, phone numbers and opening hours.

Not all the libraries covered in these directories are open to the public for casual visits. However, many will let you use their reference facilities by appointment.

If you are in, or near London you can visit or contact the:

Science Reference Library, Department of the British Library, 25 Southampton Buildings, Chancery Lane, London WC2A 1AW; 01-405 8721, ext 3344 or 3345; patent enquiries ext 3350, telex 266959. This is the national library for modern science and technology, for patents, trade marks and designs. It has the most comprehensive reference section of this type of literature in western Europe. If you have no adequate library close at hand a visit here could save you visits to several libraries. It should also be able to provide you with answers if most other places cannot do so.

The library's resources are formidable. It has 25,000 different journals, with issues back to 1960 on open shelves and the rest quickly available; 85,000 books and pamphlets and 20¼ million patents. It has a world-wide collection of journals on trade marks, together with books on law and design. Most of the major UK and European reports are held, as is trade literature and around 1,000 abstracting periodicals.

The services are equally extensive. It is open from Monday to Friday, 09.30 to 21.00, and on Saturdays, 10.00 to 13.00. You can visit without prior arrangement or a reader's ticket. Telephone requests for information, including the checking of references, are accepted. Once at the library, staff are available to help you find items and to answer general queries. Scientific staff are also on hand for specialised enquiries. There is even a linguist service to help you inspect material written in a foreign language, though for this service you must make an appointment.

The Business Information Service of the Science Reference Library; 01-404 0406. This was set up in January 1981, primarily to support the activities of other business and industrial libraries. However, it will help individual users as much as possible. Staff here can extract reference information quickly, advise on the use of business literature and suggest other organisations to contact. For extensive research you will have to call in person, but they can let you know if a visit would be worth while.

INFORMATION SERVICES

In addition to the many excellent business libraries up and down the country, there are an increasing number of organisations that will do the searching for you. The benefits to you are twofold: professionals search out the data, and can alert you to sources that you may not have thought of; they save you time, not just the time you would spend searching. If you are far from a good business reference library you may have a considerable and expensive journey to make. Mostly, these organisations have substantial libraries of their own, but Warwick, for example, will search elsewhere if they cannot find it in their stocks. They claim the second largest statistics collection in the UK, and they have access to several on-line data bases.

Organisations in the field include:

Industrial Aids Ltd, enquiry service at 14 Buckingham Palace Road, London SW1W OQP; 01-828 5036, telex 918666 CRECON G. This service is geared to supply commercial and technical information, such as who makes what/where/how much. Who is company A's agent in country X? Where are custom manufacturing sources? Details are given of company financial data, affiliations, product literature, consumption patterns, end users, prices, discounts and trading terms, as well as new legislation and standards, trade and lists of delegates. The cost is £29 per enquiry, excluding VAT. You can use the service by telephone, telex or letter, and the response is fast.

The Marketing Shop, 18 Kingly Court, Kingly Street, London W1R 5LE; 01-434 2671, telex 262284. This organisation provides a wide range of marketing services, but its information service is perhaps the most useful facility for small businesses. It can provide data on practically any topic, either using its own library or outside sources, and will also monitor the media for information on companies, products or markets. The charge is £35 an hour for ad hoc work. The more usual arrangement is for customers to take a block of hours to be used over the year. Block fees start at around £500, which works out at £30 per hour.

Warwick Statistics Service, University of Warwick Library, Coventry CV4 7AL; 0203 418938, telex 31406. Contact: Jennifer Carr or David Mart. The service offers a range of commercial and economic information based on published sources including international statistics, both official and non-official, market research, periodicals, reports, directories, company reports and on-line services. The service can be particularly helpful to a small business with information on market size and share, locating particular types of company and finding out about them, tracing recent articles on a particular product or process, on consumer expenditure data, imports and exports, economic conditions, price trends, advertising expenditure and production and sales figures.

The service will also undertake analysis of the data in question, and provide a written report on their desk research. In general, enquiries are dealt with on the telephone, telex or by post; however, personal visits are welcomed. If you telephone beforehand, documents can be assembled for you to look at.

Annual subscribers to the service pay £300 for 25 hours' search time and publication. Occasional users of the service can get information on research assistance on an ad hoc basis at a cost of £20 per hour pro rata, with a minimum charge of £5. All in all, it is very good value.

Their monthly journal, *Warwick Statistics News,* provides a regular source of information on statistical and marketing topics, and costs £25 per annum. The service holds regular one-day seminars on Information Sources for Business Planning and Market Research, costing £30.

Chapter 11

Book-keeping and Flash Reports

It is hard to believe that any businessman could hope to survive without knowing how much cash he has, and what his profit or loss on sales is. He needs these facts on at least a monthly, weekly, or occasionally even a daily basis, to survive, yet alone to grow.

And yet all too often a new business's first set of accounts are also its last, with the firm's accountant, bank manager or creditors signalling bankruptcy. While bad luck plays a part in some failures, a lack of reliable financial information plays a part in most. The chapters on financial controls show the wealth of vital facts that can be put at the decision-makers' finger-tips. That is, if only they could be bothered to assemble the basic information as it comes in.

But it is not only the owner who needs these financial facts. Bankers, shareholders, the Inland Revenue and the Customs and Excise (VAT), will be unsympathetic audiences to the businessman without well-documented facts to back him up. The Inland Revenue, for example, will present a new business with a tax demand. The onus then lies with the businessman, using his records, to either agree or dispute the sum that the IR claims. A bank manager faced with a request for an increased overdraft facility to help a small business grow, needs financial facts to work with. Without them he will generally have to say no, as he is responsible for other people's money.

Book-keeping principles

The way a business records and stores financial facts is by keeping books. The owner/manager may keep these himself at the start, if the business is small and the trading methods simple. Later on he may feel his time could be more usefully spent helping the business to expand. At that stage he may have a book-keeper in for a few hours, or days, a week. Or perhaps he could use an outside book-keeping service, sending the information to them periodically. Many small retailers now have cash tills that are programmed to analyse sales, produce product gross margin information, stock levels, and even signal when and how much new stock is needed. Finally, if the work and profits warrant it, a book-keeper (or even an accountant) may be employed full time.

In any event the owner/manager will need to appreciate the basics of the book-keeping system before it is installed. How else can he choose the best one for his purpose, and then get the best out of it?

THE RECORDS TO BE KEPT

It is essential to remember that having lots of cash, either in the till or the bank, does not mean that you are making a profit. Conversely, pursuing profitable business can often lead to cash flow problems. (A glance back at Chapter 2 will refresh your memory.) The records must keep track of all items that affect both cash and profits.

Day books

Sometimes called journals, or books of original entry, they are where every transaction is initially recorded in the order of occurrence. Each day book is used to cater for one kind of transaction, so if there are enough transactions of a particular kind, you open a day book for it. For example, there are always enough cash transactions to warrant a cash day book. If a firm sells on credit, then there will be a sales day book. Cash day books are described below.

Cash books

Many small businesses trade in both notes/coins and cheques. For book-keeping purposes these are both called cash, although initially a separate record is kept of each.

The petty cash book is used to record transactions in notes and coins. Money in is on the left-hand page and money out on the right. The money out could include such items as stamps or office coffee etc. Always keep receipts as one day you may have to verify these records. Once a week, or daily if the sums involved justify it, total the money in and out to get a cash balance. Check that it agrees with actual cash from the till or cash box.

The cash book records all receipts and payments made by cheque. Once again money in is on the left-hand page and money out on the right. Every week add up both pages to arrive at a cash at bank balance. This should be checked against your bank statement every month at least and make sure that the basic information you are working with is correct.

Sales and purchase ledgers

If your business gives credit to customers, or takes credit from suppliers, you will need a sales and a purchases ledger. Each ledger should ideally have a separate page for every business that you deal with.

On the right-hand side of the purchase ledger are listed the date, description, amount and cost of each item bought on credit. On the left-hand side a record is kept of all payments made to the supplier, with the items for which the payments were made. Each month, by deducting the left-hand total from the right, you can see how much each supplier is owed. Suppliers ought to send you a statement and you can use that to check your own view of the situation.

The sales ledger deals with customers in much the same way. One important difference is that credit sales are shown on the left-hand side of the ledger while customers' payments appear on the right. This is simply an accounting convention to deal with credits and debits. It would also be very useful to keep a note of customers' (and suppliers') addresses, telephone numbers and contacts' names, with each entry in the ledgers. This will ensure you have all the relevant information when chasing up payments, or dealing with queries.

THE CAPITAL REGISTER (or asset register)

Limited companies have to keep a capital register. This records capital items they own, such as land, buildings, equipment and vehicles, showing the cost at date of purchase. It also records the disposal of any of these items, and the cumulative depreciation.

THE NOMINAL LEDGER (or private ledger)

This is usually kept by your accountant or book-keeper. It brings together all the information from the 'primary' ledgers, as these other basic records are called. Expenses from the cash books and purchase ledger are 'posted' to the left-hand side of the nominal ledger. Income from sales (and any other income) is posted to the right. Normally each type of expense or income has a separate page, which makes subsequent analysis an easier task.

The trial balance

Every month each page in the nominal ledger is totalled, and used to prepare a 'trial balance'. In other words the sum of all the left-hand totals should end up equalling the sum of all the right-hand totals. This is the basis of double entry book-keeping, and is what gives you confidence that the figures are correctly recorded.

Monthly flash reports

Obviously, until accruals (see index for treatment of accruals) have been dealt with, a physical stock check carried out, and the business's books audited or examined, final accounts cannot be produced. However, the information from the ledgers can be used to produce a 'flash report' each month, showing how the business appears to be performing.

A Profit and Loss Account can be prepared; the cash book balances will show the cash in hand; the purchase and sales ledgers will show how much the business owes and is owed. In addition, many of the control ratios on profitability and liquidity, discussed in earlier chapters, can be prepared. All this can be compared with your plan or budget, to see if the performance is on target.

This information will let the businessman complement his natural flair with some hard facts. It will also give him time to face problems before they become unmanageable.

Review of book-keeping systems

The following is a brief survey of some of the more 'popular' book-keeping systems. They are divided into five categories: 'shoe boxes'; do-it-yourself books; halfway houses; accountants only; and computer-based systems.

'SHOE BOX' SYSTEM

This is for the simplest businesses, which need relatively little financial control beyond cash, bank accounts, accounts payable and accounts receivable.

At its simplest you need four shoe boxes, a bank paying-in book and a cheque book (the last two can tell you how much you have in the bank). You keep two boxes for unpaid invoices (one for sales, one for purchases, services and so on). You transfer the invoices into the other two boxes (one for sales, one for purchases, etc) when each invoice is paid. By adding all the invoices in one box (sales, unpaid invoices) you can find out how much you are owed, and by adding another (purchases, unpaid) you find out how much you owe. You keep every record relating to the business, too.

This is a perfectly adequate system unless you need some form of cash control or some profit information and you need it fast. It is, however, not too good on credit control. Essentially, this system is only for the smallest firms.

THE DIY SYSTEM

These are normally hardback, bound books with several sections to them, each part ruled and already laid out for the entries. Each one has a set of instructions and examples for each section.

All the systems mentioned here have some advantages and disadvantages in common:

Advantages. Each one tries to assist the small business person by allowing some measures of financial control, especially over cash and bank balances. They almost always include VAT sections and profit and loss sections. They aim, in the large part, to make an accountant unnecessary, or at least to minimise your expense in that area.

Disadvantages. None of these systems will work unless it is kept up regularly — which means weekly at a minimum, and preferably daily. As a drawback this cannot be over-emphasised. These books are probably not for you unless you currently keep a diary regularly. If not kept properly, they can cost you more in accountancy fees rather than less. Other disadvantages are that they often assume some prior knowledge from the user, even though they give instructions (which sometimes leave much to be desired, relying largely on worked examples that are difficult to follow). They compartmentalise people and business, and they tend to ignore such expenses as 'use of home as office' (for example, home telephone bills) many of which may be tax allowable. Finally, many people also find that they

161

would rather not use these books as the basis for dealing with their Inspector of Taxes, and would rather have their accountants do this. In these circumstances you are going to need an accountant anyway, and your Inspector is much more likely to pay attention to him.

The following table shows the basic information for some of the most common systems, and the conclusions as to their relative usefulness.

DIY accounting books comparison table

Name and availability	Approx Cost	Financial Control Provided	Records Provided
Ataglance Ataglance Publications 16 Sawley Avenue, Lytham St Annes, Lancs FY8 3QL; 0253 727107	£4	Bank	Payments, Receipts, VAT
Collins Self Employed Account Book W H Smith and other stationers	£9	Bank, debtors, creditors	Payments, receipts, VAT, subcontract
Collins Complete Traders Account Book W H Smith and other stationers	£9	Bank	Payments, receipts, VAT
Evrite Traders Account Book Commercial stationers or Evrite Publishing Co Ltd Hill Street Chambers, St Helier, Jersey, Channel Islands	£8	Bank, debtors	Payments, receipts, VAT
Finco Small Business Book-keeping System Casdec Ltd 11 Windermere Avenue, Garden Farm Estate, Chester-le-Street, Co Durham DH2 3DU; 0385 882906	£35	Bank, cash, debtors, creditors, wages	Receipts, payments, sales, purchases, payroll, VAT
Kalamazoo Set Up Pack Kalamazoo Business Systems Mill Lane, Northfield, Birmingham B31 2RW; 021-475 2191	£92	Bank, cash, debtors, creditors	Receipts
Simplex 'D' Cash Book Commercial stationers or George Viner (Dist Ltd) Simplex House, Mytholmbridge Mills, Mytholmbridge, Holmfirth, Huddersfield HD7 2TA	£3	Bank, cash	Receipts, payments, profit and loss

Finco Small Business Book-keeping System. At £35 this system may seem dear, but it has two years' supply of forms (compared to others which provide only one), and gives a large amount of financial control for a relatively small sum. This is first choice.

The Kalamazoo Set Up is the second choice. It would have been first choice had it not cost £92. You probably also need training to be able to use it, even with their book as support. It has been chosen because it can give the best financial control, if used properly. In addition, it can save time through being a single-write system (entering up to three records simultaneously).

GENERAL COMMENTS

Ataglance. Few instructions, mostly related to VAT. But if you are thinking of opening a fish and chip shop they have prepared a special book-keeping ledger, costing £1.98.

Collins Self Employed Account Book. This seems to be aimed at subcontractors and is reasonably comprehensive, but the instructions are a little limited, so it needs prior knowledge.

Collins Complete Traders Account Book. For retail outlets only. The instructions are somewhat limited.

Evrite Traders Account Book. Short, unclear instructions. Relies on worked examples. Assumes prior knowledge. Debtor control in total only (not by individual customers).

Finco Small Business Book-keeping System. Simple instructions, two years' supply of record sheets, loose-leaf. This is more easily adaptable to any business (there is less compartmentalisation), and gives detailed control over individual amounts outstanding, both receivable and payable. Because it is loose-leaf, your accountant can take the relevant records without depriving you of your control. It can also be used in conjunction with your accountant's minicomputer.

Kalamazoo Set Up Pack. This is the most comprehensive system (as well as the most expensive). It provides everything that all other systems give you, two years' supply of records (loose-leaf) and a debtors/creditors ledger. Your £92 also buys you a basic book-keeping book which gives information on how to keep it up (and why you need to). The book is by John Kellock, entitled *A Practical Guide to Good Book-keeping and Business Systems,* and is available separately.

Simplex 'D' Cash Book. This is the best known of this type of book. Its instructions are short, and it relies heavily on worked examples. There are separate books for VAT and wages, as well as a separate book, *Simplified Book-keeping for Small Business,* at £3.

HALFWAY HOUSE SYSTEMS

The halfway house systems lie between a simple DIY and an 'accountant only' system. Pre-printed stationery tends to be used, but in loose-leaf form. They are more flexible than the DIY, and tend to be cheaper than using an accountant only. However, they do require some knowledge by the person who keeps the books. Again, this need not be daunting, as your accountant can probably train you (or your office girl or boy) to keep them up. The major problem is that you need your accountant before you can use your records for more advanced financial control.

There are two common halfway house systems on the market: Twinlock and Kalamazoo. Twinlock is available at commercial stationers or the publishers: Twinlock Ltd, 36 Croydon Road, Beckenham, Kent BR3 4BH; 01-650 4818. Kalamazoo is available only from the publishers, Kalamazoo Ltd.

At the basic level the two systems seem remarkably similar, both in cost and financial control. The minimum systems will cost £200 to £400 and Kalamazoo offer training with their product. Both are single-write systems (where one writing can enter up to three records). You should talk to your accountant before installing one.

ACCOUNTANT ONLY SYSTEMS

The accountant only systems are those for the more complex (possibly larger) small businesses, and will be designed by your accountant. They often need trained book-keepers to run them. However, the training period can be relatively short (anything from one day upwards). The book-keeper handles the routine matters, and your accountant the non-routine.

COMPUTER SYSTEMS

There are many small computer systems that will carry out the book-keeping and accountancy functions needed by a small business. But, like all systems, they are only as good as the quality of information put in. The other major problems with computer systems are: selecting the equipment in a market with many models with claimed advantages; making sure that you have the necessary extra equipment; making sure that you have the software (programmes) capable of handling your information and record needs; and, finally, ensuring that you can use the machine efficiently. This is fine for the enthusiast, but others tend to get lost in the jungle. It would certainly be safest to start off with an accounting book-keeping practice who have their own computer-based system. This is also an area in which your nearest Microsystems Centre could be of help (see page 146).

Chapter 12
Sources of Capital for a Small Business

Small businesses need to borrow money for a variety of reasons: in order to start up, expand, re-locate, to start exporting, to innovate or carry out research and development, or to meet the unexpected, such as the collapse of a major customer or supplier. The level of borrowing that you can secure will be related in some way to your abilities, the nature of your business and how much you have put into it. Few lenders like to see themselves much more exposed to financial risk than the owner(s) who, after all, expects to make the most gain.

In the eye of most lenders, finance for the small business fits into two distinct areas: short term, which does not necessarily mean that you only want the money for a short term, but rather the life of the asset you are buying is itself relatively short; and long term, which is the converse of that. The table below may help you get a clearer picture

Term	Business need example	Financing method
Short (up to three years)	For raw materials or finished goods; to finance debtors; equipment with a short life or other working capital needs; for dealing with seasonal peaks and troughs; to start exporting; or to expand overseas sales.	Overdrafts Short-term loans Factoring Invoice discounting Bill finance Trade credit Export and import Finance
Medium to long (three years or over)	Acquiring or improving premises, buying plant and machinery with a long life; buying an existing business including a franchise; for technological innovations or developing a 'new' product or idea.	Mortgage Sale and leaseback Loan finance Long-term leasing Hire Purchase Equity and venture finance Public-sector finance

Now, of course, starting up or expanding a small business will call for a mix of short- and long-term finance. You may be able to get all this from one source; more likely, though, once you start to trade you will find that different sources are better organised to provide different types of money.

All methods of financing have important implications for your tax and financial position, and appropriate professional advice should always be taken before embarking on any financing exercise.

For most of us, borrowing money usually means contact with our local bank manager. Although he is by no means the only source of finance for a new or small business, the bank manager is a good starting point.

Choosing the form of your business

At the outset of your business venture you will have to decide in what legal form to establish your business. That form will significantly influence the types of money that are available to you. There are four main forms that a business can take, with a number of variations on two of these. The form that you choose will depend on a number of factors: commercial needs, financial risk and your tax position. All play an important part.

SOLE TRADER

If you have the facilities, cash and customers, you can start trading under your own name immediately. Unless you intend to register for VAT, there are no rules about the records you have to keep. There is no requirement for an external audit, or for financial information on your business to be filed at Companies House. You would be prudent to keep good books and to get professional advice, as you will have to declare your income to the Inland Revenue.

Without good records you will lose in any dispute over tax. You are personally liable for the debts of your business, and in the event of your business failing, your personal possessions can be sold to meet them.

A sole trader does not have access to equity capital, which has the attraction of being risk-free to the business. He must rely on loans from banks or individuals and any other non-equity source of finance.

PARTNERSHIP

There are very few restrictions to setting up in business with another person or persons in partnership. Many partnerships are formed without legal formalities, and sometimes drifted into without the parties themselves being aware that they have entered a partnership. All that is needed is for two or more people to agree to carry on a business together intending to share the profits. The law will then recognise the existence of a partnership.

Most of the points raised when considering sole tradership apply equally to partnerships. All the partners are personally liable for the debts of the business, even if those debts were incurred by one partner's mismanagement or dishonesty without the other partner's knowledge. Even death may not release a partner from his obligations, and in some circumstances his estate can remain liable. Unless you take 'public' leave of your partnership by notifying your business contacts, and advertising retirement in the *London Gazette,* you will remain liable indefinitely. So it is vital before entering a partnership to be absolutely sure of your partner and to take legal advice in drawing up a contract, which should cover the following points:

Profit sharing, responsibilities and duration. This should specify how profits and losses are to be shared, and who is to carry out which tasks. It should also set limits on partners' monthly drawings, and on how long the partnership itself is to last (either a specific period of years or indefinitely, with a cancellation period of, say, three months).

Voting rights and policy decision. Unless otherwise stated, all the partners have equal voting rights. It is advisable to get a definition of what is a policy or voting decision, and how such decisions are to be made. You must also decide how to expel or admit a new partner.

Time off. Every partner is entitled to his share of the profits, even when ill or on holiday. You will need some guidelines on the length and frequency of holidays, and on what to do if someone is absent for a long period for any other reason.

Withdrawing capital. You have to decide how each partner's share of the capital of the business will be valued in the event of a partner leaving or the partnership being dissolved.

Accountancy procedures. You do not have either to file accounts or to have accounts audited. However, it may be prudent to agree a satisfactory standard of accounting and have a firm of accountants to carry out that work. Sleeping partners may well insist on it.

Sleeping partners. A partner who has put up capital but does not intend to take an active part in running the business can protect himself against risk by having his partnership registered as a limited partnership.

LIMITED COMPANY

The main distinction between a limited company and either sole tradership or partnership is that it has a legal identity of its own separate from the people who own it. This means that, in the event of liquidation, creditors' claims are restricted to the assets of the company. The shareholders are not liable as individuals for the business debts beyond the paid-up value of their shares. This applies even if the shareholders are working directors, unless the company has been trading fraudulently.

Other advantages include the freedom to raise capital by selling shares and certain tax concessions.

The disadvantages include the legal requirement for the company's accounts to be audited by a chartered or certified accountant, and for certain records of the business trading activities to be filed annually at Companies House.

In practice, the ability to limit liability is severely restricted by the requirements of potential lenders. They often insist on personal guarantees from directors when small, new or troubled companies look for loans or credits. The personal guarantee usually takes the form of a charge on the family home. Since the Boland case in 1980, unless a wife has specifically agreed to a charge on the house, by signing a Deed of Postponement, then no lender can take possession in the case of default.

A limited company can be formed by two shareholders, one of whom must be a director. A company secretary must also be appointed, who can be a shareholder, director, or an outside person such as an accountant.

The company can be bought 'off the shelf' from a registration agent, then adapted to suit your own purposes. This will involve changing the name, shareholders and articles of association. Alternatively, you can form your own company, using your solicitor or accountant.

COOPERATIVE

There is an alternative form of business for people whose primary concern is to create a democratic work environment, sharing profits and control. If you want to control or substantially influence your own destiny, and make as large a capital gain out of your life's work as possible, then a cooperative is not for you.

The membership of the cooperative is the legal body that controls the business, and members must work in the business. Each member has one vote, and the cooperative must be registered under the Industrial and Provident Societies Act 1965, with the Chief Registrar of Friendly Societies.

Forms of business: pros and cons

Form	Advantages	Disadvantages
Sole trader	Start trading immediately Minimum formalities No set-up costs No audit fees No public disclosure of trading information Pay Schedule D Tax Profits or losses in one trade can be set off against profits or losses in any other area Past PAYE can be clawed back to help with trading losses	Unlimited personal liability for trading debts No access to equity capital Low status public image When you die, so does the business
Partnership	No audit required, though your partner may insist on one No public disclosure of trading information Pay Schedule D tax	Unlimited personal liability for your own and your partners' trading debts (except sleeping partners) Partnership contracts can be complex and costly to prepare Limited access to equity capital Death of a partner usually causes partnership to be dissolved
Limited company	Shareholders' liabilities restricted to nominal value of shares It is possible to raise equity capital High status public image If income is substantial, corporation tax for small business is lower than equivalent income tax rate	Directors are on PAYE Audit required Trading information must be disclosed Suppliers, landlords and banks will probably insist on personal guarantees from directors (except for government loan guarantee scheme)

Form	Advantages	Disadvantages
Limited company	The business has a life of its own and continues with or without the founder	You cannot start trading until you have a certificate of incorporation

Clearing banks

This is the general name given to the High Street bankers. We immediately think of the big four — Barclays, Lloyds, Midland and the National Westminster — when we think of 'clearers'. However, there are another dozen or so that fit within the general meaning of 'clearing and domestic deposit bank'.

The banks offer a wide range of services in their own right. Through wholly or partially owned subsidiaries they cover virtually every aspect of the financial market. These services include overdrafts, term loans, trade bill finance, factoring, leasing, export and import finance, the government loan guarantee scheme, and equity financing. Some of these services are described below. The others are explained later in this chapter.

Overdrafts. Bank overdrafts are the most common type of short-term finance. They are simple to arrange, you just talk to your local bank manager. They are flexible with no minimum level. Sums of money can be drawn or repaid within the total amount agreed. They are relatively cheap, with interest paid only on the outstanding daily balance.

Of course, interest rates can fluctuate, so what seemed a small sum of money one year can prove crippling the next if interest rates jump suddenly. Normally you do not repay the 'capital', you simply renew or alter the overdraft facility from time to time. However, overdrafts are theoretically repayable on demand, so you should not use short-term overdraft money to finance long-term needs, such as buying a lease or some plant and equipment. Overdrafts are more often used to finance working capital needs, stocks, customers who have not paid up, bulk purchases of materials and the like.

Term loans (short, medium and long). These are rather more formal than a simple overdraft. They cover periods of 0-3, 3-10 and 10-20 years respectively. They are usually secured against an existing fixed asset or one to be acquired, or are guaranteed personally by the directors (proprietors). As such, this may involve you in a certain amount of expense with legal fees and arrangement or consultants' fees. So it may be a little more expensive than an overdraft, but unless you default on the interest charges you can be reasonably confident of having the use of the money throughout the whole term of the borrowing.

The interest rates on the loan can either be fixed for the term or variable according to the prevailing interest rate. A fixed rate is to some extent a gamble, which may work in your favour, depending on how interest rates move over the term of the loan: if general interest rates rise you win, and if they fall you lose. However, a variable rate means that you do not take that risk. There is another benefit to a fixed rate of interest. Planning ahead is a little easier with a fixed financial commitment, unlike a variable overdraft rate, where a sudden rise can have disastrous consequences.

Government loan guarantees for small businesses were introduced in March 1981 for an initial period of three years. The 1983 Finance Act extended the life of the scheme by making a further £300m available. To be eligible for this loan, your proposition must have been looked at by an approved bank and considered viable, but should not be a proposition that the bank itself would normally support. You can be a sole trader, partnership, cooperative or limited company wanting funds to start up or to expand. The bank simply passes your application on to the Department of Industry, using an approved format.

This is an elementary business plan, which asks for some details of the directors, the business, their cash needs and profit performance or projection of the business. There are no formal rules on size, number of employees or assets, but large businesses and their subsidiaries are definitely excluded from the scheme. The other main exclusions are businesses in the following fields: agriculture, horticulture, banking, commission agents, education, forestry (except tree-harvesting and saw-milling), house and estate agents, insurance, medical and veterinary, night-clubs and licensed clubs, pubs and property, and travel agencies.

The loans can be for up to £75,000 and repayable over two to seven years. It may be possible to delay paying the capital element for up to two years from the start of the loan, however, monthly or quarterly repayments of interest will have to be made from the outset. The loan itself is likely to be expensive.

Once the proposal is approved by the Department of Trade, the bank lends you the money at bank rate plus a few per cent and the government guarantees the bank 80 per cent of its money if you cannot pay up. In return for this the government charges you a 3 per cent 'insurance' premium on the 80 per cent of the loan it has taken on risk. Borrowers would be expected to pledge all available business assets as a security for the loan, but they would not necessarily be excluded from the scheme if there were no available assets. Also on the plus side, directors will not normally be asked to give personal guarantees on security, an undertaking they may have to make for other forms of borrowing.

There are now some 30 banks operating the scheme, and by August 1983 some 12,000 loans worth £350m had been granted. The average loan is between £30,000 and £40,000.

Although there are no official figures to go on, a business failure rate of one for every 13 loans granted was the picture emerging for the scheme's first year. The rule certainly seems to be to ask for as much as you need, plus a good margin of safety. Going back for a second bite too soon is definitely frowned upon. You do not have to take all the money at once. At the discretion of your bank manager, you can take the money in up to four lots but each lot must be at least 25 per cent.

Encouraging, too, is the evidence that these loans were fairly evenly split between start-ups and growing young businesses. It is worth discussing your needs with several banks as they do not all charge the same for arranging this type of loan.

One final point on term loans. Banks tend to lump overdraft facilities and loans together into a 'total' facility, so one is often only given at the expense of the other.

In addition to providing a source of funds, the clearing banks have considerable expertise in the areas of tax, insurance and financial advice generally. Little of this expertise will rest in your local branch office. The bank's regional and main head offices are where these centralised services are provided.

As you probably have a bank account already, this may be your starting point in looking for money for business. Do not forget, however, that the banks are in competition with one another and with other lenders, so shop around if you do not get what you want first time.

The banks are becoming quite adventurous in their competition for new and small business accounts. Barclays Bank Business Start Loan is one such scheme. It is aimed exclusively at providing some, though not all, of the set-up costs of a new business. The amount needed should be between £5,000 and

£100,000. The period of the loan is three to five years, and the capital is to be repaid in full at the end of the fifth year. Not only do borrowers get the advantage of deferring capital repayments for up to five years, but interest charges are taken in the form of royalty on sales. In this way you pay only when you can best afford to, and so ease early cash flow problems. Some of the banks have a small firms specialist, one of whose tasks is to help new, small business clients get the best out of their banking services. To get an opinion from one of these specialists would be a good way of finding the possibilities of getting finance and how best to go about it.

Leasing companies

Leasing is a way of getting the use of vehicles, plant and equipment without paying the full cost at once. Operating leases are taken out where you will use the equipment for less than its full economic life — for example, a car, photocopier or vending machine. The lessor takes the risk of the equipment becoming obsolete, and assumes responsibility for repairs, maintenance and insurance. As you, the lessee, are paying for this service, it is more expensive than a finance lease, where you lease the equipment for most of its economic life and maintain and insure it yourself. Leases can normally be extended, often for fairly nominal sums, in the later years.

The obvious attractions of leasing are that no deposit is needed, leaving your working capital for more profitable use elsewhere. Also, the cost of leasing is known from the start, making forward planning more simple. There may even be some tax advantages over other forms of finance.

Leasing companies may be a little more adventurous in dealing with new and small businesses than other sources of finance. The *Equipment Leasing Association* is the main organisation in this field. It is located at 18 Upper Grosvenor Street, London W1X 6PD; 01-491 2783.

Most leasing companies are subsidiaries of much larger financial institutions, including the clearing banks. Some of them operate in specialist markets such as aircraft or agriculture, as their names imply. Many would not look at anything under £1m. A phone call to the association will put you in touch with a selection of appropriate companies. Four companies that have a spread of business between a few hundred pounds and £50,000 are:

Anglo Leasing Ltd, 2 Clerkenwell Green, London EC1R ODH; 01-253 4300.

First Cooperative Finance Ltd, 1 Balloon Street, Manchester M60 4EP; 061-832 3300.

Hamilton Leasing Ltd, Hamilton House, 80 Stokes Croft, Bristol BS1 3QW; 0272 48080.

Schroder Leasing Ltd, PO Box 99, Harrow, Middlesex HA1 2HP; 01-863 7711.

Finance houses

These provide instalment credit for short-term needs such as hire purchase. Hire purchase differs from leasing in that you have the option at the start to become the owner of the equipment after a series of payments have been made. The interest is usually fixed and often more expensive than a bank loan. However, manufacturers (notably car makers) often subsidise this interest, so it pays to shop around both for sources of hp finance and manufacturers of equipment.

The Finance Houses Association, at 18 Upper Grosvenor Street, London W1X 9PB; 01-491 2783, can give you a list of contacts. Once again, many of the clearing banks have subsidiaries in this field.

Discount houses

These are the specialist institutions that provide bill financing. A bill is rather like a post-dated cheque which can be sold to a third party for cash, but at a discount. Once you have despatched goods to your customer, you can draw a trade bill to be accepted by him on a certain date. This, in effect, is a commitment by him to settle his account on that date, and he is not expected to pay until then. You can sell this bill to a bank or a discount house and receive immediate cash. Of course, you have to pay for this service. Payment takes the form of a discount on the face value of the bill, usually directly related to the credit-worthiness of your customer. It has several advantages as a source of short-term finance.

First, it is usually competitive with bank overdrafts. Second, you can accurately calculate the cost of financing a transaction, because the discount rate is fixed and not subject to interest rate fluctuations. This is particularly important if the time between despatch of the goods and payment by the customer is likely to be several months. Third, by using bill finance, you can free overdraft facilities for other purposes. For example, you can get on with making more products for other customers — something you may not have been able to do if you were waiting for the last customer to pay up.

There are a dozen members of the *London Discount Market Association,* whose Honorary Secretary is Mr P L Shepherd, 39 Cornhill, London EC3U 3NU; 01-623 1020. Bill financing is a bit of a long shot as a source of finance for a small business. Although bills may be as little as a few thousand pounds, the average is nearer £25,000. Nevertheless, given a good proposition, discount houses will be happy to listen. Gerald Quin, Cope & Co Ltd and Page & Gwyther Ltd may be among the most responsive at the small end of the bill market.

Gerald Quin, Cope & Co Ltd, 19-21 Moorgate, London EC2R 6BX; 01-628 2771.

Page & Gwyther Ltd, 1 Founders Court, Lothbury, London EC2R 7BD; 01-606 5681.

Factoring companies

Factoring is an arrangement which allows you to receive up to 80 per cent of the cash due from your customers more quickly than they would normally pay. The factoring company buys your trade debts and provides a debtor accounting and administration service. In other words, it takes over the day-to-day work of invoicing and sending out reminders and statements. This can be a particularly helpful service to a small, expanding business. It can allow the management to concentrate on growing the business, with the factoring company providing expert guidance on credit control, 100 per cent protection against bad debts, and improved cash flow.

You will, of course, have to pay for factoring services. Having the cash before your customers pay will cost you a little more than normal overdraft rates. The factoring service will cost between ½ and 3½ per cent of turnover, depending on volume of work, the number of debtors, average invoice amount and other related factors. You can get up to 80 per cent of the value of your invoice in advance with the remainder paid when your customer settles up, less the various charges just mentioned.

If you sell direct to the public, sell complex and expensive capital equipment or expect progress payments on a long-term project, then factoring is not for you.

If you are expanding more rapidly than other sources of finance will allow, then this may be a useful service. All other things being equal, it should be possible to find a factor if your turnover exceeds £25,000 per annum, though the larger firm will look for around £100,000 as the economic cut-off point.

Invoice discounting is a variation of factoring open to businesses with a net worth of £30,000. Unlike factoring, where all your debtors are sold to the factor, in this service only selected invoices are offered. This can be particularly useful if you have a few relatively large orders to reputable, 'blue-chip' type customers in your general order book.

Up to 75 per cent of the value of the invoices can be advanced, but you remain responsible for collecting the money from your customers. This you forward to the discounting company, who in turn sends you the balance less a charge on the assigned invoices. This charge will be made up of two elements. You will pay interest on the cash advanced for the period between the date of the advance and your refunding the discount company. You will also have to pay a factoring charge of between ¼ and ¾ per cent. The snag is that, if your customer does not pay up, you have to repay the discount house their advance. Unlike normal factoring, however, your customer will never know that you discounted his invoice.

The Association of British Factors is at Moor House, London Wall, London EC2; Secretary: Mr Michael Burke.

ABF members charge between ¾ and 2½ per cent of gross turnover for the sales ledger package and around bank overdraft rate for finance charges. They will advance about 80 per cent of invoice price almost immediately the invoice is raised. They generally only consider customers with £100,000 per annum turnover, but may consider good cases from £50,000.

Another organisation in this field is the *Association of Invoice Factors,* 109-13 Royal Avenue, Belfast BT1 1FF; 0232 24522: Mr A M Selig. This may be a better bet for a small business. Their members' average client has a turnover of £100,000 per annum, and they would be prepared to look at propositions from £1,000 per month gross sales value. They advance 70 to 80 per cent of the value of the invoice, and charge between ½ and 3½ per cent for maintaining the sales ledger. Between advancing you the money and getting it in from your client, their financing rate charges are similar to overdraft rates.

Export finance and export houses

This is a specialist subject in itself. The range of possibilities open to the exporter is described in considerable detail in the Bank of England booklet *(Money for Exports,* Bank of England, Economic Intelligence Unit, London EC2R 8AW). The central feature of most forms of export financing is ECGD (Export Credits Guarantee Department) credit insurance. This is a government-backed credit insurance policy that gives cover against the failure of your foreign customers either to take up the goods you have despatched or to pay for them. The cover includes loss caused by war and trade sanctions. Although the government themselves do not provide export finance, ECGD credit insurance will put you in a highly favourable position with, for example, your bank. They in turn would be able to provide finance with a greater degree of security than they could normally expect to do.

Some banks, notably the Midland, operate a Smaller Exporters' Scheme providing ECGD-backed post-shipment finance for small exporters who may find it uneconomic to take out an ECGD policy on their own. In certain cases, an export house may be willing to manage your overseas business for you, acting as your agent in finding customers, or even as a merchant actually buying the goods from you for resale in certain overseas markets.

EXPORT HOUSES

There are some 800 export houses operating in the UK, offering almost every service possible to exporters and foreign importers. Some 230 of them belong to the British Export Houses Association, and they are actively interested in working with small firms.

Three types of company will find an export house particularly useful: first, those who are considering exporting for the first time; second, those who want to expand outside their existing overseas markets; and third, those who have to extend credit to their customers to a greater extent than they are willing or able to do (this may be to meet competition or currency problems).

Export houses are specialists in financing and servicing exports and are divided into four main types:

Export agents and managers sell a manufacturer's goods in selected countries where they have expert knowledge. They work very closely with their clients, and can in effect become the manufacturer's own export department. This can save a small company money, and provide a greater level of expertise than could realistically be afforded. Payment for these services is usually by commission, but sometimes a retainer or even a profit-sharing scheme can be used.

Confirming houses, buying or independent houses and stores buyers work as follows. Confirming houses represent foreign buyers in the UK and can confirm, as a principal, an order placed by that buyer with a British supplier. Buying or independent houses buy, pay for and ship goods for their overseas principals. A stores buyer is a particular type of buying house dealing only with departmental stores. Being linked to such houses costs you nothing but can open up many new overseas markets for your products.

Merchants, as the word implies, both buy and sell as principals. They specialise in certain products and markets. One of the largest sells in 120 different countries. Others operate in a much narrower sphere. Dealing with a merchant is little different from selling in the UK and, even better, there is no credit risk.

Finance houses can provide you with non-resource finance and allow your foreign buyer time to pay. This gives the exporter absolute security and makes the deal attractive to an overseas buyer. Normally only the foreign buyer pays a commission for the service.

The British Export Houses Association, 69 Cannon Street, London EC4N 5AB; 01-248 4444, is the best starting point for contacting an export house. The Association's secretary is Mr H W Bailey. They produce a *Directory of British Export Houses,* which tells you all about each house and its particular expertise. Alternatively, you can include full details of your requirements in the Association's monthly *Export Enquiry* circular. This will cost £25 plus VAT for the first insertion, and £10 plus VAT for each repeat. The circular goes to all members and is considered to be a very effective way of communicating quickly in a rapidly changing environment.

Public sector finance

There are over 134 different incentive schemes operating at central and local government level, offering a wide range of assistance to new and existing businesses. Two of the more authoritative publications on the subject are over 60 pages long, and a further booklet devotes 61 pages to one section of incentives alone.

New schemes are coming in all the time. One of the latest to arrive is the Small Engineering Firms Investment Scheme, which is open to engineering companies with fewer than 200 employees. It can provide a grant of one-third of the cost of new capital equipment worth between £15,000 and £200,000. For the period April 1982-1983, £20m was made available, and handed out on a first-come, first-served basis. Guidance notes for this scheme are available from the *Department of Industry,* West Midlands Regional Office, Ladywood House, Stephenson Street, Birmingham B2 4DT; 021-632 4111.

The Enterprise Allowance Scheme, recently on trial in five areas, has now been expanded to give national coverage. Under this scheme the Manpower Services Commission can pay entrepreneurs an allowance of £40 per week for up to 52 weeks, to supplement the receipts of their business.

The Cooperative Bank, through its Enterprise Plan, provides free start-up advice to selected applicants taking part in the Enterprise Allowance Scheme. The advice is given by two leading firms of chartered accountants: Deloitte, Haskins & Sells, and Thomas McLintock. The plan includes a meeting with a small business expert from one of these firms, a day's consultancy to help you prepare your business plan, and six months' commission-free banking at the Coop Bank.

In order to find out if you are eligible, your first port of call should be your nearest Small Firms Information Centre at the Department of Industry.

Your local authority Employment Development Officer will be well up on schemes that particularly apply to your area, and on schemes in general.

Merchant banks, and venture and development capital organisations

There are now a considerable number of financial institutions in this sector. Many are subsidiaries of the clearing banks, insurance companies, pension funds, overseas banks, and even the Bank of England and the government. Some of them can provide a range of services beyond equity and loan finance, although in general that is their speciality. A brief description of some of these services is given on the following pages.

Equity finance is relevant only if your business is now or shortly to become a limited company, and it refers to the sale of ordinary shares to investors. Unlike other forms of borrowing, where interest has to be paid whether or not the business makes a profit, shares usually only attract a dividend when the business is profitable. This makes it extremely important to get as large an equity base as possible at the outset. Although it does mean giving up some control, you may gain some valuable business expertise, and your reputation can be enhanced if the investors are respected themselves.

Apart from equity finance you provide yourself, you can attract investment from outside sources. These are likely to be from one of two main groups, individuals and institutions.

Individuals: Unlike publicly quoted companies, which have a Stock Exchange facility, you will have to find investors yourself. Recent tax changes — in particular, those incorporated in the government's Business Expansion Scheme (described below) — have made it attractive for high taxpayers to invest in new business. Several organisations have been established to acquire such funds and find suitable investments.

Institutions such as ICFC, subsidiaries of the clearing banks and venture capital organisations, provide equity capital, usually for companies with exceptionally high growth potential. In general, equity financing from people other than those known well by you is the most difficult money to raise.

The Business Expansion Scheme (BES) was introduced in the 1983 Finance Act, to replace the Business Start-up Scheme. The BES makes it attractive for most UK high taxpayers to invest in almost any 'unquoted' business. The investors at whom the scheme is aimed must not be connected with the business they are about to invest in. They cannot be paid directors or employees of the business, nor can they own more than 30 per cent of it. They could, however, be unpaid directors or take fees for professional services. The investor gets tax relief on up to £40,000 invested in any one year. There are, however, a number of other restrictions. For example, the minimum investment is normally £500, and it must be kept in the business for five years if the tax relief is to be retained. Your solicitor, accountant or bank manager may be able to put you in touch with interested individuals.

Alternatively, a number of financial institutions are offering 'portfolio' facilities to investors. This means that investors put their funds into an approved organisation which seeks out potential investment opportunities on their behalf. This spreads their risk, and gives them the benefit of 'professional' management. The effect of this scheme is that a top-rate taxpayer could be putting as little as £2,500 of his own money into a business in return for a £10,000 share, the balance being effectively paid by the Inland Revenue.

Venture capital is start-up capital usually associated with businesses involved in technological and technical innovation. The sums involved are usually up to £100,000 over periods of five years or more. With this capital usually comes management expertise, often in the form of a board member from the financial institution, so you will have to be able to work with him, and probably give a personal guarantee for the sums involved. Perhaps the greatest benefit coming from the provider of venture capital is their expertise at keeping your financial structure in line with your changing needs.

Development capital is funds to help established firms grow and diversify. Like venture capital, the period involved is five years or so, and the investing institution expects to be able to sell its stake either to the directors or possibly through an eventual Stock Exchange quotation. Generally you will need to have a pre-tax profit of £30,000 per annum and be looking for more than £50,000 additional finance. The investor will want to put a director on your board — as much to help you and the company as to keep an eye on its investment.

Management buy-out, though not strictly a type of money is, however, an increasingly popular activity. It involves the existing managers of a business buying out the business from its owners. As both the business and the managers will have a track record, it may be easier to find equity finance for such ventures; an increasing number of leading organisations have moved into this field. There is even a *Management Buy-Out Association,* to advise would-be buyers-out. It is at 6 George Street, Hertford, Hertfordshire.

Mortgage loans operate in much the same was as an ordinary mortgage. The money borrowed is used to buy the freehold on the business premises. That then acts as the main security for the loan, with regular repayments made up of interest charges and principal, paid to the lender.

The main suppliers are the insurance companies and pension funds, who generally prefer to deal in sums above £50,000.

Some of the smaller companies will lend as little as £5,000, particularly if the borrower is a policyholder. As well as the regular payments, a charge of about 2 per cent will be made to cover the survey, valuation and legal work in drawing up agreements.

Sale and leaseback involves selling the freehold of a property owned by a business to a financial institution, which agrees to grant you a lease on the premises.

The lender will want to be sure that you can afford the lease, so a profit track record will probably be needed, and all expenses involved in the negotiations are met by the borrower. The borrower then has the use of the value of the asset in immediate cash to plough into the business.

The tax aspects of sale and leaseback are complex and work more in the favour of some types of business than others, so professional advice is essential before entering into any arrangement. As with other forms of finance, it is a competitive market and a few quotes are worth getting.

An organisation that is heavily involved across much of this field is the Industrial and Commercial Finance Corporation. Formed in 1945, it is a division of Investors for Industry (formerly Finance for Industry). It claims to be the major source of long-term finance for new and small businesses.

ICFC's shareholders are the Bank of England (15 per cent) and the English and Scottish clearing banks (85 per cent). It operates as a private sector organisation concerned exclusively with private sector business. However, it also administers funds with low interest rates from the European Investment Bank (EIB), the European Coal and Steel Community (ECSC), and participates in the government's loan guarantee scheme.

The Corporation currently has well over £400m invested in some 3,500 companies, £100m of which was advanced to just over 1,000 businesses in 1982. Funds for individual investments range from £5,000 up to £2m and about 70 per cent of these were for £100,000. Indeed, about half of all ICFC loans are for less than £50,000.

Finance is provided through long-term loans, or in the form of ordinary or preference shares, or in any combination of these. ICFC takes an equity stake in about a third of cases, the balance being term loans. Its close relationship with the clearing banks makes the negotiation of security cover easier. This is particularly true when, for example, the clearer already has a charge on the business's assets.

ICFC's main areas of activity are financing new business, providing funds for expansion, and arranging management buy-outs. ICFC has completed over 200 buy-outs, and claims to be the pioneer of the technique. More recently it has moved into the leasing and hire purchase fields, with over £24m provided in the initial period. This spread of facilities allows ICFC to propose one of the best financial packages for a new or small business's needs.

The whole investment and lending field is extremely dynamic, so you would be well advised to look around carefully. Once you find the institution that has a package you like, find its competitor(s), and then you can negotiate the best deal for your needs.

Answers to Questions

Chapter 1

1. If your net worth is more than you thought, buy a bottle of champagne and celebrate. (If not do same and drown your sorrows.)

2. **Balance Sheet at Sunday 24 April 198X**

Net Assets employed	£	£	£
Fixed Assets			
Factory Premises		18,000	
Equipment and Machinery		7,600	25,600
Current Assets			
Stock	1,400		
Debtors	1,400		
Cash	800	3,600	
Less Current Liabilities			
Creditors	(1,800)		
Tax due	(700)	(2,500)	
Net Current Assets			1,100
			26,700
Financed by			
Owner's Capital introduced	18,700		
Less drawings	4,000		14,700
Long-term loan			12,000
			26,700

Chapter 2

		1	2	3	4	5
		£	£	£	£	£
1.	Fixed Assets	–	15,000	18,000	18,000	18,000
	Working Capital Current Assets					
	Stock	1,550	1,550	1,550	4,550	2,750
	Debtors	–	–	–	–	2,700
	Cash	13,700	12,200	12,200	12,200	12,200
		15,250	13,750	13,750	16,750	17,650
	Less Current Liabilities					
	Overdraft	5,000	5,000	5,000	5,000	5,000
	Creditors	–	–	3,000	6,000	6,000
		5,000	5,000	8,000	11,000	11,000
	Net Current Assets	10,250	8,750	5,750	5,750	6,650
	Total Assets	10,250	23,750	23,750	23,750	24,650
	Financed by					
	Share Capital	10,000	10,000	10,000	10,000	10,000
	Reserves	250	250	250	250	1,150
		10,250	10,250	10,250	10,250	11,150
	Mortgage	–	13,500	13,500	13,500	13,500
		10,250	23,750	23,750	23,750	24,650

		£
2.	Sales	174,000
	Cost of Sales	
	Opening Stock	110,000
	Purchases	90,000
		200,000
	Less Closing Stock	73,700
	Cost of Goods Sold	126,300
	Gross Profit	47,700
	Operating Expenses	
	Selling	7,000
	Administration	21,000
	Advertising	2,100
	Miscellaneous	1,900
		32,000
	Operating Profit	15,700
	Rent Received	400
		16,100
	Loan Interest Paid	3,000
		13,100
	Provision for Income Tax	5,240
	Net Profit after Tax	7,860

Chapter 3

1. High Note — Balance Sheet at end September

Fixed Assets	£	£
Fixtures and Fittings		12,500
Working Capital		
Current Assets:		
Stock	9,108	
Debtors	12,000	
Cash	–	
	21,108	
Less Current Liabilities		
Overdraft needed	4,908	
Creditors	–	
	4,908	
Net Current Assets		16,200
Total Capital Employed		28,700
Financed by		
Owner's Capital		10,000
Profit Retained		8,700
Long-term Loan		10,000
		28,700

2.

Cash Receipts in	April	May	June	July	Aug	Sept
	£	£	£	£	£	£
Sales	5,000	6,000	6,000	8,000	13,000	16,000
Owner's Capital	10,000					
Loan Capital	10,000					
Total Cash in	25,000	6,000	6,000	8,000	13,000	16,000
Cash Payments out						
Purchases	5,500	2,950	4,220	7,416	9,332	9,690
Rent, Rates etc	2,300	2,300	2,300	2,300	2,300	2,300
Wages	1,000	1,000	1,000	1,000	1,000	1,000
Advertising	250	250	250	250	250	250
Fixtures and Fittings	10,500	–	–	–	–	–
Total Cash out	19,550	6,500	7,770	10,966	12,882	13,240
Cash Balances						
Monthly Cash Balance	5,450	(500)	(1,770)	(2,966)	118	2,760
Balance brought forward	–	5,450	4,950	3,180	214	332
Balance to carry forward or Net Cash Flow	5,450	4,950	3,180	214	332	3,092

Comment. Now you can see how significant quite minor changes in assumptions can be.

3.　Part 1: Profit and Loss account unchanged.
　　Part 2: Balance Sheet

Fixed Assets	£	£
Fixtures and Fittings		10,500
Working Capital		
Current Assets		
Stock	9,108	
Debtors	6,000	
Cash	3,092	
	18,200	
Less Current Liabilities		
Creditors	—	
Net Current Assets		18,200
Total Capital Employed		28,700
Financed by		
Owner's Capital		10,000
Profit Retained		8,700
Long-term Loan		10,000
		28,700

4. From Parkwood & Company accounts:

Sources and Applications of Funds Statement

		£
Cash and liquid funds at start of year (Cash + Overdraft = £4,340 − £5,000)		(660)

Sources of Funds	£	
Trading, ie, last year's profit before tax	15,530	
New long-term loan	8,000	23,530
		22,870

Applications (uses of funds)

Purchase of Fixed Assets	11,500	
Tax paid	2,960	

Increases in Working Capital	£	
Stock (14,650 − 9,920)	4,730	
Debtors (38,800 − 24,730)	14,070	
Creditors* (29,140 − 24,000)	(5,140)	13,660
		28,120

	£
Cash and liquid funds at year end (Cash + Overdraft = £750 − £6,000)	(5,250)
	22,870

* Don't forget creditors are people you have borrowed from so we have to knock that extra source of money off new working capital to see how much more funds are tied up.

Chapter 4

1. To make a satisfactory return on capital employed and to maintain a sound financial position.

2. (a) Lower expenses; (b) Lower finance charges and tax; (c) Lower fixed assets; (d) Lower working capital.

3. (a) A personal goal — or budget; (b) This year against last; (c) Another business's performance — or an industry average.

4. (a) Unadjusted Sales Ratios.

Year	Sales	Sales Growth	Sales Growth Ratio
	£	£	%
1	100,000	—	—
2	130,000	30,000	30
3	160,000	30,000	23

(b) *Sales growth, adjusted for inflation*

(i) For year 1 sales now become 140/106 x £100,000 = £132,075

                2   140/124 x £130,000 = £146,774

                3   140/140 x £160,000 = £160,000

(ii) Year	Adjusted Sales	Adjusted Sales Growth	Adjusted Sales Growth Ratio
	£	£	%
1	132,075	—	—
2	146,774	14,699	11.1
3	160,000	13,226	9.0

Chapter 5

		Year 1	Year 2
1. (a) Return on total capital employed	=	13,222	17,690
		25,700	41,730
	=	51.4%	42.4%
Return on shareholders' capital	=	7,213	11,030
		15,700	26,730
	=	46%	41%
Gearing	=	10,000	18,000
		15,700	26,730
	=	0.64:1	0.67:1
Times interest earned	=	13,222	17,690
		1,200	2,160
	=	11X	8X
Gross profit	=	39,890	55,450
		249,340	336,030
	=	15.9%	16.5%
Operating profit	=	13,222	17,690
		249,340	336,030
	=	5.3%	5.2%
Net profit after tax	=	7,213	11,030
		249,340	336,030
	=	2.9%	3.4%

Chapter 6

1. Overtrading is the term used to describe a business which is expanding beyond its capacity to get additional working capital resources. As sales expand, the money tied up in stocks and customers' credit grows rapidly. Pressure also comes from suppliers who want payment for the ever increasing supply of raw materials. The natural escape valve for pressures on working capital is an overdraft (or a substantial increase in the current one). Unfortunately, many small or expanding businesses do not have a financial planning or control system, so steps to secure additional working capital are often not taken until too late.

2. (a) The current ratio = $\dfrac{38,990}{31,960}$ = 1.22:1; $\dfrac{54,200}{39,640}$ = 1.37:1

   (b) The quick ratio = $\dfrac{29,070}{31,960}$ = 0.91:1; $\dfrac{39,550}{39,640}$ = 0.99:1

   (c) The average collection period =

   $\dfrac{24,730}{249,340}$ x 365 = 36 days; $\dfrac{38,800}{336,030}$ x 365 = 42 days

   (d) Average days' stock held =

   $\dfrac{9,920}{209,450}$ x 365 = 17 days; $\dfrac{14,650}{280,580}$ x 365 = 19 days

   (e) Circulation of working capital =

   $\dfrac{249,340}{7,030}$ = 35X $\dfrac{336,030}{14,560}$ = 23X

3. Without knowing the nature of the business any comment is conjectural. The facts, however, are that working capital has increased, largely as a result of having to finance higher stock levels and more debtors. The debtors are, on average, taking six days longer to pay. This represents an extra working capital requirement of £5,524 in the second year $\dfrac{(336,030 \times 6)}{365}$.

   As this sum is a fifth of the whole capital base of the business in the preceding year (£25,700), it seems too much to accept from 'careless' control of working capital. It has also contributed to the lower ROCE figures. (See question 1 in Chapter 5.)

Chapter 7

1. Testing the Internal Rate of Return deduced by Interpolation:

Year	Net Cash Flow	Present Value Factor at 23%	Net Present Value
	£		£
0	(7,646)	1.000	(7,646)
1	3,000	0.813	2,439
2	4,000	0.661	2,644
3	5,000	0.538	2,690
		Present Value	7,773
		Net Present Value	127

Year	Net Cash Flow	Present Value Factor	Net Present Value
	£		£
0	(7,646)	1.000	(7,646)
1	3,000	0.806	2,418
2	4,000	0.650	2,600
3	5,000	0.524	2,620
		Present Value	7,638
		Net Present Value	(− 8)

This proves the IRR is between 23 and 24 per cent, which is quite accurate enough for capital appraisal purposes.

2. Using the 10 per cent trial rate would produce the following:

$$\text{IRR} = 10 + \left[\frac{(2,140)}{2,140 + 126} \times (25 - 10) \right] \%$$

$$= 10 + 14.2 = 24.2.$$

This is above the proven IRR rate of 23 per cent and so demonstrates that the wider the interest band used for interpolation, the less accurate the calculated IRR. The converse must also be true. Nevertheless this degree of accuracy would be quite satisfactory for most capital appraisal work.

3. (a) **Machine A**

Year	Cash out	Cash in	Net	10%	Net Present Value	15%	Net Present Value
	£	£	£		£		£
0	12,500	—	(12,500)	1.000	(12,500)	1.000	(12,500)
1		2,000	2,000	0.909	1,818	0.870	1,740
2		4,000	4,000	0.826	3,304	0.756	3,024
3		5,000	5,000	0.751	3,755	0.658	3,290
4		2,500	2,500	0.683	1,708	0.572	1,430
5		3,500	3,500	0.621	2,173	0.497	1,739
					12,758		11,223
				NPV	258		(1,277)

Machine B

Year	Cash out	Cash in	Net	10%	Net Present Value	15%	Net Present Value
	£	£	£		£		£
0	15,000	–	(15,000)	1.000	(15,000)	1.000	(15,000)
1		3,000	3,000	0.909	2,727	0.870	2,610
2		6,000	6,000	0.826	4,956	0.765	4,590
3		5,000	5,000	0.751	3,755	0.658	3,290
4		3,000	3,000	0.683	2,049	0.572	1,716
5		4,500	4,500	0.621	2,794	0.497	2,236
					16,281		14,442
				NPV	1,281		(558)

(b) **Machine A**

Internal Rate of Return = 10% + $\left[\dfrac{258}{258 + 1277} \times (15 - 10) \right]$

= 10% + (0.168 x 5) = 10% + 0.84% = 10.84%.

Machine B

Internal Rate of Return = 10% + $\left[\dfrac{1281}{1281 + 558} \times (15 - 10) \right]$

= 10% + (0.697 x 5) = 10% + 3.4% = 13.4%

(c) The Profitability Index for Machine A = $\dfrac{12,758}{12,500}$ = 1.02

The Profitability Index for Machine B = $\dfrac{16,281}{15,000}$ = 1.09

(d) Machine B is the choice. It comes ahead in all financial considerations: higher positive net present value at the 10 per cent discount level, lower negative net present value at the 15 per cent discount level, higher internal rate of return. And finally, as the projects call for different sizes of initial investment, the profitability index must be taken into consideration. Once again Machine B comes out better.

Chapter 8

1. Margin of safety calculations:

	Company A	Company B
	£	£
Total Sales	100,000	100,000
− Break-even point	53,333	36,360
= Margin of safety	46,667	63,640
Margin of safety as a percentage of sales	46.7%	63.6%

2. (a) *Break-even Point*

Fixed Costs	£	Unit Variable Costs	£
Car	1,500	Sales Commission	5
Salary*	5,000	Unit Buy in Price	30
Office	3,500	Unit Installation Cost	10
Other	4,500	Sundry Variable Costs	5
Advertising	2,000		
Total	16,500	Total	50

$$\text{BEP} = \frac{\text{Fixed Costs}}{\text{Selling Price} - \text{Unit Variable Costs}}$$

$$= \frac{16,500}{100 - 50} = \frac{16,500}{50} = 330 \text{ units.}$$

(b) *Break-even Profit Point*

$$\text{BEPP} = \frac{\text{Fixed Cost} + \text{Profitability Objective}}{\text{Selling Price} - \text{Variable Costs}}$$

$$= \frac{16,500 + 10,000}{100 - 50} = \frac{26,500}{50}$$

$$= 530 \text{ units.}$$

(c) *Calculating New Selling Price*

$$400 = \frac{26,500}{\text{Selling Price} - 50}$$

$$\text{Selling Price} = 50 + \frac{26,500}{400} = £116.25$$

(d) *New Cost Structure*

Fixed	£	Variable	£
Car	2,500	Unit Buy in Price	30
Sales Salary	8,000	Sundry Variable Costs	5
Office	3,500		
Advertising	2,000		
Installation Engineer	6,000		
Other	4,500		
Total	26,500		35

i. *Break-even Point*

$$BEP = \frac{26,500}{100-35} = 407 \text{ units}$$

ii. *Break-even Profit Point*

$$BEPP = \frac{36,500}{65} = 561 \text{ units}$$

iii. *Calculating New Selling Price*

$$400 = \frac{36,500}{\text{Selling Price} - 35}$$

$$\text{Selling Price} = 35 + \frac{36,500}{400} = £126.25$$

Comment. Taking on these extra fixed costs may be profitable in the long run. For example, paying the salesman a flat £8,000 per annum is more economic than paying commission if sales exceed 300 units. Unfortunately, in the short run, all these extra fixed costs look like killing the business off very early.

---

* The business depends on the success or failure of this key post, so over most of the first year this must be viewed as a fixed cost even if the salesperson is changed.

Useful Organisations for Help and Advice

Small Firms Service

This service is provided by the Department of Industry and operates through a nationwide network of Small Firms Centres. It provides information and counselling services to help owners and managers of small businesses with their plans and problems. It also helps those thinking of starting up, and there is no limit to the sorts of business the service will help. The range of advice available is wide, covering such fields as finance, training, marketing, exporting, diversification and new technology.

The service can also put you in contact with the right people in government departments, local authorities, chambers of commerce, the professions or any other body that can play a part in solving your problems. It can also find national and international sources of information. The centres are manned by experienced businessmen who can probably answer your questions on the spot or tell you whom to speak to.

If your problem cannot be settled on the telephone you will be invited to meet your local counsellor. There are some 50 Area Counselling Offices around the country, so you will not have to travel far. Each centre is backed by the full resources of the Department of Industry, whose aim is to help you get the right answers. In the end, however, the decisions you make on the basis of advice given are your responsibility and yours alone, so you must also consult your own professional advisers before acting on that advice.

To contact your nearest Small Firms Centre dial 100 and ask the operator for the national Freefone number 2444, or you can make contact direct. They provide a range of free leaflets both on their services and on various aspects of running a business.

Birmingham: Small Firms Centre, 6th Floor, Ladywood House, Stephenson Street, Birmingham B2 4DT; 021-643 3344. Contact: Mr J Colclough.

Bristol: Small Firms Centre, 5th Floor, The Pithay, Bristol BS1 2NB; 0272 294546. Contact: Mr A S W Corbridge.

Cambridge: Small Firms Centre, 24 Brooklands Avenue, Cambridge CB2 2BU; 0223 63312. Contact: Mr R Fenley.

Cardiff: Small Firms Centre, 16 St David's House, Wood Street, Cardiff CF1 1ER; 0222 396116. Contact: Mr D Pendlebury.

Glasgow: Small Firms Centre, 57 Bothwell Street, Glasgow G2 6TU; 041-248 6014. Contact: Mr L Baston.

Leeds: Small Firms Centre, 1 Park Row, City Square, Leeds LS1 5NR; 0532 445151. Contact: Mr R Mawhinney.

Liverpool: Small Firms Centre, 1 Old Hall Street, Liverpool L3 9HJ; 051-236 5756. Contact: Mr A Monk.

London: Small Firms Centre, Ebury Bridge House, 2-18 Ebury Bridge Road, London SW1W 8QD; 01-730 8451. Contact: Mr N J Turner.

Manchester: Small Firms Centre, 3rd Floor, 320-25 Royal Exchange Buildings, St Ann's Square, Manchester M2 7AH; 061-832 5282. Contact: Mr R Curry.

Newcastle: Small Firms Centre, 22 Newgate Shopping Centre, Newcastle upon Tyne NE1 1ZP; 0632 325353. Contact: Mr C J Mather.

Nottingham: Small Firms Centre, 48-50 Maid Marian Way, Nottingham NG1 6GF; 0602 49791. Contact: Mr J T Gibbon.

Centre points outside England

Details of the services provided for their respective communities (including those of CoSIRA) can be found at:

Wales: The Welsh Development Agency (Small Business Unit), Treforest Industrial Estate, Pontypridd, Mid Glamorgan CF37 5UT; 044 385 2666. Contact: John Collins.

Scotland: The Scottish Development Agency (Small Business Division), 102 Telford Road, Edinburgh EN4 2NP; 031 343 1911. Contact: Mr Campbell-Russell.

Northern Ireland: The Local Enterprise Development Unit, Lamont House, Purdys Lane, Newtownbreda, Belfast BT8 4AR; 0232 691031. Contacts: K Gilbert and G Briggs.

Other organisations

Alliance of Small Firms and Self-Employed People Ltd, 42 Vine Road, East Molesey, Surrey KT8 9LF; 01-979 2293. Members can use the enquiry services which can give advice on tax and accountancy matters.

The Association of Authorised Public Accountants, 10 Cornfield Road, Eastbourne, East Sussex BN21 4QE; 0323 641514.

The Association of British Factors, Moor House, London Wall, London EC2Y 5HE; 01-638 4090.

The Association of Certified Accountants, 29 Lincoln's Inn Fields, London WC2A 3EE: 01-242 6855.

The Association of Invoice Factors, 109-13 Royal Avenue, Belfast BT1 1FF; 0232 24522.

The British Export Houses Association, 69 Cannon Street, London EC4N 5AB; 01-248 4444.

The Co-operative Development Agency, Broadmead House, 21 Panton Street, London SW1Y 4DR; 01-839 2985.

Can give advice on sources of finance, legal, accounting and taxation problems for cooperatives, both existing and planned.

Corporation of Mortgage, Finance & Life Assurance Brokers Ltd., PO Box 101, Guildford, Surrey GU1 2HZ; 0483 35784/39126.

Council for Small Industries in Rural Areas (CoSIRA) is the main agent of the Development Commission, whose aim is to encourage small rural businesses in England. They define rural areas as anywhere with a central population under 10,000. Most small manufacturing and service businesses employing fewer than 20 people are eligible to use CoSIRA's services, as are small tourism businesses that provide overnight accommodation, but in certain areas only. There are a few limitations and exceptions: agriculture, horticulture and the professions are not eligible; retail businesses such as village shops, post offices and so on can use the advisory service but are not eligible for financial aid.

CoSIRA concentrates on providing consultancy advice, training and finance.

Consultancy advice is coordinated by local Small Industries organisers. It covers the areas common to all businesses such as finance, accountancy and marketing, and it extends to specialist areas such as engineering, wood-working and plastics.

Training courses are provided in a wide range of skills either locally or in CoSIRA's own workshops. They cater for everyone from experienced craftsmen to the absolute beginner.

Finance and funding propositions can be drawn up for presentation to the banks, ICFC (Industrial and Commercial Finance Corporation) or another lender. CoSIRA has some funds of its own. These are used in certain cases to 'top up' the money needed to get a new business started or to help a business through the first year or two of its life. This money will be provided in the form of a loan over a maximum of 20 years for buildings, and five years for plant and equipment. Loans can range from a minimum of £250 to a maximum of £50,000.

The Equipment Leasing Association, 18 Upper Grosvenor Street, London W1X 9PB; 01-491 2783.

Export Credits Guarantee Department (ECGD), Headquarters at: Aldermanbury House, Aldermanbury, London EC2P 2EL; 01-606 6699.

Institute of Chartered Accountants in England and Wales, PO Box 433, Chartered Accountants Hall, Moorgate Place, London EC2P 2BJ; 01-628 7060.

The Institute of Chartered Accounts of Scotland, 27 Queen Street, Edinburgh EH1 1LA; 031-225 5673.

The Institute of Cost and Management Accountants, 63 Portland Place, London W1N 6AB; 01-580 6542.

The Institute of Directors, 116 Pall Mall, London SW1Y 5ED; 01-839 1233. They represent the interests of both large company directors and the owner/directors of smaller ones. They run schemes from time to time, putting those with funds in touch with those that need them.

Local Enterprise Agencies. About 200 local enterprise agencies have been set up specifically to help people starting or already running a small business. These agencies frequently have a small full-time staff seconded from industry or the financial sector. They can offer advice on book-keeping methods, preparing business plans, raising finance and perhaps even local business courses. The BBC publication, *The Small Business Guide,* lists and describes these agencies' services. Alternatively, you can contact the Industrial Development Officer at your town hall, who will either advise personally or suggest someone else who can.

London Discount Market Association, Hon Secretary, Mr P L Shepherd, 39 Cornhill, London EC3L 3NU; 01-623 1020.

The London Society of Chartered Accountants, 38 Finsbury Square, London EC2A 1PX; 01-628 2467. The Society provides a free booklet, 'You Need a Chartered Accountant', and will put you in touch with an accountant if you ring its client information service.

Manpower Services Commission, Training Division, Moorfoot, Sheffield S1 4PQ; 0742 753275. The MSC supports a wide range of courses designed specifically to help people who are thinking of setting up a new business. Many of their courses include a substantial element of financial training, book-keeping, costing and planning, and raising money. The courses are run at colleges and business schools throughout the country and over the whole year. They run for around 16 weeks and are not only free, but participants are paid a training allowance.

The National Federation of Self-employed and Small Businesses Ltd, 32 St Anne's Road West, Lytham St Annes, Lancashire FY8 1NY; 0253 720911. It has over 50,000 members in 300 branches throughout the UK.

The Small Business Bureau, 32 Smith Square, London SW1P 3HH; 01-222 9000. They run an advisory service and have a monthly newspaper, *Small Business.* Membership costs around £15 per annum.

Small Firms Information Service, of the British Institute of Management, Parker Street, London WC2B 5PT. The BIM runs this service and provides a package of articles, pamphlets, checklists and reading lists called 'Setting up in Business'. The service is basically for members, though non-members can have some information sent to them, for a modest fee.

The Society of Company & Commercial Accountants, 11 Portland Road, Edgbaston, Birmingham B16 9HW; 021-454 8791.

Other useful organisations are listed in the appropriate chapters.

Further Reading

Chapters 1 to 3

Management Accounting, Tax and Cases by Robert Anthony, published by Irwin. An expensive but extremely well written American book — a recognised classic and used by many business schools as their standard text.

Understanding Company Financial Statements by R H Parker, published by Penguin, 1982.

Chapters 4 to 6

The Hambro Tax Guide, annual publication from Macdonald General Books, Paulton House, 8 Shepherdess Walk, London N1.

An Insight into Management Accounting by John Sizer, published by Penguin, 2nd edn 1979 — a minor classic.

Management Accounting by Brian Murphy, published by Teach Yourself Books, 2nd edn 1978.

Chapter 7

Finance and Analysis of Capital Projects by A J Merrett and Allen Sykes, published by Longman. One of the definitive books on this subject.

Chapter 8

Cost Accounting by A J Tubb, published by Teach Yourself Books.

Also *An Insight into Management Accounting* listed above.

Chapters 9 to 10

Basic Marketing by Tom Cannon, published by Holt.

Marketing Management Analysis, Planning and Control by Philip Kotler, published by Prentice Hall. One of the most lucid and comprehensive books on the subject.

Sales Forecasting by Albert Battersby, published by Pelican.

Chapter 11

Principles of Accounts by E F Castle and H P Owens, published by Macdonald and Evans.

The Small Business Guide, published by BBC Publications.

Tolley's Survival Kit for Small Businesses, from Tolley Publishing Company, 102-4 High Street, Croydon, Surrey CRO 1HD.

Chapter 12

Financial Incentives and Assistance for Industry — a comprehensive guide published by Arthur Young, McClelland Moor and Co, Rolls House, 7 Rolls Buildings, Fetter Lane, London EC4A 1NL; 01-831 7131.

Industrial Aids in the UK, a Businessman's Guide by Lisa Walker and Kevin Allen, available from the Centre for Study of Public Policy, McCance Building, University of Strathclyde, Glasgow G1 1XQ.

Official Sources of Finance and Aid for Industry in the UK by the National Westminster Bank, Market Intelligence Unit, 41 Lothbury, London EC2P ZBP.

Raising Finance, the Guardian Guide for the Small Business by Clive Woodcock, published by Kogan Page, 1982.

The Small Business Guide listed above.

Glossary of Accounting Terms

Cross references within entries are shown in **bold type**.

Account. Page in the ledger recording the common aspects of different transactions, cash books, sales and purchase budgets, for example.

Accounting. Art of preparing reports from book-keeping records, based on accounting concepts and measurement conventions.

Accounting concepts. Accounting principles. Practical rules which enable book-keeping records of transactions to be converted into accounting reports. See Chapter 1.

Accounting language. Special accounting meaning rather than the layman's meaning of words, and used in this glossary.

Accounting period. Period of time from one **balance sheet** to the next. Period of the **profit and loss account**.

Accounting reports. **Balance sheet**, **profit and loss account**, and **cash flow** forecasts.

Account payable. Creditor. Money owed by a business. **Current liability.**

Account receivable. Debtor. Money owed to the business.

Accumulated depreciation. Extent to which the **fixed asset** cost has been allocated to **depreciation expense**, since the asset was originally acquired. Deducted from fixed assets.

Accumulated profit. Retained earnings. Balance of **profit** retained in the business. Increase in **owner's equity** due to profit earned but not paid out in dividends. Profit and loss account balance carried forward. *Not* the profit for one year only, but for whole business life.

Accrual. Liability. Creditor. Payable. Current liability. Accounting concept: income and expense for the accounting period must be included whether for cash or credit.

Administrative expense. Cost of directing and controlling a business. Includes directors' fees, office salaries, office rent, lighting, heating, legal fees, auditors' fees, accounting services, etc. *Not* research, manufacturing, sales or distribution expenses.

Amortisation. Depreciation.

Appropriation account. Statement of **accumulated profit**.

Asset. Something owned by the business which has a measurable cost. Fixed, current or other assets. See Chapter 1.

Authorised capital. Share capital of the business authorised by law. May be only partly issued for cash. Ordinary or preference shares.

Bad debt. Debtor who fails to pay. Amount written off to **expense**.

Balance. Difference between the debits and credits in a ledger account.

Balance sheet. Accounting report. Statement of **assets** owned by a business and the way they are financed from liabilities and **owner's equity**.

Does *not* indicate the market value of the business. See Chapter 1.

Bonds. Debentures. Long-term loans. Often secured on the assets. *Not* current liabilities.

Book-keeping. Recording of transactions in debits and credits. Posting of transactions from journals to ledgers to provide data for **accounting reports**. See Chapter 11.

Book value. Two meanings: (a) Value of assets in the books; (b) Value of ordinary shares in the books. (Computed: owner's equity less preference shares, divided by the number of ordinary shares.)

Buildings. **Fixed assets** unless acquired for resale. Depreciated to expense over their working life. Balance sheet value at cost less depreciation. *Not* market value. Sometimes revalued periodically. Land is *not* depreciated.

Capital. Several meanings: (a) **Share capital**; (b) **Owner's equity** (net worth); (c) **Working capital**; (d) **Fixed asset** (as apart from expense); (e) Assets of the business.

Capital allowance. An allowance given against taxable profit by the Inland Revenue instead of depreciation.

Capital reserve. Capital surplus. Capital profit. *Not* available for normal dividend. *Not* accumulated profit. Includes share premium. *Not* cash.

Cash. Money asset of a business. Includes both cash in hand and cash at bank. Balance sheet current asset.

Cash discount. Discount allowed to a debtor for early payment of the debt. Terms may be, '2½ per cent for payment within 10 days or net (no discount) for payment within one month'.

Cash flow. The pattern and extent of cash payments and receipts by a business over a particular period. Also used to describe the differences between total cash inflow and total cash outflow for a specific project. See Chapters 3 and 7.

Cash transactions. Receipt or payment of cash.

Claims. Claims against the assets of business. Owners or creditors. Total claims equal total assets. Creditors' claims are called liabilities. Owners' claims are called **owner's equity**.

Closing stock. Stock at end of the accounting period. Part of the computation of cost of goods sold.

Collateral. Security.

Company. Legal entity. Limited or unlimited. Regulated by the Companies Acts.

Conservatism. Accounting concept. Accounting reports avoid overstating the financial position. **Profits** usually not recognised until realised. **Losses** usually recognised as soon as they are known.

Consistency. Accounting concept. Accounting methods are not changed frequently, and if changed, only for good stated reasons.

Contingent liability. Liability not yet recorded on the **balance sheet.** May or may not become an actual liability.

Cooperative. A legal business structure, where the members who own the business must also work in the business. Each member has one vote.

Cost. Several meanings: (a) Expenditure on a given thing; (b) To compute the cost of something; (c) Direct or indirect cost (indirect cost is overhead). See Chapter 8.

Cost accounting. Recording of cost data and preparation of cost statements.

Cost concept. Accounting concept. Assets valued at cost, *not* market value. Exceptions: (a) Fixed assets valued at cost less depreciation; (b) Current assets normally valued at the *lower* of cost or market value.

Cost of goods sold. Cost of goods *actually* sold during the accounting period. Excludes cost of goods left unsold. Excludes all overhead except manufacturing overhead. Charged in the income statement. Sales less cost of goods sold equal gross profit. Cost of sales. See Chapter 2.

Creditor. Payable. Account payable. Liability. Money owed to other parties. *Not* owner's equity. Current or long-term liability.

Credit transaction. Transaction which incurs (accrues) liability. No cash is paid or received until later.

Cumulative preference shares. Preference shares whose unpaid dividends accumulate until they are eventually paid by the company. Some preference shares are specifically non-cumulative.

Current asset. Something owned by a business that is either cash or can be turned into a known amount of cash quickly; or is owned with the intention of selling it for cash within one year. See Chapter 1.

Current liability. Liability due for payment within one operating period, normally one year. Does not include long-term liabilities or **owner's equity.**

Current tax liability. Current liability for income tax. Due within one year. See also **future tax liability.**

Debenture. A document that shows the debenture owner has lent money to the business for a specific period of time, at an annual rate of interest. In some cases the capital sum is secured against certain of the business's assets.

Debt capital. Money loaned to a business for more than one year.

Debtor. Receivable. Account receivable. Money due to business. Current asset.

Deferred income. Income received in advance of being earned and recognised. Normally left as a theoretical **current liability** in the **balance sheet,** until the sale is made and the income recognised.

Deferred shares. Shares of a company ranking for dividend after preference and ordinary shares. Deferred stock.

Depreciation (on buildings, vehicles etc). Allocation of the cost of a **fixed asset** to **expense** over its working life. Measure of the *cost* of using the fixed asset. Land does not depreciate. See also **accumulated depreciation, depreciation expense, straight line depreciation** and **diminishing balance depreciation.**

Depreciation expense. Depreciation (at cost) during the accounting period. *Not* the same as accumulated depreciation except in the first year of the fixed asset. See **depreciation.**

Diminishing balance depreciation. Depreciation method charging off the cost of a fixed asset by *level percentage* of the reducing balance over its working life. The percentage remains the *same* but the depreciation charge decreases.

Director. Officer of a **limited company.** Member of the board of directors. *Not* a partner.

Dual aspect. Accounting concept. Two aspects of each transaction. Basis of double-entry book-keeping. Debit and credit.

Earnings. Income. Profit. Revenue.

Entity. **Accounting concept.** A business has an entity separate from the owners or managers. It is to this entity that the **accounting reports** are addressed.

Equipment. Fixed asset if acquired for *long-term use* and *not* for resale. Recorded in the balance sheet at cost less depreciation, not at market value.

Equity. The capital of a business that comes from the issue of shares. See Chapter 1.

Expenditure. Money paid for cost, expense, asset or other purposes.

Expense. **Expenditure** properly chargeable in the **profit and loss account.** Amount used up during the accounting period. Indirect cost. Manufacturing, selling or administrative expense. Includes **depreciation** of fixed assets. Expenses are 'matched' against revenues during the accounting period to compute the figure of profit. Not **fixed asset.**

Note. Purchases of small, low value **fixed assets** (eg, under £5 each) are often charged as expense, to avoid depreciation calculations and show a conservative financial position.

Face value. Nominal value of **shares.** Not the book (**owner's equity**) value or market value.

Fixed assets. **Assets** such as land, plant and equipment acquired for long-term *use* in the business and *not* for resale. Charged to overhead expense periodically as **depreciation.** Recorded in the balance sheet at cost less depreciation, not market value. Sometimes revalued periodically. Land is *not* depreciated. See also **expense.**

Fixtures and fittings. Fixed assets if acquired for use and *not* for resale.

Furniture and fixtures. Fixed assets if acquired for use and *not* for resale.

Future tax liability. Reserve for future income tax. Tax computed on the current year's profit not due for payment until a future date. Normally becomes the **current tax liability** in the following year.

Gearing. The relationship between a firm's **debt capital** and its **equity.** The higher the proportion of debt, the more highly geared is the business. See Chapter 5.

General expense. **Expense** of the business which is *not* part of manufacturing, selling or administrative expense. Sometimes grouped with administrative expense in the income statement. Includes audit fees, legal expenses etc.

General reserve. Part of accumulated profit set aside in the **owner's equity** section of the balance sheet. Avoids distribution of profits as dividends. *Not* an asset. *Not* cash. Merely part of owner's equity shown separately on the claims side of the balance sheet.

Going concern. **Accounting concept.** All accounting reports and values assume that the business is continuing and not about to liquidate (end). In accounting, *market* values are therefore based upon those expected in the *normal* course of business.

Goodwill. Value of the name, reputation or intangible assets of a business. In accounting it is only recorded (at cost) when it is *purchased.* Not depreciated. Often written off to nil. Never valued at market price. Generally a hidden asset of the business.

Gross profit. Difference between **sales** and **cost of goods sold.** Profit computed before charging for selling and administrative expenses etc.

Income. Earnings. Profit. Revenue. Sometimes used to mean sales and all forms of incoming benefits, not necessarily in cash.

Income statement. Profit and loss account. See Chapter 2.

Income tax liability. See **current tax liability** or **future tax liability.**

Incomplete transaction. Transaction incomplete at the end of the accounting period. Cause of uncertainty in accounting. Concept of profit recognition must be employed to determine in which accounting period the profit is earned or loss sustained.

Inflation accounting. Accounts are based on historical values, assuming the purchasing power of money to be stable from one year to the next. However, because of inflation this is untrue and various methods of accounting attempt to reconcile this with useful accounting information.

Intangible asset. Asset which cannot be actually touched eg, **goodwill.** Normally 'other' asset. *Not* fixed or current asset.

Inventory. Stock.

Investment. Amount invested in stocks, shares, bonds, debentures or any asset. See also **trade investment.**

Issued capital. Share capital actually issued by a **company.** Part of **owner's equity** in the **balance sheet.** See also **authorised capital.** Price at which a share is first sold by a company. Normally the nominal value plus share premium or less *share* discount. May be ordinary, preference or deferred shares.

Issue price of a share. Price at which a **share** is first sold by a **company.** Normally the nominal value plus share premium or less share discount.

Land. Freehold or leasehold property owned by a business. Normally **fixed asset.** Recorded at cost. *Not* depreciated. Sometimes land and buildings revalued to market value. Difference between cost and revaluation, increases fixed assets and increases capital reserve.

Leverage. See **gearing.**

Limitations of accounting. Accounting reports show a limited picture of a business because: (a) Some important facts cannot be stated in money terms; (b) Accounting periods at fixed intervals involve uncertainty due to incomplete transactions; (c) Accounting reports depend on concepts; (d) Accounting is not scientific but depends upon judgement.

Limited company. Company whose shareholders have limited their liability to the amounts they subscribe to the shares they hold. Regulated by the Companies Acts.

Liquidity. Availability of cash or **assets** easily turned into cash.

Loan capital. See **debt capital.**

Long-term liability. Liability *not* due for payment within one year. **Bonds, debentures** or loans. Holders are **creditors** and receive interest. They are not shareholders. *Not* current liability. *Not* owner's equity.

Loss. Opposite of profit or income. Excess of costs and expenses over sales. Reduces owner's equity. May not affect the cash balance.

Loss on disposal of fixed assets. Loss due to sale or disposal of fixed assets. Excess of fixed asset cost over accumulated depreciation, and scrap or sale proceeds. Treated as 'other income and expense' in the income statement. Significant losses or profits sometimes charged to capital reserve.

Machinery. Fixed asset if acquired for *use* and not for resale. Valued at cost less depreciation. Machinery manufactured or acquired for *resale* is **inventory.** See **depreciation.**

Maintenance cost. Expense of| maintaining or repairing the fixed assets of the business. Charged as expense in the income statement.

Matching. Accounting concept. Costs and revenues in the accounting period should be 'matched' in order that the computed profit may be true and fair. Matching means 'appropriate to' not 'equal to'.

Manufacturing expenses. Overheads for manufacturing. Part of cost of goods sold. *Not* sales or administrative expense.

Mortgage. Long-term loan normally *secured* on a fixed asset. Long-term liability. *Not* a current liability.

Net. Two meanings: (a) Figure after deduction, eg *gross* sales less sales returns, equals *net* sales; (b) Payment of the full amount with no allowance for cash discount (2½ per cent 10 days, net 30 days).

Net current assets. See **working capital.**

Net profit. Profit for the accounting period after income tax. Net income. Net earnings. Increases owner's equity. Does *not* necessarily affect cash balance.

Net worth. Owner's equity. Assets less liabilities. Balance sheet value of owner's claims based on accounting concepts. Does not indicate the market value of a business.

Nominal value. Face value of **shares.** Authorised and issued share capital in the balance sheet shows the nominal value of the shares separately from any premium or discount. *Not* the book value or market value of shares.

Non-operating expense. Expense not directly related to *normal* operations, eg, loss on sales of fixed assets, interest paid etc.

Non-operating income. Income not arising from *normal* operations, eg, profit on sale of fixed assets, dividends received etc.

Notes to financial statements. Notes attached to the **balance sheet** and **income statement** which explain: (a) Significant accounting adjustments: (b) Information required by law, if not disclosed in the financial statements; (c) Accounting concepts used to prepare the financial statement; (d) Exceptions to consistency with previous figure; (e) Contingent liabilities; (f) Commitments.

Opening stock. Inventory at the beginning of the accounting period.

Operating expenses. All **overheads** of the business. Sometimes restricted to mean only selling, administrative and general expenses.

Operating profit. Gross profit less operating expense in the income statement.

Order. Purchase order to a supplier for delivery of goods and services.

Ordinary shares. Share capital. *Part* of **owner's equity** in the balance sheet. Holders entitled to dividends recommended by the directors. *Not* preferred shares. Possible values: (a) Face or nominal value; (b) Market value; (c) Issue price (including any premium); (d) Book value (total owner's equity less the nominal value of preference shares). See also **deferred shares.**

Other assets. Assets which are not fixed or current assets. Normally **goodwill, research cost** carried forward, **trade investments** etc. Valued at cost not market value, unless *losses* are exceptional.

Other creditors. Creditors or accruals for services. *Not* trade creditors for purchase of material and supplies. **Current liabilities.**

Overhead. Overhead expense. Indirect cost which cannot be conveniently associated with a unit of production.

Owner's equity. Owner's claims. Net worth. Amount due to owners of the business, increased by profits, reduced by losses and dividends. *Note:* Assets less liabilities equal owner's equity.

Package of accounting reports. Set of financial statements. **Balance sheet, income statement,** statement of **accumulated profit.**

Pari passu. Ranking equal, as in the rights of different shareholders.

Partnership. When two or more people agree to carry on a business together intending to share the profits.

Patent. Legal right to exploit an invention. **Asset** in the balance sheet. Recorded at cost less depreciation under the heading **other assets.**

Payable. Creditor. Liability. Account payable.

Plant. Equipment and machinery. **Fixed asset** if acquired for use and *not* for resale.

Preference share. Share which entitles the holder to fixed dividends (only) in preference to the dividends for ordinary shares. On liquidation, normally entitled only to the nominal value. *No* right to share in excess profits. Preference stock.

Prepaid expense. Expense paid in advance for more than one accounting period.

Profit. Income. Earnings. Excess of sales over costs and expenses, during an accounting period. Does not necessarily increase cash — it may be reflected in increased assets or decreased liabilities. See also **net profit.**

Profit and loss account. Income statement. *Not* a **balance sheet.** Statement showing sales, costs, expenses and profit for an accounting period. See Chapter 2.

Profit and loss appropriation account. Statement of **accumulated profit.** Retained earnings. Balance of profit and loss account.

Profit before tax. Operating profit less non-operating expenses plus non-operating income, in the income statement. *Not* **net profit.**

Provision. Strictly means liability, but often has several different meanings: (a) Reserve, eg, future income tax liability; (b) Accumulation, ie, accumulated depreciation; (c) Expense, eg, depreciation expense; (d) Accrual, eg, accrued expense, liability.

Published financial statements. Balance sheet, profit and loss account and statement of **accumulated profit,** with comparative figures and notes disclosing the information required under the Companies Acts. Less informative than internal statements. See **notes to financial statements.**

R and D. Research and development cost. Normally **expense.** Sometimes treated as 'other asset'.

Receivable. Account Receivable. Debtor. Current asset.

Redeemable preference shares. Preference shares which may be repurchased by the company from the shareholders. Part of **owner's equity.** *Not* ordinary shares.

Research cost. Cost of research. Separate overhead or part of manufacturing overhead. **Expense.** Sometimes carried forward as an 'other asset' if it is of specific future benefit for a future limited period.

Reserve. Vague term. Strictly means **accumulated profit**. See **revenue reserve, capital reserve, provision.**

Retained earnings. Accumulated profit. Available for dividend. *Not* capital reserve. *Not* capital surplus. Part of **owner's equity.**

Revaluation. Sometimes **fixed assets** revalued from cost to current values. Difference credited to capital reserve.

Revenue. Earnings. Income. Profit. Sometimes also used to mean sales.

Revenue reserve. Profit available for dividend. Accumulated profit and general reserve. Retained earnings. *Not* capital reserve. *Not* liability.

Sales. Total of amounts sold. Recognised normally when goods are shipped to customer.

Sales allowance. Special allowance to a customer against the amount due for goods sold. Often allowed for damaged goods or shortages.

Sales discount. Trade or cash discount on sales.

Sales expense. Cost of promoting sales and retaining custom. Indirect cost. Overhead expense. *Not* manufacturing, administrative or general expense. Includes advertising, sales literature, sales salaries, travelling expenses, depreciation of sales cars etc.

Security. Assets claimable by some creditors in priority to others. **Collateral.**

Share. Document certifying ownership of shares in a **company. Share capital.** Part of **owner's equity.**

Share capital. Capital stock. Part of **owner's equity.** Money put into a business by the owners. Ordinary, preference or deferred shares.

Shareholder. Owner of part of the **share capital** and **owner's equity.** Stockholder.

Share premium. Excess of original sales price of a share over its face or nominal value. **Owner's equity. Capital reserve.** *Not* available for dividend.

Sleeping partner. Is one who puts **capital** into a **partnership** but does not intend to take an active part in running the business.

Sole trader. Simplest type of business. No shareholders, just the owner's money and borrowings.

Stock. Inventory. Goods on hand for resale or manufacture. Stores. Raw material, work in process, finished goods. Valued at the lower of manufacturing cost or market value.

Straight line depreciation. Depreciation method charging off the cost of a fixed asset equally over the years of its working life. See also **depreciation, diminishing balance depreciation.**

Tangible asset. Asset which can be physically identified or touched. Sometimes means only those assets which have a definite value, ie, excludes **intangible assets, goodwill** and **R and D** expenditures carried forward.

Trade creditor. Account payable. Money owed for credit purchases. **Current liability.**

Trade discount. Deduction from the selling price of an invoice because the buyer is in the same trade as the seller. *Not* a cash discount.

Trade investment. Investment in shares or debentures of another company in the same trade or industry. Long-term investment. *Not* a marketable security. **Other asset** in the balance sheet. Valued at cost, unless there is a substantial loss.

211

Transaction. Change in two items in the balance sheet. Cash or credit transaction. May be sale, purchase, cash receipt, cash payment or accounting adjustment. Translated into debits and credits in the book-keeping records.

True and fair. Accounting concept. Balance sheet and income statement show a 'true and fair' view of the business, in accordance with generally accepted accounting principles.

Uncertainty. Limitation of accounting. Uncertainty at the end of each accounting period makes it difficult to determine the 'true and fair' position. Uncertainty arises from: (a) Incomplete transactions; (b) Market value of inventory; (c) Working life of fixed assets for depreciation calculations; (d) Realisable values of current assets; (e) Contingent liabilities not yet known or calculable.

Unpaid dividends. Dividends declared as due to shareholders but *not* yet paid in cash. Shown as **current liability** in the **balance sheet**. Deducted from **accumulated profit** in the **owner's equity**.

Value. Several meanings: (a) Accounting value — value according to accounting concepts, appropriate to the particular asset. Fixed assets valued at cost less depreciation. Current assets generally valued at cost or *lower* realisable value; (b) Market value — realisable value of inventory in the normal course of business *(not* in liquidation); (c) Real value — *not* known in accounting.

Working capital. Special meaning: **current assets** less **current liabilities**. *Not* the same as 'capital'. See Chapter 6.

Work in process. Inventory. **Stock.** Work partially completed. Valued at the lower of manufacturing cost or market value.

Appendices

GL-GQ 32	ROBERT GLEW & CO. LTD	GLE

MANUFACTURERS AND WHOLESALERS OF YARNS.

Reg. Dec. 1933 as a Private Co. Reg. No. 282741.

Reg. Office: Robin Mills, Idle, Bradford, BD10 9TE. Tel.: 0274 612561. Telex: 517069

Principal activities of Group are manufacture and wholesaling of hand knitting yarns.

SUB. COS.: DIRECT: *Grosvenor China Ltd; Robert Glew Wool Industries Ltd; *Robin Knitwear Ltd; INDIRECT: *Dales Spinning Co. Ltd; *Emu Wools Ltd; Robert Glew Wool Industries (Ireland) Ltd (Eire); *Emu Wools (South Africa) Pty Ltd (South Africa); Robert Glew Yarns Ltd. *Emu International Ltd.;

*Jackson & Gosling Ltd; *Robin Wools Ltd; Studley Wools Ltd *Non-trading.

DIRECTORS: R W Glew (Chairman); D M Sidney; J M Glew; G N Hunter; R M W Naylor; P Howarth; R A Wright; Mrs J Glew; A G Martin.

SECRETARY: N G Watherill.   AUDITORS: Peat, Marwick, Mitchell & Co.

CAPITAL

	AUTHORISED	ISSUED
4.2% (formerly 6% gross) Cum. Pref. shares of £1	£40,000	£20,000
Ord. Shares of 25p	£2,460,000	£1,560,000

In Sept. 1977, existing Ord. shares of £1 were sub-divided into four Ord. shares of 25p. Followed by Scrip issue of 2,880,000 Ord. shares of 25p (12 for one). In Dec. 1979, Scrip issue of 6,000,000 Ord. shares at 25p (one for one).

VOTING: One vote per share, Pref. only in certain circumstances.

RANKING RIGHTS: Pref. rank in priority for dividend and in a winding up for repayment of capital plus arrears of dividend (if any), but no further participation of profits.

CLOSE CO. (Income & Corpn Taxes Act, 1970): Yes.

DIRECTORS' INTERESTS in shares of Co. at 19-12-81: Beneficial: R W Glew, 1,086,800 ORD.; J M Glew, 789,464 ORD. and 3,322 PREF. Other: R W Glew, 1,664,000 Ord.

BORROWING POWERS: Unlimited.

HCA CONSOLIDATED PROFIT AND LOSS ACCOUNT

YEAR ENDED DEC. 15 (a)	ISSUED ORD. £	T'OVER £	INVEST INC £	INT RECD £	GOVT GRANTS £	NET PROF BEF. TAX £	CORPN TAX £	TAX RATE %	ACT £
1972	60,000	3,055,546	87	10,263	–	338,203	150,366	40	–
1973	60,000	4,363,612	87	8,391	–	232,781	122,400	48.5	–
1974	60,000	6,153,946	63	1,952	–	Le 61,004	Cr. 1,750	–	g 1,500
1975	60,000	6,428,240	71	336	–	122,095	80,450	52	–
1976	60,000	6,861,046	71	882	–	337,755	1,091	52	5,842
k1977	780,000	9,781,073	45	304	–	837,207	8,400	52	11,010
1978	780,000	11,732,703	51	7,420	–	601,363	–	–	12,235
1979	1,560,000	12,500,002	69	421	–	808,463	50,317	52	11,683
1980	1,560,000	12,245,901	780	–	18,628	1,089,824	346,500	52	–
1981	1,560,000	13,536,705	1,383	–	10,274	1,435,659	350,820	52	–

YEAR ENDED (a) DEC. 15	DTR £	DEFD TAX £	O'SEAS TAX £	TOTAL TAXN £	NET PROF. AFT. TAX £	PREF. DIV. £	PROF. AFT. PREF. DIV. £	COST OF ORD. DIVS. £	*RETD PROF £	DEPN CHARGED £	EXPORTS £	EMPLOYEES AV NO	REMN £
1972	–	Cr.5,000	–	145,366	192,887	1,200	191,637	10,500	181,137	39,035	166,816	473	571,002
1973	–	–	–	122,400	110,381	840	109,541	d 7,875	101,666	46,799	513,915	861	784,608
1974	–	48,000	–	47,750	L108,754	840	L 109,594	–	M 109,594	53,888	848,564	773	1,361,060
1975	–	Cr.25,250	–	55,155	66,940	840	66,100	–	66,100	51,542	852,532	649	1,285,040
1976	–	187,043	–	193,976	143,779	840	142,939	10,500	132,439	52,134	564,256	598	1,322,980
k1977	Cr.3,600	–	3,600	19,410	817,797	840	816,957	21,000	795,957	48,788	925,925	665	1,665,248
1978	–	–	Cr.4,338	7,897	593,466	840	592,626	24,000	568,626	70,575	1,281,309	801	2,273,078
1979	–	–	–	62,000	741,463	840	740,623	r 26,425	714,198	118,775	1,708,720	793	2,325,276
1980	–	–	–	346,500	743,324	850	742,484	r 33,675	708,809	140,497	1,578,376	621	2,619,205
1981	–	–	–	350,820	1,084,839	840	1,083,999	60,000	1,023,999	207,204	t	588	2,880,920

CHARGES (CONTD)

YEAR ENDED (a) DEC. 15	INT £	PLANT HIRE £	DIRS' EMLTS £	**EXCEPTIONAL ITEMS EXCLUDED £			EX'ORD. ITEMS £
1972	6,319	23,795	17,159	Dr.b 1,041	Dr.c 8,965		–
1973	46,766	46,331	18,091	Cr.b 473	Cr.c 262		–
1974	161,640	61,920	17,529	Cr.b 10,581	Cr.c 31,903		–
1975	160,563	42,952	23,896	Dr.b 85	Cr.c 1,034	Cr.h 7,740	Dr.2,000
1976	137,967	83,154	27,647	Cr.b 9,297	Cr.c 22,151	Cr.j 1,049	Dr.39,090
k1977	146,201	134,395	30,561	Cr.b 33,709	–	Cr.j 29	Dr.37,687
1978	179,624	164,553	n 49,324	Cr.b 41,190	Cr.c 4,427	Dr.p 11,393	Dr.q 127,570
1979	323,659	183,458	s 181,617	Cr.b 8,885	Cr.c 11,099	Dr.p 4,000	Dr.q 137,845
1980	268,521	142,887	86,864	Cr.b 2,473	Cr.c 32,755	Cr.j 731	–
1981	113,494	159,538	118,877	Cr.b 9,672	Cr.c 41,067		–

*Before exceptional and extraordinary items. **Exceptional items excluded from profit shown in accounts. (a) Approx. (b) Profit or loss on sale of fixed assets. (c) Tax adjustments (including £9,664 ACT in 1976; £15,000 in 1979 and £25,573 in 1980). (d) Originally declared as £10,500, but subsequently reduced. (e) After charging £11,580 provision for losses on contracts and £8,079 provision for investment in Robin GmbH. (g) Irrecoverable ACT. (h) Provision for contract losses written back. (j) Profit on sale of investments. (k) Figures not comparable to previous year due to change in accounting policy re Defd tax in compliance with ED 19. Had new policy been implemented in previous year, tax charge would have decreased by £187,043. (n) Including £10,000 compensation for loss of office to former Director of Sub. Cos. (p) Office relocation costs. (q) Data-processing facility reorganisation. (r) After deducting £3,575 dividend waived in 1979 and £6,325 in 1980 (disclosed in following year's accounts). (s) Including £50,000 Chairman's pension contribution. (t) Not disclosed. L-Loss. M-Minus.

CCA CONSOLIDATED PROFIT AND LOSS ACCOUNT – Supplementary

	HCA Net Prof. Bef. Tax £000	Addl Depn £000	CCA Adjustments Cost of Sales £000	Wkg Cap £000	Gearing £000	CCA Net Prof. Bef.Tax £000	Taxn £000	Net Prof. Aft. Tax £000	Prof.Aft. Pref.Divs. £000	Cost of Ord.Divs. £000	*Retd Prof. £000	**Excpl Items Excluded £000			Ex'ord. Items £000
1981	1,436	40	72	Cr.27	Cr.10	1,360	851	509	508	60	448	Cr.a 10	Cr.b 1	Cr.c 41	–

*Before exceptional and extraordinary items. **Exceptional items excluded from profit shown in accounts. (a) Profit on sale of investments. (b) Profit on sale of fixed assets. (c) Tax adjustments.

ROBERT GLEW & CO. LTD
STATEMENT OF SOURCE AND APPLICATION OF FUNDS – Summarised

	Source of Funds							Application of Funds						Increase/Decrease Net Liquid Funds
	Ops £000	Asset Disposal £000	Invest Disposal £000	Total £000	Loans £000	Grants £000	Divs. £000	Fixed Assets £000	Taxn £000	Loan Repmts £000	Invests £000	*Wkg Cap. £	Total £000	£000
1977	936	-	-	936	-		11	115	6	209	-	895	1,236	- 300
1978	533	69	-	1,038	350	86	22	766	2	90	-	937	1,817	- 779
1979	781	76	-	921	24	40	25	362	13	140	-	(148)	392	+ 529
1980	1,215	17	-	1,291	-	59	27	311	23	353	46	(1)	759	+ 532
1981	1,632	18	47	1,703	-	6	34	740	149	21	-	434	1,378	+ 325

*Excluding net liquid funds.

CONSOLIDATED BALANCE SHEETS (£000)

	HCA			CCA–
	Dec. 15 1979	Dec. 20 1980	Dec. 19 1981	Dec. 19 1981
CURRENT ASSETS				
Stocks	2,909	2,750	2,958	3,029
Debtors	3,249	3,445	3,604	3,604
Tax Recovble	-	17	40	40
Cash	57	14	26	25
	6,215	6,226	6,628	6,698
CURRENT LIABILITIES				
Creditors	2,124	2,164	2,096	2,096
Bank Advances	221	211	136	136
Group Bank A/c.	1,143	578	340	340
Tax	24	211	550	550
Dividend	30	40	60	60
	3,542	3,204	3,182	3,182
NET CURRENT ASSETS	2,673	3,022	3,446	3,516
FIXED ASSETS	1,090	1,243	1,767	1,873
LISTED INVESTS	-	47	1	1
	3,763	4,312	5,214	5,390

	HCA			CCA–
	Dec. 15 1979	Dec. 20 1980	Dec. 19 1981	Dec. 19 1981
a FREEHOLD LAND & BUILDINGS				
At Cost or Valuation 1973	1,190	1,207	1,210	1,210
At replacement cost	-	-	-	-
Depreciation	348	398	449	449
	842	809	761	761
PLANT, MCHY & VEHS.				
At cost	783	1,024	1,472	2,037
At replacement cost	-	-	-	-
Depreciation	535	590	466	925
	248	434	1,006	1,112
b Market value	1	33	1	
CAPITAL COMMITMENTS				
Committed	130	406	9	
Not contracted	-	150	-	

CAPITAL	1,580	1,580	1,580
P. & L. A/C	1,615	2,356	3,438	3,105
CURRENT COST RESERVE	—	166	—	509
DEVELOPMENT GRANT	125	—	162	162
EMPLOYEES BENVLT FUND	34	34	34	34
LOANS	374	21	—	—
FUTURE TAX	35	155	—	—
	3,763	4,312	5,214	5,390

CONTINGENT LIABILITY: Under a group registration Co. is jointly and severally liable for value added tax due by other group companies. At 19-12-81 contingent liability of Co. amounted to £201,801.

NET ASSET VALUE, excluding intangibles, at B/s. date per 25p Ord. share — 1981: HCA 77.5p; CCA 82.9p.

REPORT FOR Year ended 19-12-81.

LAND & BUILDINGS: Based on advice of professional valuers. Directors have formed opinion aggregate market value of Group's interest in land & buildings is not significantly different from their net book amounts. 16-9-82.

Extel undertakes Companies House Searches —

once-off or on a regular up-dating basis

Ring Search Section 01—253 3400

Extel is the registered trade mark of The Exchange Telegraph Company Limited.
Extel Statistical Services Limited 1982.

2. ICC Information Group Limited

Principal Activities

Directors

Secretary

Reg Office

Ultimate Holding Co.

	30/09/82	30/09/81	30/09/80	30/09/79
Date of Accounts				
Number of Weeks	52	52	52	52
	£000	£000	£000	£000
Fixed Assets	1935	1682	1960	1927
Intangible Assets	0	0	0	0
Intermed Assets	8	8	2737	2610
Stocks	669	449	594	972
Debtors	1082	727	578	1127
Other Current Assets	158	2	3	4
Total Current Assets	**1909**	**1178**	**1175**	**2103**
Creditors	1762	1122	1012	1634
Short Term Loans	100	41	1651	1496
Other Current Liabl.	8	8	300	126
Total Current Liabl.	**1870**	**1171**	**2963**	**3256**
Net Assets	**1982**	**1697**	**2909**	**3384**
Shareholders Funds	1382	997	1409	1884
Long Term Loans	600	700	1500	1500
Other Long Term Liab.	0	0	0	0
Capital Employed	**1982**	**1697**	**2909**	**3384**
Sales	**9423**	**5939**	**10235**	**12900**
Exports	83	32	92	97
Non-Trading Income	–	–	–	–
Depreciation	–	–	–	–
Interest Paid	134	234	312	312
Profits	**416**	**595–**	**475–**	**589–**
Directors Remun.	54	31	31	31
Employee Remuneration	1801	–	–	–
No. of Employees	503	–	–	–
Profitability Ratios				
Return on Capital	21.0	35.1–	16.3–	17.4–
Profitability	10.8	20.7–	8.1–	8.9–
Profit Margin	4.4	10.0–	4.6–	4.6–
Return on Shrhlds Funds	30.1	59.7–	33.7–	31.3–

Asset Utilisation				
Asset Utilisation	244.6	207.1	174.3	194.3
Sales / Fixed Assets	4.9	3.5	5.2	6.7
Stock Turnover	14.1	13.2	17.2	13.3
Credit Period	42	45	21	32
Liquidity Ratios				
Liquidity	1.0	1.0	0.4	0.6
Quick Ratio	0.7	0.6	0.2	0.3
Gearing Ratios				
Gearing Ratio I	0.5	0.7	2.2	1.6
Gearing Ratio II	0.4	0.3	0.2	0.3
Gearing Ratio III	24.4	64.8–	191.4–	112.6–
Employee Ratios				
Average Remuneration	3581	–	–	–
Profit / Employee	827	–	–	–
Sales / Employee	18734	–	–	–
Cap. Emp. per Employee	3940	–	–	–
Fixed Assets / Employee	3847	–	–	–
Export Ratio	0.9	0.5	0.9	0.8

	Latest Date of Accs.	SALES £000		
		81/82	80/81	79/80
BATLEYS OF YORKSHIRE PLC *	05.82	103947	89123	60942
STOCKPRT & DISTRICT WHSLE GRS LTD *	03.81	4982	4474	4229
PHILLIP MORRIS (CAST & CRY) LTD	01.82	7722	6499	5271
A E PARR AND SON LTD	12.81	15338	12283	11403
U SAVE CASH & CARRY LTD *	06.81	8213	6365	5280
A W TURPIN AND SONS LTD	07.81	14535	13294	11116
CATERWAY (CASH & CARRY) LTD	04.81	841	746	646
EVANS (CASH AND CARRY) LTD	12.81	2019	1676	1355
W HUSBAND AND SONS LTD	04.82	3690	4199	4077
J W SMALLEY (CASH AND CARRY) LTD	09.81	17585	15497	12511
A G WRIGHT & CO LTD	03.82	2014	–	1674
A J ANDERTON & SONS LTD	03.81	9148	7447	6012
W S GIBBINS AND CO. LTD	12.81	8473	7372	6566
J R GITTINS AND SON LTD	03.81	2009	1935	1932
R T WILLIS (FOOD DISTRS) LTD *	05.81	15686	13398	12674
WEYMOUTH GROCERS LTD	03.82	843	857	875
R A INSTONE AND SON LTD	03.81	4560	4375	4129
MISSELBROOK & WESTON LTD	09.81	35722	33638	27948
JOSHUA WILSON & BROS LTD	04.81	166368	156585	115512
LONSDALE & THOMPSON LTD	01.82	109463	91769	70165
JOHN RUSSELL & SON (GROCERS) LTD	03.82	4451	4495	4495
WATSON & PHILLIPS PLC	10.81	81767	70754	64358
H AND W (CASH AND CARRY) LTD	08.81	12149	4061	3377
JOHN EDWARDS (WHSLE GROCERS) LTD	03.81	2644	2179	1846
NURDIN & PEACOCK PLC *	01.82	400345	338831	281258
LEIGH LINEHAM LTD	10.81	2023	2390	2618
T PHILLIPS AND SONS LTD	01.82	1734	816	1080
MAKRO SELF SERVICE WHLESALRS LTD	12.81	307996	264629	224256
G T OWEN AND SON (CHESTER) LTD	01.82	10998	9939	9124
MOJO CARRYWAY LTD	03.81	47268	44103	42245
BOOKER BELMONT WHOLESALE LTD	12.81	611352	347278	316194
ARTHUR BADDELEY LTD	04.81	12971	14524	12046
HEWINS (LEAMINGTON SPA) LTD	12.81	3535	3277	2909
R HICKS AND SONS LTD	06.81	2739	2855	2540
A AND H LTD	05.81	1681	1371	1326
RDFG LTD *	04.81	33680	28443	23474
THOMAS LINNELL & SONS LTD *	04.81	55907	88479	77530
CONTINENTAL WINE SPLY (S.WLS) LTD	08.81	1091	941	943
G & F PERRY (CASH & CARRY LTD	03.81	1459	1367	973
L E SANSOM'S CASH & CARRY LTD	05.81	2161	1883	2035
A G PETERS LTD	06.81	2953	2536	2783
ORBRO CASH AND CARRY LTD	12.81	10642	10119	9256
IAN YATES LTD	09.81	12490	9797	8834
THREE PEARS WHOLESALE C & C LTD	03.81	7008	4961	5439
C C RYAN (WHLE CASH & CARRY) LTD	04.81	1722	1827	1826
L GARVIN & CO LTD	12.81	1764	1872	1748
THREE COUNTIES CASH & CRY CO LTD	02.81	–	3440	3245
WALTER CLARKE LTD	01.81	–	5214	4257
W AND G (CASH AND CARRY) LTD	04.80	–	48527	42358
DHAMECHA FOODS LTD	03.80	–	2670	1887
H E BATTY LTD	12.80	–	5083	4742
H B T TRADEMARKETS LTD	02.81	–	39229	35593
M6 CASH & CARRY LTD *	01.81	–	30007	24918
MARKS CASH AND CARRY LTD *	12.80	–	16146	14221
BROOK & CO (WHSALE GROCERS) LTD	04.80	–	9296	8814
T & G (DISCOUNT STORES) LTD	04.80	–	3147	2786
PENWITHIAN WHOLESALERS LTD	01.81	–	2821	2551
J R CLARKE AND SONS LTD	12.80	–	4549	4164
CLAREMONT CASH & CARRY LTD	10.80	–	11717	6790
ROY HALL (CASH AND CARRY) LTD	12.80	–	4004	3415
Totals & Averages for 45 companies £M		2166	1735	1467
Percentage change between years			24.8	18.3

TOTAL ASSETS £000			SALES / TOTAL ASSETS RATIO			
81/82	80/81	79/80	Later Ratio	81/82	80/81	79/80
11602	11539	7665	8.6	9.0	7.7	8.0
583	549	504		8.5	8.1	8.4
967	856	692		8.0	7.6	7.6
1974	1745	1670		7.8	7.0	6.8
1078	884	664		7.6	7.2	8.0
1970	1581	1373		7.4	8.4	8.1
120	113	83		7.0	6.6	7.8
290	240	218		7.0	7.0	6.2
546	722	667	6.1	6.8	5.8	6.1
2667	2109	1564		6.6	7.3	8.0
313	–	229	7.0	6.4	–	7.3
1431	1196	947		6.4	6.2	6.3
1333	1052	923		6.4	7.0	7.1
319	318	368		6.3	6.1	5.3
2547	2280	2213		6.2	5.9	5.7
138	149	173	5.4	6.1	5.8	5.1
748	780	771		6.1	5.6	5.4
5903	5212	4907		6.1	6.5	5.7
27856	24814	23019		6.0	6.3	5.0
18493	15752	12368		5.9	5.8	5.7
765	726	726	5.6	5.8	6.2	6.2
14435	14127	12280		5.7	5.0	5.2
2165	643	519		5.6	6.3	6.5
478	416	175		5.5	5.2	10.5
74079	64679	56788		5.4	5.2	5.0
378	365	356		5.4	6.5	7.4
331	297	193		5.2	2.7	5.6
60810	27688	38097		5.1	9.6	5.9
2259	2053	1911		4.9	4.8	4.8
10355	12523	10733		4.6	3.5	3.9
140499	94515	86100		4.4	3.7	3.7
3204	4313	3339		4.0	3.4	3.6
912	775	710		3.9	4.2	4.1
713	428	391		3.8	6.7	6.5
444	416	399		3.8	3.3	3.3
9029	7026	5760		3.7	4.0	4.1
15377	20924	15302		3.6	4.2	5.1
308	235	190		3.5	4.0	5.0
413	389	251		3.5	3.5	3.9
630	655	628		3.4	2.9	3.2
1010	867	751		2.9	2.9	3.7
4220	3713	3817		2.5	2.7	2.4
4974	4320	2340		2.5	2.3	3.8
3008	2751	1537		2.3	1.8	3.5
763	674	567		2.3	2.7	3.2
913	800	787		1.9	2.3	2.2
–	388	394		–	8.9	8.2
–	678	920		–	7.7	4.6
–	8103	7644		–	6.0	5.5
–	459	329		–	5.8	5.7
–	878	897		–	5.8	5.3
–	6784	7358		–	5.8	4.8
–	5190	3412		–	5.8	7.3
–	2853	2952		–	5.7	4.8
–	1738	1272		–	5.3	6.9
–	671	668		–	4.7	4.2
–	627	524		–	4.5	4.9
–	1090	972		–	4.2	4.3
–	3113	1501		–	3.8	4.5
–	1607	1308		–	2.5	2.6
433	338	305		5.0	5.1	4.8
	28.0	10.7			2.5–	6.8

CREDIT RATING REPORT
R P HUGHES LIMITED

Ref. No.	444444	Customer Name:	Mr M Droy
Reg Office	Castlemill		
	11 Station Road		ICC LIMITED
	Newtown		
	NT13 2LP		
Trading Address	2 High Street	Ref No	I 44
	Newtown		
	NT4 1BR		

STATUTORY INFORMATION

Date of Incorporation	April 4th 1944
and Change of Name	No Change of Name
Principal Activities	Printers, Manufacturers, Wholesalers and Retailers of Stationery. Suppliers of Office Equipment. Photographers, Advertising and Design Consultants
Directors	B C Hughes, P A Hughes, Mrs E F Hughes, R H Thompson
Company Secretary	K G Stanley
Issued Share Capital	£100 made up of 100 Ordinary Shares of £1 each
Major Shareholders	Hughes & Son (Holdings) Ltd (80%)
	B C Hughes (20%)
Ultimate Holdings Company	Hughes & Son Plc
Charged Indebtedness	£44,000
Outstanding Charges	Copy of Mortgage Register enclosed
Employee Remuneration	£950,000
Number of Employees	200
SIC Code Numbers	

SUMMARY OF PROFIT & LOSS ACCOUNT + BALANCE SHEET

	31/03/82	31/03/81
Date of Accounts	31/03/82	31/03/81
No of Weeks	52	52
Consolidated	NO	NO
Profit & Loss Account	*£000*	*£000*
Turnover	7197	6638
Profit before tax	32–	122
Interest paid	15	10
Directors and emoluments	45	46
Depreciation		
Non trading income		
Balance Sheet		
Assets:		
Fixed Assets	961	997
Intangible Assets	3	3
Intermediate Assets	11	11
Current Assets:		
Stocks	1200	1095
Debtors	1804	1447
Other Current Assets	70	61
Total Current Assets	3074	2603

Current Liabilities

Creditors	1744	1507
Bank Overdraft & Short Term Loans	955	718
Other Current Liabilities	110	115
Total Current Liabilities	2809	2340
Net Current Assets:	265	263
Total Net Assets:	1240	1274

Financed by:

Long Term Loan	105	104
Shareholders Funds	1135	1170
Other Capital Employed		
Total Capital Employed	1240	1274

Note: Full particulars of the accounting procedures adopted are printed on the attached page. The financial extracts in this report are from the 31/03/82 accounts, a copy of which can be forwarded on request. This report can be automatically updated, immediately later accounts are lodged at Companies House. Please quote reference I 44.

CREDIT RATIOS		COMPANY RESULTS		*INDUSTRY AVERAGES		
		This Year	(Last Year)	Low	Median	High
Current Ratio	Ratio	1.1	(1.1)	1.2	1.5	1.9
Liquidity Ratio	Ratio	0.7	(0.6)	0.6	0.8	1.1
Profit Margin	%	− 0.4	(0.0)	0.6	3.9	7.4
Profitability	%	− 0.8	(0.0)	1.2	6.4	13.1
Stock Turnover	Ratio	6.0	(6.0)	4.1	6.1	8.8
Credit Period	Days	92	(80)	84	68	60
Debt Equity	%	9.3	(9.0)	20	0	0
Borrowing Ratio	%	94	(70)	70	30	10

* Taken from the ICC Business Ratio Report on _____
   or taken from the ICC Database of Companies in the _____ industry

Credit Score Out of 100   35

Calculated Upper Credit Limit   £5,500

Commentary. The company has a rather low credit score and care should be taken to ensure the correct credit decision is reached. Although Sales have risen during the period under review, the Company has moved from a Profit to a Loss making situation. It should be noted that the accounting data has changed due to Stock Sheets being lost in a burglary, and a stock check was retaken on 20/7/81. The Company's Current & Liquidity Ratios are poor both in absolute and relative terms, and the long Credit Period has arisen from the growth in Debtors. It would be prudent to refer to the accounts of the parent company before deciding on the amount of credit to be extended.

Copyright © ICC Information Group Limited

3. Key Note Publication Limited Data Sheet

FINANCIAL DATA (£000s)	Yr. End	Sales	Exports	Pre-tax Profits	Credit Period	Stock Turnover	Profit/ Sales%	Rtn. on Capital %	C. Assets/ C. Liabs
Travenol Laboratories Ltd UHC: Baxter Travenol Laboratories Inc (USA)	11-80 11-79 11-78	49519 36650 25885	9995 5633 3268	2210 4566 3554	54.0 54.3 73.3	4.3 3.3 3.7	5.4 13.6 13.7	12.3 29.0 30.1	1.8 2.1 2.1
Abbot Laboratories Ltd	11-79 11-78 11-77	24047 21242 17006	4171 4298 3509	2918 3290 2074	69.3 75.4 79.4	5.0 4.1 3.6	12.1 15.2 12.2	18.6 24.7 23.3	2.1 2.1 2.2
Downs Surgical Ltd	3-81 3-80 3-79 (65W)	16243 14359 18135	6529 5517 6956	275 849 1781	94.4 84.2 79.0	2.6 2.3 2.8	1.7 5.9 9.8	3.8 12.2 21.3	1.6 1.9 2.1
A D International Ltd UHC: Dentsply International Inc (USA)	11-80 11-79 11-78	15657 13039 11775	5444 2871 2849	-1844 161 -579	* 102.3 106.4	* 2.2 4.5	-11.8 1.2 -4.9	-35.6 1.6 -6.8	* 1.6 1.4
GEC Medical Equipment Ltd UHC: General Electric Co Ltd	3-81 3-80 3-79	14588 13528 15259	4937 3867 4841	720 473 1125	58.1 66.4 67.7	3.1 2.7 3.1	4.9 3.5 7.4	12.6 7.5 21.6	2.1 2.4 1.7
Eschmann Bros & Walsh Ltd UHC: Glaxo Holdings Ltd	6-81 6-80 6-79	12155 10755 11046	6882 6524 5956	538 -420 104	87.6 92.4 114.2	9.4 9.0 2.4	4.6 -3.9 0.9	14.6 -8.6 1.4	1.6 2.0 3.3
OEC Europe Ltd (Formerly Zimmer Orthopaedic) UHC: OEC Intl Inc (USA)	10-80 9-79 (39WK) 12-78	11818 7776 10312	6661 4334 5326	336 17 427	80.0 80.2 72.9	2.1 2.1 2.1	2.8 0.2 4.1	4.7 0.4 9.1	1.5 2.3 1.9
Portex Ltd UHC: Smiths Industries Ltd	8-80 8-79 8-78 (53WK)	8785 7684 6357	6231 5281 5475	1436 1340 1257	98.2 68.1 72.3	2.9 3.2 4.2	16.3 17.4 19.8	27.5 37.0 44.7	3.9 3.4 4.1
S S White Ltd UHC: Pennwatt Corp (USA)	12-80 12-79 (56WK) 11-78	8095 8131 6422	1692 1450 1921	215 399 323	109.0 184.7 114.8	3.0 3.3 3.3	2.7 4.9 5.0	6.4 13.5 12.6	2.1 1.9 2.2
Vessa Ltd UHC: Thomas Tilling Ltd	12-80 12-79 12-78	8060 7404 6079	718 802 515	703 791 666	24.6 39.2 30.1	5.1 4.9 4.6	8.7 10.7 11.0	51.0 60.0 53.2	1.3 1.2 1.3
C R Bard International Ltd UHC: C R Bard Inc (USA)	11-80 11-79 11-78	5955 5810 4443	3307 2809 2218	-61 627 635	91.9 80.8 77.9	2.6 4.7 4.2	-1.0 10.8 14.3	-1.6 35.7 43.7	1.8 1.8 1.6
Howmedical (UK) Ltd UHC: Pfizer Inc (USA)	11-80 11-79 11-78	4873 4614 4169	1917 1818 1789	200 246 209	70.7 88.8 83.9	3.7 3.6 3.6	4.1 5.3 5.0	15.5 22.6 24.8	1.5 1.3 1.3
Medelec Ltd UHC: Vickers Ltd	12-80 12-79 12-78	4060 3553 3375	3326 2999 2700	57 -586 312	88.6 107.3 144.9	3.0 3.3 4.7	1.4 -16.5 9.3	2.6 -28.3 23.0	1.3 2.6 1.6
Credit period = days						*Stock turnover = times per annum		*See Financial Appraisal	

This information, though believed to be accurate, is not guaranteed. © 1982 Key Note Publications Ltd.

4. Business Plan for a New Business

Business Plan for a New Business
The following is a summary plan for a hotel toiletries business.

Introduction

The business

Kew Cosmetics will be supplying attractively packaged soaps and shampoos to hotels in the medium price range to luxury bracket. The business itself is solely concerned with the assembly of the materials involved in this package and the marketing and selling of the product. In the first two years of trading the business will be confining its product range to soap and shampoo; in the future it is hoped to provide a complete range of toiletries for the hotel bathroom.

Raw material purchases will be soap and shampoo from pharmaceutical companies and plastic shampoo bottles and soap boxes from plastic moulding companies. In addition to these products, there is the adhesive label to be stuck on the face of the soap boxes and shampoo bottles. These labels are to be designed by Kew Cosmetics' designer who will tailor the label to depict the image of the individual hotel. High design content with up to four colours used on the label is central to the product.

The component parts of the package are to be assembled by the business and distributed by transport companies to the purchasers.

Personal résumé

Name:	W R H Tudhope (Bill)
Address:	c/o Margo Kyle, Graduate Enterprise, Stirling University
Date of Birth:	1 February 1959
Qualifications:	BA (History) Victoria University, New Zealand. B Comm (Public Admin) Victoria University. MA (Law) Cambridge University, England.
Relevant work experience:	James Cook Hotel, Wellington, New Zealand. From 1978 to 1980 I worked full-time in my university vacations and part-time during the term in this large (300 room) 4-star hotel. During this time I became well acquainted with all the departments of a large hotel. I have also had a very brief opportunity to study at first hand the small hotel toiletries supply firm in London which will be my main competition once the business is established.
Past business experience:	I have set up numerous 'small scale' business ventures in the past — all typical student enterprise eg: — showing hired films to the boarders at college for a

small profit.
— acquiring advertising revenue for the university 'rag' magazine.

Relevant courses attended: Starting Your Own Business
A course run by Stoy, Hayward & Co (CAS)
Introduction to Management
A course run by Cambridge University Careers Service.
Graduate Enterprise
An intensive three-month course on setting up a small business run by Stirling University.

Business plan

The product

(a) SOAP

The soap is packaged in plastic cartons with an adhesive label on the top. The soap itself will have the name of the product line (eg, Lux) rather than that of the hotel stamped on it. This is to enable the purchase of cheap, standard units from the manufacturer.

	SOAP SIZE:	50gm
Cost of materials:	*SOAP:	4p each (3-5p depending on quality)
	**CONTAINER:	1p
	***LABEL:	1p

(b)SHAMPOO

The shampoo is packaged in a plastic bottle with an attractive top. An adhesive label is placed on the front of the bottle.

	SHAMPOO QUANTITY:	50ml
Cost of materials:	*SHAMPOO:	4p for 50ml
	**CONTAINER:	1p
	**TOP:	1p
	***LABEL:	1p

Total cost of materials per unit:	Soap	6p — Selling Price: 20p
	Shampoo	7p — Selling Price: 20p

Price quotes from:	*	Boots Ltd, Nottingham
	**	ICI, Teeside
	***	Willets Ltd, Slough

(The above firms gave these prices as the average one should expect to pay rather than as actual quotes.)

Business potential

The number of hotels, guest houses and conference centres in the medium to luxury price range has increased rapidly in recent years. However, because of the recession, the increase in the number of patrons has not kept pace with the increased number of rooms available. Consequently, competition among hoteliers has never been keener.

With this resulting competition, standards of guest-room comfort have risen as each hotel has tried to offer amenities superior to its competitors. Bathroom toiletries is one area in which a hotel manifests its standard of comfort. My product is one intended to give the bathroom a more luxuriant impression for a minimal extra cost (the 40p price tag for both products is one easily passed on to the customer in a bill which may be upwards of £40 a night).

Thus the selling features of the product are:

(a) It raises the standard of the hotel for a negligible increase in cost.
(b) It is attractive to the guest and thereby improves his impression of the hotel.
(c) It will most likely be taken by the guest and thereby develop in him a further appreciation of the hotel.
(d) In the event of (c) it is most likely that others will acquire the packages eventually and consequently develop a favourable awareness of the hotel, which may in turn lead to their patronage.
(e) It appeals to the hotelier's vanity to have his 'own' soap and shampoo brand.

Most importantly (a), (b) and (c) combine to create the all-important 'repeat guest'.

The market

In the first two years, limited resources necessitate that I confine my attention to the smaller, private hotels in Scotland and the North of England. I have not, as yet, visited any hotels in this area in order to ascertain the extent of the market; however, if I am successful with an application to the MSC for a grant, systematic market research will be undertaken in November 1983.

Although I haven't studied the market in Scotland, my experience with a small London firm supplying the south-east of England with hotel toiletries revealed a rich market for a product such as I will be producing. It is not an unreasonable assumption that such a product will be equally well received in the north.

Competitors

The success of my future product in the south has been ascribed to two factors in particular. First, design strength and the rare use in packaging of four colours; and second, the lack of competition.

At present the area of hotel toiletries is dominated by two product types:

1. The single piece of cheaply wrapped soap costing the hotelier between 2p and 5p.
2. The complete array of expensive French toiletries eg, Roger & Gallet's set of soap, shampoo, cologne, bath foam and other accessories which costs the hotelier over £1.50 for the set.

There would appear to be nothing on the market for between 5p and £1. Consequently, the package which gives the impression of a high quality hotel, but sells to the hotelier for only around 20p a unit, has been highly successful in the south-east of England.

Fortunately, the firm with which I am acquainted has had such success with the product in the south-east that it has directed its attention almost exclusively to large hotel chains, particularly in the US where the strength of the dollar and cut-throat freight charges over the Atlantic has allowed for very successful market penetration. The Scottish market for medium-priced hotel toiletries is, it would appear, largely untapped.

Customers

Year 1. In the first year, sales to 15 hotels in Scotland and the north of England are estimated. Each order comprises enough soap to last 12 months. Twenty orders are estimated for the whole of year 1 as five hotels are expected to re-order towards the end of the 12 months for year 2.

The target market is the small to medium-size hotels in the north with a 3- to 5-star rating, the reason for this being that such hotels have been largely neglected by what few hotel supply firms there are in this product area; their efforts have tended to be directed more at the profitable hotel chains and metropolitan giants.

The average value of each soap order in year 1 is estimated at being £1,000:

Average size of hotel	40	rooms
No of rooms available in a year (40 x 365) rounded figure	14,000	
Average occupancy rate of hotels	70	per cent
No of rooms occupied in a year (14,000 x 0.7) rounded figure	10,000	
No of days each soap lasts before being replaced	2	
No of units required by a hotel in a year	5,000	
= 5,000 units at 20p each: £1,000		

Total soap sales in year 1 (£1,000 x 20 orders) = £20,000

In addition it is estimated that six of these hotels will buy the shampoo with a further two year-end re-orders, making an additional eight sales of shampoo at 20p each also, at an average of £1,000 per sale.

Hence total estimated sales in year 1 amount to £28,000:

Soap	£20,000
Shampoo	£8,000

Year 2. During the first year I would have built up a portfolio of sales which would have greatly enhanced my credibility in the market, not to mention giving me invaluable experience, material for sophisticated sales literature and a better understanding of my market and the competitors. As a result of these benefits, combined with the increased size of my business, I will be in a position to approach large hotels throughout the UK in year 2.

It is thus estimated that in year 2 I will make sales to 12 large hotels during the year at an average value of £5,000 a sale:

Average size of hotel	200	rooms
No of rooms available in a year (200 x 365)	73,000	
Average occupancy rate of hotels	70	per cent
No of rooms occupied in a year (73,000 x 0.7; rounded)	50,000	
No of days each soap lasts before being replaced	2	
No of units required by a hotel in a year	25,000	
= 25,000 units at 20p each: £5,000		

Total soap sales to the 12 new large hotels	£60,000

In addition it is also estimated that 12 of the 15 hotels who purchased the product in year 1 will continue with the product at the same level of sales, ie:

12 orders at £1,000 each: £12,000.

Similarly, as in year 1, it is estimated that between a third and half the hotels will want to add the shampoo to their soap package:

4 sales to large hotels at £5,000 per order =	£20,000
8 sales to the smaller hotels at £1,000 =	£8,000

Hence total estimated sales in year 2 amount to £100,000:

Soap sales to large hotels	£60,000
Soap sales to small hotels	£12,000
Shampoo sales to large hotels	£20,000
Shampoo sales to small hotels	£ 8,000
	£100,000

Personnel

Year 1. In the first year I will be employing an unskilled labourer to package the goods once the first order has been secured, ie, in month 2. As demand picks up towards the end of the year, another labourer will be employed on the same work.

Secretarial services will be used to provide a business address and telephone service for incoming calls while I'm away (the figure used being an estimate by Reception Secretarial Services of Edinburgh). A designer, employed on a job basis, will be employed at £13 per hour, and I will be paying myself £410 a month:

1 unskilled labourer − 11 months @ £420 per month	£4,620
1 unskilled labourer − 2 months @ £420 per month	£840
1 designer − 15 jobs / 10hrs a job @ £13 per hour	£1,950
Reception services for one year	£370
Myself − £410 per month	£4,920
	£12,700

Year 2. The second year sees a steady increase of packagers as the volume of sales builds up; all unskilled, one will be performing a warehousing function by the end of the year and will be paid a little more. Secretarial services will still be adequate without having to employ a secretary or receptionist. Designer fees are raised to £20 per hour.

2 unskilled labourers − 12 months @ £450 per month	£10,800
2 unskilled labourers − 8 months @ £420 per month	£6,720
1 unskilled labourer − 4 months @ £420 per month	£1,680
1 unskilled warehouseman − 4 months @ £500 per month	£2,000
1 designer − 12 jobs / 10hrs a job @ £20 per hour	£2,400
Myself − £500 per month	£6,000
Reception services for one year	£400
	£30,000

Marketing

In year 1 I will be making personal contact with a large proportion of the hotels in Scotland and the North of England which fit into my target market: the small 3- − 5-star hotels which are generally not part of a chain. All product promotion will be undertaken in year 1 by personal visits to the hotels. General advertising in trade magazines, mail shots and selling to large hotels or chains will not be undertaken in year 1 while resources could not be stretched to cope with large orders and inexperience would make the possibility of such a major sale highly unlikely anyway.

During the market research phase of development in November and December 1983 I hope to establish contact with at least 20 hotels. This will enable me to establish a rapport with the buyers in these hotels which will greatly facilitate my subsequent sales mission in 1984.

In year 2 I will be approaching the larger hotels armed with sales literature comprising glossy photos of the most attractive sales in year 1. As well as the market credibility which such a presentation gives, my experience in the market in year 1 will leave me much better equipped to secure major deals. Towards the end of the year as my production base expands and the size of the premises increases, I will be in a position to advertise in trade journals and invest in a mail shot with my promotional literature enclosed.

Funding

The business is not one which requires major capital investment. All the assembly of the raw materials into the completed package is to be done by hand. Consequently, the overwhelming proportion of expenditure will be on labour and raw materials. This means that a surprisingly low amount of capital needs to be introduced in comparison with the large amounts normally required for manufacturing industries.

In year 1 £10,000 will be introduced from my own resources. A further £4,000 overdraft facility will need to be obtained from the bank. I have a further £2,000 of my own in investments which can be used to secure this facility.

The £12,000 of my own resources which are being made available to the firm in year 1 is the sum total of a recent legacy which I received and which represents my total assets, excluding my motor vehicle which is also being made available to the business.

Location

Approximately 700 square feet of leased property in the Kinning Park or Kingston area in Glasgow will be sought. It need not be a prime industrial site and non-ground floor accommodation is quite acceptable.

The reasons for the siting are:

1. Glasgow offers big city services.
2. Proximity to my intended markets.
3. Availability of government assistance in the region.
4. Cheap rentals and availability of labour in times of expansion.
5. Proximity to desired residential area: Queen's Park/Shawlands.
6. Familial reasons.

Estimated rental charge for industrial property in Kinning Park:

- £2.50 (inclusive of rates) per square foot.
- 700 square feet @ £2.50: £1,750 in year 1.

In year 2 an allowance is made for an increase in square footage required to 1,000 square feet.

Profitability and growth

See Profit and Loss Account.

Year 1. In the first year, start-up costs, the size and number of customers, and an inability to buy raw materials in any large discounted quantities will result in negligible profits.

Year 2. In the second year all the stifling influences in year 1 disappear and consequently, there results an after-tax profit of £17,000. Economies of scale used in buying in bulk and selling to large hotels will be the principal contributor to the greatly increased profits.

Year 3. The third year sees the expansion of the product range to include bath salts and eau de cologne. By the end of the year nearly all the 3- — 5-star hotels in the country should have been visited. Also investigation into the possibility of acting as an agent for a French manufacturer of luxury toiletries will be undertaken in order to expand my potential market.

With increased market penetration it is estimated that sales to another 10 large hotels will be secured and at least one order from a metropolitan giant (400+ rooms). The resulting profit level, working on the margins used in years 1 and 2, will ensure a profit level in year 3 which will necessitate the changing of the legal status of the company for tax reasons.

Sundry information

Accountant — Arthur Young, McClelland Moores & Co.
Bank — Lloyds (John Simmonds)
Lawyer — Stitt & Co. (Peter Crawford)
The business will be registered for VAT.
Legal status — Sole trader.

Profit and Loss (Years 1 and 2)

		Year 1		Year 2	
		£	£	£	£
1.	**INCOME**				
	Car	2,000			
	Sales	28,000	30,000		100,000
2.	**MANUFACTURING COSTS**				
	Opening Stock	–		1,900	
	Purchases	10,700		34,000	
		10,700		35,900	
	–Closing Stock	1,900		4,400	
	Cost of Materials used	8,800		31,500	
	Direct Labour	12,700		30,000	
	Workshop Power	500	22,000	500	62,000
3.	**GROSS PROFIT**		8,000		38,000
4.	**OPERATING EXPENSES**				
	Vehicle expenses (including depreciation)	2,000		2,000	
	Travel and Entertainment	500		1,000	
	Distribution	600		2,000	
	Equipment (depreciation cost)	600		1,600	
	Telephone and Post	600		1,000	
	Rent (including rates)	1,700	6,000	2,400	10,000
5.	**OPERATING PROFIT**		2,000		28,000
6.	**NON-OPERATING EXPENSES**				
	Insurance	500		1,000	
	Stationery	200		500	
	Cash Purchases	200		600	
	Legal and Professional	600		600	
	Advertising	500	2,000	1,300	4,000
7.	**PROFIT BEFORE TAX**		0		24,000
	+ Enterprise Allowance		2,000		–
8.	**TAX**		700		7,000
9.	**PROFIT AFTER TAX**		1,300		17,000

P AND L ACCOUNT EXPLANATIONS

Sales: Explanation of how the sales figures are arrived at on pages 227-8 under 'CUSTOMERS'.

Cost of materials used:
    (a) Cost of materials per unit soap package (page 226)   6p
    (b) Cost of materials per unit shampoo package (page 226)   7p
    (c) Total unit sales of soap: 100,000 (year 1) 360,000 (year 2)
    (d) Total unit sales of shampoo: 40,000 (year 1) 140,000 (year 2)
Cost of materials used in year 1:
    Soap – (a) x (c)   £6,000
    Shampoo – (b) x (d)   £2,800
                      £8,800
Cost of materials used in year 2:
    Soap – (a) x (c)   £21,700
    Shampoo – (b) x (d)   £9,800
                      £31,500

Direct Labour: Explanation on pages   and   under PERSONNEL.

Vehicle Expenses: £1,400 plus £600 depreciation — £2,000.

Distribution: quote from National Carriers — £25 per 400 cwt for 100 miles.

> Year 1 — 20 orders, each going an average of 100 miles
> — £500 + £100 miscellaneous
> — £600
> Year 2 — 24 orders, each going an average of 150 miles (ie, £40 for 400 cwt)
> — average weight 800 cwt
> — (24 x £40) x 2
> — £1,900 + £100 miscellaneous
> — £2,000

Equipment: the capital purchases are very small for a manufacturing business. This is because all raw materials are purchased from suppliers and the business performs a simple, labour intensive, packaging function. Consequently, very little equipment will be needed other than something on which to assemble the product, glues, pouring receptacles, desk, chairs and lights:

> Year 1 — Expenditure on equipment: £1,800 – depreciation cost: 1/3   £600
> Year 2 — Expenditure on equipment: £3,000 – depreciation cost: 1/3   £1,000
> + depreciation of year 1 equipment   −£600
>
> £1,600

Rent and Rates: see page 230 under LOCATION.

Insurance:

Car — £150 per annum (quote Halstead Insurance brokers — including two years no claim bonus).

Public liability — £50 pa for manual light worker employed @ £5,000.*
> — Year 1: £100 Public liability insurance.
> — Year 2: £300 Public liability insurance.

Year 1			Year 2	
— Car insurance	— £150			— £150
— Public liability insurance	— £100			— £300
— Sundry other insurance	— £250			— £550
	£500			£1,000

Legal and Professional: quote from Arthur, Young, McClelland, Moore.

Advertising: figures for year 1 represent expenditure on sales literature. Figures for year 2 represent further expenditure on sales literature and preliminary advertisements in trade magazines.

Tax: for convenience a rough 30 per cent figure was used, but I am aware that a certain amount of income is not taxable and that profits over £14,600 are taxable at a higher rate.

* Quote from Midland Bank Insurance Services.

Balance Sheet (Years 1 and 2)

Year 1 at 31 December 1984

NET ASSETS EMPLOYED	£	£	£
Fixed Assets			
Car	2,000		
–Depreciation	600	1,400	
Fixtures and Fittings	1,800		
–Depreciation	600	1,200	2,600
Current Assets			
Stock	1,900		
Debtors	8,000		
Prepaid rent	400		
Cash	(900)	9,400	
Current Liabilities			
Tax	700	700	
Net Current Assets (Working Capital)			8,700
			11,300
FINANCED BY			
Owner's Capital Introduced			10,000
Net Profit			1,300
			11,300

Year 2 at 31 December 1985

NET ASSETS EMPLOYED	£	£	£
Fixed Assets			
Car	1,400		
–Depreciation	500	900	
Fixtures and Fittings	4,200		
–Depreciation	1,600	2,600	3,500
Current Assets			
Stock	4,400		
Debtors	25,900		
Cash	1,500	31,800	
Current Liabilities			
Tax	7,000	7,000	
Net Current Assets (Working Capital)			24,800
			28,300
FINANCED BY			
Owner's Capital Introduced			10,000
Net Profit			17,000
Retained Earnings			1,300
			28,300

Cash Flow Forecast

	Jan £	Feb £	Mar £	Apr £	May £	Jun £	Jul £	Aug £	Sep £	Oct £	Nov £	Dec £	Total £
RECEIPT ITEMS													
Collection from debtors:													
Soap				1,000	1,000	1,000	1,000	2,000	2,000	2,000	2,000	2,000	14,000
Shampoo				1,000		1,000	1,000		1,000		1,000	1,000	6,000
Enterprise Allowance	160	160	160	160	160	160	160	160	160	160	160	240	2,000
Capital Introduced	10,000												10,000
TOTAL RECEIPTS (a)	10,160	160	160	2,160	1,160	2,160	2,160	2,160	3,160	2,160	3,160	3,240	32,000
PAYMENTS													
Payments to Creditors		950	950	4,400					4,400				10,700
Cash Purchases	50			50			50			50			200
Gross Wages	540	940	940	960	1,060	1,060	1,060	1,060	1,060	1,060	1,480	1,480	12,700
Rent (including Rates)	425			425			425			425		400	2,100
Insurance	400							100					500
Workshop Power	150				80		100	50	120				500
Printing and Stationery							80				120		200
Legal and Professional	100		100	200								200	600
Post and Telephone			150			150			150			150	600
Vehicle Running Costs	120	120	120	120	110	110	110	110	120	120	120	120	1,400
Travel and Entertainment	50	50	50		50	50		50	50	50	50	50	500
Distribution		30	30	30	30	60	70	70	70	70	70	70	600
Advertising								500					500
Capital Purchases	1,200				600								1,800
TOTAL PAYMENTS (b)	3,035	2,090	2,340	6,185	1,930	1,430	1,895	1,940	5,970	1,775	1,840	2,470	32,900
MONTHLY SURPLUS DEFICIT (a−b)	7,125	(1,930)	(2,180)	(4,025)	(770)	730	265	220	(2,810)	385	1,320	770	
OPENING BANK BALANCE	–	7,125	5,195	3,015	(1,010)	(1,780)	(1,050)	(785)	(565)	(3,375)	(2,990)	(1,670)	
CLOSING BANK BALANCE	7,125	5,195	3,015	(1,010)	(1,780)	(1,050)	(785)	(565)	(3,375)	(2,990)	(1,670)	(900)	

	First Quarter £	Second Quarter £	Third Quarter £	Fourth Quarter £
RECEIPTS				
Collection from debtors:				
Soap	6,000	18,000	18,000	18,000
Shampoo	2,000	6,000	6,000	7,000
TOTAL RECEIPTS (a)	8,000	24,000	24,000	25,000
PAYMENTS				
Payments to Creditors	5,000	5,000	10,000	14,000
Cash Purchases	150	150	150	150
Gross Wages	5,000	7,000	8,000	10,000
Rent (including Rates)	600	600	600	600
Insurance	900		100	
Workshop Power	150	100	100	150
Printing and Stationery		100		400
Legal and Professional		400	100	100
Postage and Telephone	250	250	250	250
Vehicle Running Costs	500	500	500	500
Entertaining and Travel	250	250	250	250
Advertising		400	400	500
Capital Purchases			2,000	1,000
Tax	700			
TOTAL PAYMENTS (b)	13,500	14,750	22,450	27,900
MONTHLY SURPLUS/DEFICIT (a–b)	(5,500)	9,250	1,550	(2,900)
OPENING BANK BALANCE	(900)	(6,400)	2,850	4,400
CLOSING BANK BALANCE	(6,400)	2,850	4,400	1,500

Index